Juvenile Justice Today: Essays on Programs and Policies

American Correctional Association
Lanham, Maryland

Printed in the United States of America by Magnet Print Brokers, Alexandria, Virginia.

For information on publications and videos available from ACA, contact our worldwide web home page at: http://www.aca.org

ISBN 1-56991-151-7
This publication may be ordered from:
American Correctional Association
4380 Forbes Boulevard
Lanham, Maryland 20706-4322
1-800-222-5646

Library of Congress Cataloging-in-Publication Data

Juvenile justice today: essays on programs and policies.
    p.cm.
  Includes bibliographical references and index.
  ISBN 1-56991-151-7
    1. Juvenile justice, Administration of–United States. 2. Juvenile corrections–United States. I. American Correctional Association.

HV9104.J8734 2002
364. 36–dc21   2002025363

10|02

Table of Contents

Preface
James A. Gondles, Jr, CAE..*vii*

Introduction — Juvenile Corrections
in a Changing American Landscape
Charles J. Kehoe..**1**

Chapter 1 — Programming, Staffing, and Managing
the Violent Juvenile Offender
Frank Alarcon..**3**

Chapter 2 — Six Elements that Form a
Context for Staff Safety
Jesse W. Doyle..**13**

Chapter 3 — Overrepresentation of Youth
with Disabilities in Corrections
*Robert B. Rutherford, Jr., Mary Magee Quinn,
Jeffrey Poirier, and Lili Garfinkel*..**19**

Chapter 4 — Civil Rights in Juvenile
Correctional Facilities
Steven H. Rosenbaum..**27**

Chapter 5 — Reentry at the Point of Entry
Kit Glover and Kurt Bumby..**39**

Chapter 6 — The Ventura Youth Correctional Facility:
Providing Needed Treatment Programs
to Youthful Female Offenders
Al Palomino..**47**

Chapter 7 — Juvenile Corrections in Indiana:
The Dawning of a New Era
Brent Matthews and Ron Leffler...**53**

Chapter 8 — Watching Grassroots Grow in Louisiana:
The Children's Initiatives
Anne Hasselbrack...**61**

Chapter 9 — Turning the Tables:
The Safer Foundation's
Youth Empowerment Program
Ron Tonn...**67**

Chapter 10 — Writing Our Stories: An Update on the
Antiviolence Creative Writing Program for Juveniles
Anne Hasselbrack...**77**

Chapter 11 — Managing Juveniles in Adult Facilities:
Identifying Population and Institutional
Characteristics to Determine Staff Training Needs
Salvador A. Godinez...**83**

Chapter 12 —
Developing a Security Envelope for a
Youthful Offender Program
William "Bill" Sturgeon..**89**

Chapter 13 — Increasing Collaboration Between
Family Courts and Juvenile Justice
Gina E. Wood...**97**

Chapter 14 — Youth Courts:
A National Youth Justice Movement
Scott B. Peterson and Michael J. Elmendorf, II......................**103**

Chapter 15 — WorkBridge:
Employing and Providing Community
Service Opportunities for Court-involved Youth
Claudia Thorne, Dan Zarecky, Earlene Green,
Jennifer O'Mara, and Kathryn Scott......................**111**

Chapter 16 — Restorative Justice Conferences as an Early
Response to Young Offenders
Edmund F. McGarrell......................**121**

Chapter 17 — Mobilizing Partners:
The Kansas Community Experience
Albert Murray......................**143**

Chapter 18 — The Oregon Youth Authority's
Gangbusters Program and the Office of Minority Services
Lonnie Jackson......................**151**

Chapter 19 — Identifying Juvenile
Offenders with Mental Health Disorders
Lisa Melanie Boesky, Ph.D.......................**175**

About the Authors......................**187**

Index......................**193**

Preface

According to the Office of Juvenile Justice and Delinquency Prevention (OJJDP), the arrest rate for violent juvenile crime in the United States dropped 36 percent between 1994 and 1999. However, the overall juvenile population increased 8 percent between 1993 and 1999 even though juvenile arrests went down in every category of violent crime in that same period, and the juvenile arrest rate for murder dropped 68 percent.

Insightful research and innovative programs are making a difference. We continue to seek out what works and apply that growing body of knowledge to our response to juvenile delinquency. Juvenile Justice Today: Essays on Programs and Policies is a reflection of the increasingly effective efforts of the juvenile justice system. These essays address various topics focusing in the management and treatment of juvenile offenders from jurisdictions all over the country. Juvenile offenders present unique challenges that require a specialized response from corrections professionals. This book spotlights crucial areas that need to be considered when administering services to the juvenile population including programming, staff training, staff safety, security, civil rights, mental health, court programs, and family involvement.

These essays were written by practitioners and academics. Those who work with juvenile offenders on a day-to-day basis will appreciate reading about what works in other jurisdictions. Professors of criminal justice will find this a useful teaching tool for introducing their students to the practical workings of juvenile corrections. We have seen some encouraging progress in juvenile justice over the last few years. The American Correctional Association is proud to share some of the most recent efforts that have gone into continuing that success.

James A. Gondles, Jr., CAE
Executive Director
American Correctional Association

Introduction

Juvenile Corrections in a Changing American Landscape

Charles J. Kehoe
President-elect
American Correctional Association
and Vice President, Securicor New Century,LLC, Richmond, Virginia

The world changes minute by minute. Some changes are hardly noticeable, while others can alter the course of international relations and the world itself. It has been said that 80 to 90 percent of what a person must know to be successful in corrections actually is happening outside of corrections. That is why adult and juvenile correctional employees and volunteers must be committed to lifelong learning and increasing their knowledge base in corrections and in a broader range of subjects as well.

Understanding how our country and the world are changing is very important in anticipating the trends that are shaping juvenile and adult corrections. In the United States, for example, the 2000 U.S. Census indicates that the country is becoming a nation of people who declare themselves to be of more than one race. The Hispanic population is the fastest-growing ethnic group in the country. By 2020, the number of Hispanic teens will increase by 62 percent, compared to an overall increase of teens of 10 percent. According to sources such as *USA Today* and *The Futurist*, Hispanic children and adolescents often are considered at-risk. Fewer Hispanic youths graduate from high school than white non-Hispanic or African-American youths. Female Hispanic teens have the nation's highest dropout rate. While teen pregnancy has declined overall during the last several years, the decrease has been less for Hispanic teens and the pregnancy rate has actually increased for Mexican-American females.

These are serious risk indicators and they are sounding the alarm that unless juvenile justice systems act responsibly now, we will be seeing a "second generation" of minority overrepresentation, but this time it will involve Hispanic youths. The juvenile justice system did not proactively watch the increasing trend of African-American youths in juvenile correctional facilities until it was too late. It cannot afford to make that mistake again.

The United States is growing older, and during the next nine years, baby boomers will reach sixty-five, after which most will leave the workforce or change jobs for more flexibility. This loss of so many workers will have a great impact on the workforce. All indications are that during the next seven to eight years, the United States will have 5 to 7 million more jobs than qualified workers. Most of these jobs will demand knowledge and skills rather than physical strength. Correctional education will have to be funded at levels equal to or better than public schools to overcome the educational deficits most juvenile offenders bring to correctional programs.

Juvenile correctional agencies have an opportunity to take advantage of these trends by teaching juvenile offenders vocational and job skills that will be needed in the next three to five years. Due to the great demands in the workforce, businesses and industries will be willing to consider employing juveniles "with records," provided they are knowledgeable, skilled, and drug-free.

Some states will have such a large increase in the older population that juvenile correctional agencies will have to compete for limited tax dollars with services for senior citizens. This competition will mean that juvenile correctional programs need to create "value-addedness" to their programs. Juvenile correctional programs and services that are able to form alliances with senior citizen programs will be in a better position to receive needed funding.

The greatest challenge juvenile correctional agencies most likely will face is one they will share with adult corrections and the private sector—hiring and retaining qualified workers. Given the current situation, it is even more likely that juvenile correctional agencies will have to work harder to hire and retain qualified workers. This can be accomplished only if the public image of corrections is positive.

As you read this volume of essays, you will find articles that cover the entire spectrum of juvenile services. Consider the programs and services described herein and the promise they hold for the future. And finally, think about how these programs complement the information about our changing world that you receive from sources outside of corrections. When you make that connection, you can help shape the future of juvenile corrections in a changing American landscape.

Chapter One

Programming, Staffing, and Managing the Violent Juvenile Offender

Frank Alarcon
Deputy Secretary
Florida Department of Juvenile Justice
Tallahassee, Florida

March 7, 2001—Caucasian eighth-grader Elizabeth Catherine Bush of Williamsport, Pennsylvania, was arrested and held in custody after allegedly shooting her classmate in the shoulder.

March 13, 2001—At the request of Florida's Department of Corrections, the Department of Juvenile Justice agreed to accept and place fourteen-year-old African-American Lionel Tate in a maximum-security juvenile facility. Tate was sentenced to life imprisonment for the murder of a six-year-old girl.

March 26, 2001—A judge postponed the arraignment of fifteen-year-old Caucasian Charles "Andy" Williams, charged with killing two students and injuring thirteen others in a suburban San Diego high school, to give his attorneys time to challenge a California law requiring youths to be tried as adults.

From California, to a small town in Pennsylvania, to Florida, the media is obsessed with the seemingly mindless, heartless, and emotionless violent acts of juveniles—male or female, white, black, and other races—who, one would surmise, at a minimum, lack spiritual guidance and respect for human life. A review of the media coverage of these juveniles and violent events reveals that all reports and stories focus on one or more of the following:

- Why some children snap and who is to blame
- Should youths who commit violent crimes be tried and sentenced as adults?
- The prevalence of ethnic minority children in the criminal justice system
- The long-lasting effect violent acts have on victims

Those issues certainly are important and debates may improve policies or systemwide developments. However, we hold few discussions about another important consequence of violent juvenile crime and sentencing—how to manage violent juvenile offenders once they have been committed or sentenced to a residential or correctional facility.

Growing Concern

Discussions about the issues corrections professionals face in juvenile or adult systems typically are absent from media reports. Journalists rarely show an interest in or an understanding of the challenges corrections personnel deal with every day. Despite the correctional setting, whether it is a juvenile correctional facility or an adult prison that houses young violent offenders, correctional staff, administrators, and policymakers nationwide struggle to find ways to best manage this difficult population.

From 1986 to 1995, violent personal offenses handled by U.S. juvenile courts increased 98 percent, according to the Office of Juvenile Justice and Delinquency Prevention (Office of Juvenile Justice and Delinquency Prevention, 1998). The good news is that most states have been experiencing a decline in such offenses in recent years. The bad news is that the numbers still are much higher than earlier decades, and the number of juvenile arrests for violent index crimes still is 43 percent above 1986 figures.

The Josephson Institute of Ethics conducted a national survey in 2000 of 15,000 teens. The study found that one out of five high school boys carried a weapon to school, one out of three high school students are afraid at school, 27 percent of middle school students and 31 percent of high school students say they think it is okay to hit or threaten someone, and 70 percent have hit someone at least once in the past year. These statistics, along with the fact that the at-risk youth population is expected to continue to increase this decade, prove that addressing management strategies for violent juvenile offenders is essential.

Assessments

A review of existing literature suggests there is not one significant cause for violent juvenile offenders and that until someone discovers a magic pill, any attempt to treat such offenders should be multidimensional and individualized. Such treatment would increase the potential for success, however it may be measured. Dr. Hans Steiner, professor of child psychiatry and child development at Stanford University Medical Center, in Palo Alto, California, and an advocate for improving research in this area, says, "When you call someone a violent offender, you are talking about an extremely heterogeneous group of people."

Treatment experts contend that a comprehensive approach will consider all four dimensions of young people—biological, psychological, social/emotional, and spiritual. This asks the question: How do corrections professionals get to know offenders? A sequential diagnostic/assessment system that identifies variables unique to each offender and then accurately tracks treatment progress is the best way to get to know juvenile offenders and prescribe appropriate changes to subsequent treatment and sanctions. Authorities should not treat each assessment as an isolated event, but as information that they can connect with previous knowledge and assessments so that decisions about managing violent juvenile offenders can be well informed. That approach allows corrections professionals to adjust the intensity of treatment, the level of security, and the severity of sanctions with full knowledge of each individual's history and changing condition.

Unfortunately, many factors often limit corrections professionals' abilities to be that comprehensive. This includes use of outdated or inappropriate instruments, lack of staff training on the application and use of assessment tools, real or perceived costs associated with a systematic approach, and the failure of some administrators and policymakers to recognize the value of quality screening, assessment, and diagnosis.

Specialized Treatment

Assessments reveal that specialized program units with reduced staff-to-offender ratios are the preferred program approach to managing violent juvenile offenders. Frequent face-to-face contact between staff and offenders should be an important component of programs or facilities designed for violent juvenile offenders. Program managers should pay critical attention to staff selection for specialized units, programs, and facilities that manage violent juvenile offenders, particularly when assessments suggest the existence of significant biological impairments among juvenile offenders. "Some individuals may have an organic impairment that contributes to their violent offending," says Dr. William Davidson, a staff psychiatrist for the Virginia and Washington, D.C., departments of correction.

Correctional staff in such programs must have a high tolerance for frustration, exhibit emotional stability, and present a calm demeanor. Staff should receive special training and be knowledgeable in all aspects of domestic violence, since it is a common occurrence in violent juvenile offender histories.

Scientific knowledge about the potential biological causes and other causes of violence is increasing rapidly. Yet, tremendous gaps requiring more research still exist. The treatment implications of scientific advancements are enormous for corrections. Maternal exposure to toxic substances, poor prenatal nutrition, and extreme stress during pregnancy can have a damaging influence on the developing brain. Davidson believes that, "A deadly triad of increased noradrenaline, decreased serotonin, and increased testosterone results in chronic, uncontrolled violence."

Forensic psychiatrist Dr. Albert Globus suggests that abnormal temporal lobe functioning is involved in violent offending and he has found statistically significant differences in temporal lobe activity between violent and nonviolent research subjects. Many treatment professionals see the use of psychotropic drug treatments, though highly controversial, as promising. Steiner has reported on the effective use of antikindling/antiseizure medications to combat "short-fuse syndrome."

Treatment Targets

A comprehensive approach to treatment establishes goals for treatment interventions with the understanding that many factors may contribute to violent offending. John Platt, a juvenile justice consultant and former youth correctional administrator in Illinois, suggests ten targets for treatment:

- Change antisocial attitudes.
- Change antisocial emotions.
- Increase self-control, self-management and problem-solving skills.
- Replace aggression, lying, and stealing "skills" with prosocial alternatives.
- Remove chemical dependencies and substance abuse.
- Shift costs and rewards so that youths view noncriminal activities as more rewarding than criminal activities.
- Ensure offenders can recognize situations that promote criminal behavior and have a plan for dealing with those situations.
- Reduce antisocial peer associations.
- Promote family affection and communication.
- Promote identification and association with noncriminal role models.

Recidivism studies of the Family Services Research Center of the Medical University of South Carolina (1996) support goals for treatment interventions and the multitargeted approach.

Educational efforts within specialized program units that teach offenders parenting skills, and attempt to reduce domestic violence and other behaviors that lead to childhood trauma, may reduce intergenerational transmission of violent offending. Many correctional administrators report other programs have made a positive impact on violent juvenile offenders. These include programs on anger management, conflict resolution training, gang awareness, and the impact of crime on victims—pioneered in the California Youth Authority and used in facilities nationwide.

Reality of Transition

With the relatively rare exception of offenders sentenced to life in prison without the possibility of parole or release, violent juvenile offenders eventually reenter their communities. Case management and community corrections supervision takes over responsibility for successful reintegration into a society and, according to Platt, "is a very strong protective mechanism against future violent acts."

Program components to enhance violent offender transition to the community should include continuation of targeted treatment interventions; intense supervision to ensure maximum compliance with aftercare, parole, and conditional release requirements; gradual reduction of structure with an opportunity for increased responsibility and self-control; services consistent with individualized case planning; activities to develop competencies and skills; and opportunities for offenders to recognize obligations to victims; and to repay their debts to society.

Competent Staff

The key to any effective treatment program for violent juvenile offenders is competent staff. Clearly, staff members with certain personality types are preferred over others in managing such difficult offenders. However, once the staff has been selected, retaining, training, developing, testing, and evaluating them regularly is of equal or even greater importance.

Dealing with the increasing numbers of violent juvenile offenders in juvenile and adult facilities requires a new set of skills for staff. This is true even for those who, until now, have been extremely effective in dealing with other nonviolent juvenile offenders. We need a new training paradigm to address curriculum development, competency testing, and training evaluation. This shift in thinking should begin with a thorough review of the training methods and curriculum. This includes an occupational analysis to determine the actual tasks and skills associated with each job that manages violent offenders. Involving individuals from all organizational levels will engage everyone in quality assurance, and it will take into account a variety of experiences. Such insights will improve training curriculum.

Professionals have a growing realization that even with significant advancements in correctional training academies in some states and improved use of technologies, most learning in corrections takes place outside the classroom and, by necessity and practice, probably always will. This suggests that structured on-the-job experiences are extremely important and should be linked to classroom-based instruction whenever possible. Many staff members have not been exposed to violent individuals. Training and education about the causes and treatment of violent offenders and course work in human development, criminal personality, and domestic violence will help staff gain a basic understanding and insight into this population.

Teaming new staff with veteran staff who are role models will make structured on-the-job experiences both real and constructive. Cross-training staff from different classifications and disciplines, who work with violent juvenile offenders, reinforces the teamwork necessary to accomplish objectives and further strengthens learning opportunities. It also helps everyone gain a better appreciation for the big picture.

Training efforts should not overlook the needs of veteran staff members. Some existing staff may have the most difficulty adjusting to changes in the level of violence exhibited by offenders. Competency standards will help define job expectations and give veteran staff the opportunity to identify their strengths and weaknesses. A system should be established that officially recognizes participants for successfully attaining new competencies.

The issue of staff safety and wellness must be addressed. Obviously a safe and secure operation is going to be more conducive to effective staff and programming. Even in the best circumstances, these specialized units or facilities can be very stressful. Strong evidence suggests that individuals who work with violent offenders are at risk of becoming involved in domestic violence or other inappropriate coping responses. Training efforts should help staff understand and appropriately manage job stress. This will help to promote a psychologically well-adjusted and healthy staff.

Facility Design

Just as it is important to assess and know violent juvenile offenders and review training curriculum, techniques, and tasks in programs, it is as important to conduct comprehensive facility assessments. While the federal Violent Offender Incarceration and Truth-in-Sentencing programs and some state funding have provided opportunities to construct new facilities with violent juvenile offenders in mind, the vast majority of facilities throughout the country are facilities built in prior decades for a much different population. That makes it necessary to assess existing facilities to manage violent offenders. Again, assessments should involve a broad cross section of staff who work with violent offenders.

While safety and security are foremost considerations, flexibility also is important. The ideal facility for the treatment and management of violent juvenile offenders would provide a range of correctional environments, from group living to individual lockups. The challenge is to provide facilities that respond to difficult security issues and assure the public's safety, while providing space that supports education and treatment programming. Whether constructing a new facility or unit, or retrofitting an existing structure, facility living environments that the public, staff, and offenders perceive to be safe, stable, and consistent, provide the best opportunities for violent offenders to respond favorably to in-custody treatment. Establishing basic standards for facility security, designing program space, recognizing environmental factors, having flexibility in space that encourges staff and offender interaction are all important.

Juvenile Differences

Obviously, secure perimeters, entries, and internal movement control are essential components of operating correctional facilities whether designed for juveniles or adults. However, juvenile facilities should not be merely carbon copies of their adult counterparts. Juvenile offenders have different programmatic needs and facilities should reflect that. The American Correctional Association recognized these differences in 2001, when the standards committee adopted new accreditation standards for adult prisons that house juveniles. Juvenile offenders are prepared for their return to society through substance abuse treatment, education, job training, and other programs. Design flexibility and adaptability in these programs are very important. Many corrections professionals believe that transferring violent juvenile offenders from facility to facility may be damaging and reinforce established patterns of destructive behavior. Facilities with a range of security options and living space arrangements may reduce the need for transfers and promote effective treatment. Experience also has shown that violent juvenile offenders can be very creative in their misuse and possible destruction of equipment and facilities. Thus, planners should consider designing durable interiors (Witke, 1999).

Another design priority is consideration of staff. Interaction should be encouraged in the design of control centers and other staff areas. Natural light, varied and interesting workplaces, comfortable furnishings, and acoustically buffered areas all contribute to functional work space. Staff must always be able to see, hear, and communicate with juveniles. Staff must perceive the facility design as useful and convenient or they will modify its use.

A discussion of facility design considerations in managing violent juvenile offenders would not be complete without mentioning parole, conditional release, and aftercare office space. Violent juvenile offenders are increasingly less likely to be accepted into traditional community-based programs due to public safety concerns. Existing facilities, programs, and services typically cannot meet their complex needs. A significant and important option is to lease or construct postcommitment supervision offices to accommodate multiple services for violent youths, such as educational assistance, job training, and substance abuse counseling. Multiservice facilities can meet violent juvenile offenders needs while allowing for an increased level of accountability and supervision.

Technology as an Aid

The National Law Enforcement and Corrections Technology Advisory Committee of the National Institute of Justice's Office of Science and Technology has been researching, developing, and evaluating ways that technology can make correctional staff's jobs easier. Despite the enormous impact technology can have on the design and operations of correctional facilities that house violent juvenile offenders, technology cannot replace well-trained staff. It is nevertheless common for rapidly advancing technology to have an impact on the ability of correctional practitioners to keep pace.

Correctional managers looking for solutions to better manage violent juvenile offenders sometimes are viewed as easy prey for aggressive vendors selling the latest gadgets. Correctional decision makers must establish guidelines for considering new technologies to avoid purchasing products that have limited value. Technology should be viewed as an aid and not as a replacement for competent staff. Of course, this also applies to good information and tracking systems. The more comprehensive data systems are designed the greater is the opportunity to improve research and evaluation of violent juvenile offender programs. And better research and evaluation should ultimately lead to better treatment and increased accountability and public safety.

Conclusion

Youths like Elizabeth Bush, Lionel Tate, and Andy Williams pose significant dilemmas for society, generate *Newsweek* and *Time* covers, and provide much fodder for local and national media and talk shows. While those forums and discussions flow with the ebb and tide of the latest crime of the day, thousands of dedicated corrections professionals wake up every day knowing their job is to make a difference with violent juvenile offenders. Their efforts contribute greatly to public safety and often go unheralded. The corrections industry can best show its appreciation to staff by continually improving.

To do so, it is first necessary to make managing violent juvenile offenders a priority. Then, it is essential to comprehensively assess offenders, staff training, and facilities. Agencies are encouraged to establish properly designed specialized units, programs, or facilities for violent juvenile offenders with targeted treatment interventions and carefully selected competent staff. These structures should be flexible and recognize the different needs of juveniles. These same principles should apply to postcommitment supervision offices that are part of the violent juvenile offenders transition back to the community. Finally, every effort should be made to take advantage of appropriately selected technology as a potential aid in managing violent juvenile offenders, but always with the clear understanding that competent staff is still the most valuable resource.

References

American Psychological Association. 1997. Is Youth Violence Just Another Fact of Life? A Briefing Paper. Washington, D.C.: American Psychological Association.

Armstrong, T. L. 1991. *Intensive Interventions with High-risk Youths*. Monsey, New York: Criminal Justice Press.

Blanchette, K. 1996. *Sex Offender Assessment, Treatment and Recidivism: A Literature Review*. Ottawa, Ontario: Correctional Service Canada.

Blumstein, A. 1995. Violence by Young People. *National Institute of Justice Journal*. 229.

California Youth Authority. 1998. *Violent Youthful Offenders*. Sacramento, California. September.

Crime and Violence Prevention Center. 1995. *Violence Prevention: A Vision of Hope*. Sacramento, California: Crime and Violence Prevention Center

Davidson, W. 1997. Staff psychiatrist, Washington, D.C. Violent Offender Programming. Paper presented at Fred C. Nelles Youth Correctional Facility to Statewide Violent Offender Panel.

Elliott, D. 1994. Youth Violence: An Overview. Paper presented at the Aspen Institute's Children's Policy Forum: Children and Violence Conference.

Family Services Research Center. 1996. Multisystemic Therapy Using Home-based Services. Charleston, South Carolina: Medical University of South Carolina, Department of Psychiatry and Behavioral Sciences.

Globus, A. 1997. Forensic psychiatrist. Presentation to violence panel: Abnormal temporal lobe metabolism in violent subjects: Correlation of imaging and neuropsychiatric findings. Stockton, California.

Inciardi, J. A. 1996. A Corrections-based Continuum of Effective Drug Abuse Treatment. Paper presented at the National Institute of Research in Progress Seminar Series.

Josephson Institute of Ethics. 2000. Nationwide study of 15,000 teens (results reported in numerous media accounts).

Komure, S. 1981. Follow-up Evaluation of the Cambria Program for Violent Offenders. Sacramento, California: Department of Youth Authority.

Office of Juvenile Justice and Delinquency Prevention. 1993. *Comprehensive Strategy for Serious, Violent and Chronic Juvenile Offenders*. Washington, D.C.: U.S. Department of Justice.

_____. 1998. Juvenile Court Statistics. Washington, D.C.: U.S. Department of Justice.

Platt, J. 1997. Consultant. Architectural Interface with Corrections Programming–Form Follows Function, But Does It Function? Remarks presented to a violent offender task force in Whittier, California.

Sekel, J. P. and J. K. Turner. 1980. *Institutional Violence Reduction Project*. Sacramento, California: Department of Youth Authority.

Steiner, H. 1995 and 1997. Professor of psychiatry, Stanford University School of Medicine. Assessing and Treating Serious and Violent Juvenile Offenders. Papers presented to the California Task Force to Review Juvenile Crime and the Juvenile Justice Response in San Jose, California, and a National Panel on Violent Offenders in Sacramento, California.

Witke, L., ed. 1999. *Planning and Design Guide for Secure Adult and Juvenile Facilities*. Lanham, Maryland: American Correctional Association.

Chapter Two

Six Elements That Form a Context for Staff Safety

Jesse W. Doyle
Vice President,
Youthtrack Inc.
Western Region Operations
Littleton, Colorado

One important element of maintaining an effective correctional organization is to address key staff concerns. Throughout my twenty-five-year career in juvenile corrections, one issue that has consistently concerned staff, particularly those who work the front line, is personal safety.

In times when a facility becomes unstable and the number of staff injuries begin to rise, many staff begin to look to someone other than themselves to make their environment feel safer. Whether perceived threats to safety are real, such as several documented group disturbances, or unreal, including false stories of a group disturbance or a riot that occurred five years ago in an otherwise trouble-free environment, staff look to management for answers. More often than not, management reacts to staff concerns by addressing them piecemeal. For example, if staff on a particular unit have been involved in many resident restraints and some staff have expressed concern for their safety, an immediate response may be to transfer those employees to another location or temporarily increase staffing on the unit until the problems subside.

Managers are often reactive, rather than proactive, when it comes to staff safety. Although addressing an immediate problem is a quick fix, management periodically must step back to look at staff safety from a systemic view. Managers must consider the fact that staff safety occurs within the context of the organization's total environment.

Likewise, the context for staff safety in a juvenile correctional facility is the environment in which the facility operates. The various structures that we create within the facility support all its elements, including staff safety. In this article, we discuss six elements of environmental structures that form a context for staff safety: physical plant, behavior management, staff relationship with youths, policy and procedures, supervision, and staff training.

Physical Plant

Building. The building defines structure by limiting the movement of residents within its walls. A well-designed building will enhance staff safety in

13

many ways. One example is that we may use the building's structure to separate occupants into small groups, which will reduce contagion behavior that may occur when an isolated incident affects the larger groups. In a dormitory type situation, even a small disturbance can lead to everyone in the dormitory getting involved. We can use living quarters with individual rooms to isolate residents. On the other hand, a poorly designed building may diminish staff safety. If the building is designed with blind spots, inmates may conspire away from staff supervision behind blind corners or walls that are not designed with a good sight line. Staff also can be isolated and overpowered in places where blind spots exist. Many older institutions were inadvertently designed with blind spots.

Security system. In this section, we describe the physical security system as part of the physical plant because it generally is attached to the building's structure. These devices extend the listening and viewing range of security personnel. Visual and audio equipment can enhance staff safety by adding an additional pair of eyes and ears to a work area. The presence of video cameras allows staff to monitor inmate activities in real time. As a result, they can reduce their response time during emergencies.

Perimeter barriers. Whether a wall or a fence, a perimeter barrier keeps residents in a defined space and keeps out unwanted intruders. Perimeter barriers define the spatial limits of those enclosed by the defined physical boundaries. The barriers greatly reduce attempted escapes, while reducing the chance that staff will get hurt running after and stopping attempted escapees.

Rooms, doors, and locks. Rooms, doors, and locks serve as limited defined structural barriers. As with perimeter barriers, doors and locks help keep inmates in and intruders out. For safety, doors and locks protect staff from out-of-control residents. When used wisely, they help to modify residents' behavior and help them conform to social standards espoused in their environment.

Behavior management system. A behavior management system helps structure the juveniles' or inmates' environment and achieve desired outcomes. A behavior management system gives its participants rewards for socially accepted behavior. A good system provides clear guidelines for socially acceptable behavior and provides rewards to reinforce expected behavior. When residents buy into the behavior management system, they learn to delay gratification to achieve external rewards. Their ability to repeatedly delay immediate gratification lays the groundwork for self-discipline, which will lead to an ordered way of life once they internalize discipline.

Behavior management systems help improve staff safety by having juveniles take part in their own behavior control. In a well-implemented system, the authority of all staff to authorize desired rewards for positive behavior equalizes their worth across the board. This means that regardless of the staff member, staff has an equal opportunity to authorize rewards and sanctions as stated in the behavior management system.

Long ago, when people entered the juvenile corrections field, we interviewed them and gave them start dates. When they first reported to work, we gave them keys and directions to a residential unit, which did not have a behavior management system. All too often in such an environment, a person's success depended on his or her size and physical prowess. What counted was the ability to stand up to youths and, if necessary, overpower them if they got out of control. For the people who did not have brute strength or street skills, their authority and value were limited.

During that time, a well-implemented behavior management system would have been beneficial. Staff gained value by virtue of the organization. We increase staff safety when residents view them as having value. Further, the tangible and intangible rewards given to residents support a stable environmental structure.

Staff and resident relationships. The structure of staff relationships with the juvenile offenders in their care is the most critical component for staff safety in a juvenile corrections environment. Unlike the adult system, in which an abundance of aids supports the structure of the environment, such as cell extraction devices, and weapons, such as stun guns, we exclude the juvenile system, often by law or public mandate, from using many such items. They also do not use lethal weapons, such as firearms, and although the use of chemicals, such as pepper spray, is on the rise throughout the country, a small minority of organizations allows the use of such agents.

For the most part, juvenile corrections staff must depend on their relationships with offenders to create a safe environment for themselves and others. Healthy relationships between staff and juveniles form the basis of a safe and secure environment. No matter how much correctional knowledge staff has, they must be able to generate the warmth and strength needed to make contact with juveniles. Most juveniles will gravitate toward their peer group and bond with staff if staff value them.

Staff can encourage juvenile offenders to value them without violating policies and procedures or personal integrity. The type of relationship staff form with the juveniles depends on the role the individual staff members play—the expected behavior they agreed to display when they were hired. The operational idea is the appropriateness of behavior.

How do staff behave in a juvenile corrections setting? As soon as the juveniles meet staff, they begin to define their relationship with staff in their environment. The juveniles determine what we expect of them and if they would be able to "get one over" on staff.

As juveniles increase their interactions with staff, their uncertainty diminishes as they receive feedback from staff and their peers. Exchange of information between staff and juveniles clarifies and structures the relationship accordingly. Staff often develop relationships based on role behavior. For example, a juvenile may ask a staff member to make a phone call. Although the staff member knows the youth does not deserve the privilege, he or she will allow it based on fear or an inability to handle conflict. As a result, the staff member has acted "out of role" or outside the expected behavior associated with his or her position. As actors learn roles in theatrical productions,

15

staff can teach juveniles how to function as members of a juvenile corrections institution.

Correctional staff must treat juveniles with respect, dignity, and compassion. Simultaneously, they must set appropriate limits and enforce the organization's rules and procedures. When staff enforce expected roles for juveniles and treat them with respect, they make it possible for youths to conform to rules and behave even before they can understand and control their behavior. For example, a youth may not understand the value of an education but may attend a class because he or she has a friendly relationship with a supervising staff member. We cannot understate the importance of relationships in juvenile corrections settings.

Unfortunately, some staff are verbally and physically abusive to juveniles throughout their stays in institutions. Those people wonder why the juveniles return the abuse whenever given the opportunity. For example, a staff member in a juvenile correctional facility complained during a staff meeting that he feared for his safety in the community. He said he had encountered several juveniles whom he had supervised before they were released. He explained that the juveniles had accosted him outside a store, shouted expletives at him, and reminded him of how he treated them while they were in custody. Although several other staff members stated they had positive experiences with juveniles they ran into outside the facility, this staff member refused to acknowledge that his treatment of the juveniles inside the facility had a direct bearing on their attitudes toward him in the community.

Staff's role is to set boundaries for juveniles and to hold them responsible for their behavior while maintaining a safe environment, which must be done humanely and with caring. Staff must discipline the juveniles, but they also can help the youths acquire new skills that will help them be successful in the facility and eventually in the community.

Another staff role is to help juveniles develop confidence. Staff who model appropriate behavior for youths to emulate help youths embrace the organization's way of life and follow its values. The development of interpersonal competencies helps youths negotiate their needs. As juveniles increasingly meet their needs because of their interpersonal competence, they are less likely to risk their gains by going against facility norms. Youths need a sense of worth and belonging, and values clarification—a sense of right and wrong.

Experiences with staff and other youths influence and shape their behavior along with attitudes about themselves and others. The experience teaches youths how to be responsible and relate to others in their environment, both adults and peers. When staff relate to juveniles positively by setting limits and demonstrating fairness, consistency, and caring, juveniles develop healthy interpersonal skills which lead to competence. Competence leads to confidence and confidence helps youths try newly learned skills. Acquisition of skills begets more competence and confidence and leads to increased skill acquisition. When staff develop relationships with juveniles that reinforce this cyclical process, they help to create and maintain a safe environment for themselves and everyone around them.

Policies and Procedures

Every organization must develop policies and procedures to maintain a standard for consistent implementation of rules and regulations. A policies and procedures manual provides staff with a systematic method for carrying out the mission, goals, and objectives of the organization. Policies reflect organization philosophy, provide a framework and structure for the activities of the facility, and guide decision making. Procedures determine the tasks which will be completed, define who will carry out the tasks and when we will start them, and provide the step-by-step process of how to complete the policy. It also ensures conformity in the organization. Further, a policies and procedures manual is the authority on how things are done, eliminating guesswork. Policies and procedures provide structure to the organization by minimizing potential conflicts among staff. For example, each staff member brings a different set of values, beliefs, and behaviors to the job. Without the guidance provided by policies and procedures, staff are left to make their own varied decisions. They begin to create their own rules and behaviors. This situation creates the perfect environment for juveniles to manipulate staff and eventually leads to unsafe conditions. Clear and consistent communication between staff and juveniles is essential. Clearly written, thoughtful, thorough, and consistently implemented policies and procedures enhance the opportunity for safe conditions.

Supervision and Training

Effective supervisors must reflect a guiding vision, strong values, and organizational beliefs. Their job is to remind staff of the rules needed to shape their behavior for their benefit and the organization's. The supervisor must consistently and clearly communicate what the system requires to maintain its structure, form, and stability. This task is deceptively simple: It is easy to articulate but difficult to carry out. For example, in many organizations, each time a crisis occurs, the tendency is to create a new policy or change parts of the system.

In most cases, when we complete an in-depth review of a crisis, we see that it is not the lack of written policies that created the crisis. Instead, it is the failure of supervisors to effectively and consistently direct staff to carry out system processes. Before an organization can move forward, it must have an adequate number of well-trained staff and supervisors, particularly at critical junctures, such as the nexus between front-line staff and first-line supervisors.

Effective recruitment is the best way to develop a well-trained staff. If we hire self-centered, ill-tempered, abusive people, no amount of training will make them effective. After we carefully screen and hire them, we must train

17

them. First, we must complete a proper assessment of the knowledge, skills, and abilities needed for juvenile corrections. Once we have figured out training needs, we have found that use of adjunct trainers from the organization's various disciplines is effective.

Classroom training enables staff to gain knowledge and, to a smaller degree, skills and abilities, but it does not fully prepare them for the day-to-day events they will face when placed in the actual workplace. The dilemma is how do staff transfer learning in the classroom to practical application?

Two methods used to transfer learning are on-the-job training and direct supervision. On-the-job training allows staff to complete tasks under the supervision of more experienced staff and receive direct feedback. Also, it allows them to observe the more experienced staff. For the organization to work well, it must generate replication. On-the-job training and continuous supervision help to support this process.

Conclusion

When we develop large organizational structures as a context for staff safety, staff are able to look at emerging themes and patterns and isolated causes. Viewed this way, they begin to see how multiple forces work together to shape the organization. Effective implementation of the structures of the organization is an integral part of its safety. When we design and put effective structures in place, the organization replicates itself on all levels. Setting up systems to develop structures helps staff come together in their various disciplines to perform their jobs effectively and efficiently. It also creates a context for staff safety.

References

Wheatley, Margaret J. 1992. *Leadership and the New Science*. San Francisco: Clear Communication/The Graphic Solution.

Chapter Three

Overrepresentation of Youth with Disabilities in Corrections

Robert B. Rutherford Jr., Ph.D.
Professor of Special Education and Associate Director of
Research and Graduate Programs in Curriculum and Instruction
Arizona State University

Mary Magee Quinn, Ph.D.
Senior Research Analyst
American Institutes for Research
Washington, D.C.

Jeffrey Poirier
American Institutes for Research
Washington, D.C.

Lili Garfinkel,
PACER Center
Minneapolis, Minnesota

Children and youths with disabilities are those whose intellectual, physical, learning, emotional, and academic-skill deficits are significant enough to entitle them to special education services. The Education for All Handicapped Children Act (PL-94-194, 1975), and subsequently the Individuals with Disabilities Education Act (IDEA, 1997), mandate that all disabled individuals under the age of twenty-two have the right to a free and appropriate public education adapted to meet their individual needs. Furthermore, juveniles and youthful offenders with disabilities in the justice system are guaranteed special education services in accordance with IDEA, the Americans with Disabilities Act (ADA, 1990), Section 504 of the Rehabilitation Act of 1973, the Fourteenth Amendment to the U.S. Constitution, and various state laws (Rutherford, Griller-Clark, and Anderson, 2001).

Prevalence estimates vary considerably with regard to the number of youths with special education disabilities who are in corrections. Rutherford, Nelson, and Wolford (1985), in a national survey of state directors of juvenile and adult correctional education, found an overall estimated prevalence rate for youths with learning disabilities, emotional disturbance, and mental retardation of 24 percent of the incarcerated population. The variation of state estimates of special education students as a percent of the total incarcerated population, however, ranged from 4 to 99 percent for juvenile corrections and 1 to 84 percent for youthful offenders in adult corrections. This tremendous

19

variation in estimates of the number of offenders with disabilities, coupled with the fact that state education directors of seven juvenile systems and nineteen adult systems failed to identify any inmates with disabilities, suggests that the actual number of special education students in corrections in the United States has not been determined.

Edgar and Hayden (1985) suggest that between 7 and 10 percent of all children and youths in public education can be considered to have some type of special education disability. Bullock and McArthur (1994) contend that the prevalence of special education disabilities in corrections typically is four to five times greater than the rate of special education disabilities in the general population. Therefore, it follows that somewhere between 30 and 50 percent of youths in the correctional system have a special education disability. This extrapolation is roughly congruent with studies that estimate that between 20 and 60 percent of youths in juvenile and adult correctional facilities are disabled (Fejes-Mendoza and Rutherford, 1987; Hugo and Rutherford, 1992; Lewis, Schwartz, and Ianacone, 1988; Murphy, 1986).

The variability in identifying and labeling offenders with disabilities limits the conclusions that may be drawn from existing prevalence rates (Bullock and McArthur, 1994). In fact, because of the problems noted above, the rates reported in the professional literature may actually understate the prevalence of disabilities among incarcerated youths (Leone, 1994; Warboys, Burrell, Peters, and Ramiu, 1994).

Although the full range of disabilities exists among youths placed in the correctional system, by far the most common special education conditions are specific learning disabilities, emotional disturbance, and mental retardation (Nelson, Rutherford, and Wolford, 1987; Rutherford and Wolford, 1992).

Prevalence of specific learning disabilities in the general population. Currently more students in the public school system are identified as having specific learning disabilities than those in any other special education category. The U.S. Department of Education (1999) reports that during the 1997-98 school year, more than 5.4 million children, ages six through twenty-one, were being served nationally through special education in the public school system. Of this number, 51 percent of the children and youths received services for specific learning disabilities, compared with 19.8 percent who were being served for speech or language impairments, 11.2 percent being served for mental retardation, 8.4 percent being served for emotional disturbance, and 9.6 percent for other disabilities.

According to the Sixteenth Annual Report to Congress on the Implementation of the Individuals with Disabilities Education Act (U.S. Department of Education, 1994), 10 percent of school-age children were identified as disabled, and more than 50 percent of the total disabled population had specific learning disabilities. During the last two decades, the number of students identified as learning disabled has increased substantially.

Prevalence of specific learning disabilities among youths in the justice system. Studies on the prevalence of youth with special education disabilities in the correctional system demonstrate that there has been great variance in prevalence estimates of persons with learning disabilities in the correctional system. Morgan (1979), in a survey of administrators from 204 state juvenile correctional facilities, found the overall prevalence rate of learning disabilities to be 10.59 percent. Nelson and Rutherford (1989), however, reported the percentage of learning disabled students in special education programs in juvenile corrections ranged from 9 to 76 percent. Furthermore, Casey and Keilitz (1990), in an analysis of twenty-two studies of the prevalence of specific learning disabilities among juvenile offenders, estimated a prevalence of 35.6 percent. As previously noted, a wide disparity exists in the estimated prevalence of specific learning disabilities among youths in the correctional system.

Prevalence of emotional disturbance in the general population. Estimates of the prevalence of emotional or behavioral disorders vary greatly, ranging from 0.5 percent to 20 percent or more of the school-age population (Kauffman, 1997). Kauffman (1997) contends that 3 to 6 percent of the school-aged population need specialized services because of emotional and behavioral disorders. The U.S. Department of Education (1997) reported, however, that only 0.74 percent of all students in U.S. schools were identified as emotionally disturbed.

Prevalence of emotional disturbance among youth in the justice system. Even though there is no direct relationship between emotional disturbance and delinquency, a large number of delinquents and youthful offenders are diagnosed as having a serious emotional disturbance. Morgan's (1979) survey of 204 correctional administrators showed that 16 percent of juvenile offenders in custody at that time were identified as emotionally disturbed. Warboys, et al. (1994) reported that the estimated prevalence of emotional and behavioral disorders is 20 percent in the juvenile offender population. Other studies have provided varied estimates of the prevalence of emotional disturbance in juvenile offenders. Murphy (1986), for example, reported a rate of emotional disturbance in juvenile corrections between 16 and 50 percent of the incarcerated population.

Youths who are adjudicated tend to exhibit more emotional and behavioral disorders than individuals who do not come under the purview of the criminal justice system (Bullis and Walker, 1995; Rutherford, et al., 1985). Rutherford and Wolford (1992) posit that the overrepresentation of youths with emotional disturbance in the correctional system is a result of the fact that those who exhibit antisocial or acting-out behaviors are more likely to come into contact with the juvenile or adult criminal justice system. A number of characteristics of delinquent youths are strongly correlated with emotional disturbance. These characteristics include: substance abuse; school failure and dropping out; low verbal intelligence; family reliance on welfare or poor management of income; single parent families (or lack of male parent in the home); overcrowded or chaotic homes; erratic and inadequate parental supervision; parental or sibling indifference or hostility toward the youth; parental history of mental illness; and having a parent or sibling in the corrections system (Kauffman, 1997; McIntyre, 1993).

Prevalence of mental retardation in the general population. The prevalence of mental retardation in the general population is reported to be between 1 and 3 percent. Differing prevalence rates depend on the definition of mental retardation used, the method of assessment, the population studied, the age of the population, and the severity of mental retardation. More individuals are identified with mental retardation between the ages of ten and fourteen years than after adolescence and the prevalence of mental retardation decreases as the severity increases. More individuals are diagnosed with mild mental retardation than severe and profound retardation. While most published studies define mental retardation strictly by IQ, more recent definitions of mental retardation focus on adaptive behavior, the developmental period, and systems of support and intellectual functioning. Estimates using this expanded definition report the prevalence of mental retardation to be 1.61 percent of the school-age population (Sikorski, 1991).

Prevalence of mental retardation among youth in the justice system. Offenders with mild to moderate mental retardation have historically been overrepresented in the criminal justice system. Individuals with severe and profound developmental disabilities, on the other hand, are unlikely to have the opportunity to commit criminal offenses and be incarcerated and, if arrested, are rarely found in correctional facilities because they are diverted to community and residential programs (Nelson, 1987).

Santamour and West (1979) found that the prevalence of mild to moderate mental retardation in corrections was three times that found in the general population. Morgan (1979) found a similar prevalence rate of 9.5 percent in state correctional facilities, based on the criterion of "significantly sub average general intellectual functioning existing concurrently with deficits in adaptive behavior." More recently, an analysis of the literature on the prevalence of juvenile offenders with disabilities found the overall weighted prevalence estimate for offenders with mental retardation to be 12.6 percent (Casey and Keilitz, 1990). Other studies estimate the prevalence rate of offenders with mental retardation to be between 6 and 8 percent of the incarcerated population (Day and Joyce, 1982; Prescott and Van Houten, 1982; Warboys, et al., 1994).

The difference between the rate of mental retardation in society as a whole versus the rate of mental retardation in the juvenile and adult correctional system has ignited concern in the form of legislation, standards, and greater attention to the issue, and has provided some education and treatment support for offenders with mental retardation. However, Santamour (1987) contends that the majority of individuals with mental retardation who encounter the criminal justice system still suffer gross injustice. He states, " . . . people with mental retardation are more likely than those without retardation to be arrested, to be convicted, to be sentenced to prison, and to be victimized in prison" (p. 106).

Compared with disability prevalence figures in the general population, a disproportionate number of adults and youths with these disabilities are in the correctional system. Any effort to establish accurate prevalence rates requires an examination of a census of youth with disabilities already in custody. States are required to report special education census data to the federal government on a yearly basis. Establishing a national census of youths with disabilities who are in custody could eliminate the wide-ranging prevalence estimates found in the literature. Replacing estimates (Rutherford et al., 1985) with actual figures should minimize difficulties in determining the resources to be allocated based on the number of youths with disabilities in custody and sharpen national plans for specific intervention initiatives to these populations. Over time, yearly census data should reflect changes and improvements in identifying and serving youths with disabilities.

Conclusion

The reasons for the discrepancies between the numbers of youths with disabilities served in correctional education programs and disability prevalence estimates may be due to a number of factors. These include: inconsistent definitions of disabilities; inadequate special education screening and assessment procedures available in correctional facilities; reluctance to identify offenders with disabilities as a result of inadequate staffing and funding for special education; inability to implement effective special education programs in correctional settings (Foley, 2001); and failure to obtain, and/or difficulty in obtaining, prior school records to determine the presence of a special education label (Leone, 1994; Leone, Rutherford, and Nelson, 1991; Rutherford, Bullis, Anderson, Griller-Clark, in press; Rutherford et al., 1985).

Awareness of these statistics, and acknowledgment of the issues surrounding the overrepresentation of youths with disabilities placed in the correctional system, are not enough to serve these individuals effectively. There is considerable work to be done to improve the services designed to prevent youths with disabilities from entering the justice system, provide appropriate special education and related services to youths while they are in custody, and provide for effective transition and aftercare services when they return to their communities. The information presented here is critical for system-level administrative planning, personnel recruitment, and structuring intervention programs for youths with disabilities.

References

Bullis, M., and H. M. Walker. 1995. Characteristics and Causal Factors of Troubled Youth. In C. M. Nelson, B. I. Wolford, and R. B. Rutherford, eds. *Comprehensive and Collaborative Systems that Work for Troubled Youth: A National Agenda*, pp. 15-28. Richmond, Kentucky: National Coalition for Juvenile Justice Services.

Bullock, L. M. and P. McArthur. 1994. Correctional Special Education: Disability Prevalence Estimates and Teacher Preparation Programs. *Education and Treatment of Children*. 17: 347-355.

Casey, K. and I. Keilitz. 1990. Estimating the Prevalence of Learning Disabled and Mentally Retarded Juvenile Offenders: A Meta-analysis. In P. E. Leone, ed. *Understanding Troubled and Troubling Youth*, pp. 82-101. Newbury Park, California: Sage Publications.

Day, E. and K. Joyce. 1982. Mentally Retarded Youth in Cuyahoga County Juvenile Court: Juvenile Court Work Research Group. In M. B. Santamour and P. S. Watson, eds. *The Retarded Offender*, pp. 141-165. New York: Praeger.

Edgar, E. and A. M. Hayden. 1985. Who Are the Children Special Education Should Serve: And How Many Such Children Are There? *Journal of Special Education*. 18: 523-539.

Fejes-Mendoza, K. and R. B. Rutherford. 1987. Learning Handicapped and Non-learning Handicapped Female Juvenile Offenders' Education and Criminal Profiles. *Journal of Correctional Education*. 38: 148-153.

Foley, R. M. 2001. Academic Characteristics of Incarcerated Youth and Correctional Educational Programs: A Literature Review. *Journal of Emotional and Behavioral Disorders*. 94: 248-259.

Gaddes, W. H. and D. Edgell. 1993. *Learning Disabilities and Brain Function, 3rd ed*. New York: Springer-Verlag.

Hugo, K. E. and R. B. Rutherford. 1992. Issues in Identifying Educational Disabilities among Female Juvenile Offenders. *Journal of Correctional Education*. 43: 124-127.

Individuals with Disabilities Education Act Amendments. 1997. P.L. 105-17.

Kauffman, J. M. 1997. *Characteristics of Emotional and Behavioral Disorders of Children and Youth, 6th ed*. Upper Saddle River, New Jersey: Prentice-Hall.

Leone, P. E. 1994. Education Services for Youth with Disabilities in a State-operated Juvenile Correctional System: Case Study and Analysis. *Journal of Special Education*. 28: 1, 43-58.

Leone, P. E., R. B. Rutherford, and C. M. Nelson. 1991. *Special Education in Juvenile Corrections*. Reston, Virginia: Council for Exceptional Children.

Lewis, K. S., G. M. Schwartz, and R. N. Ianacone. 1988. Service Coordination Between Correctional and Public School Systems for Handicapped Juvenile Offenders. *Exceptional Children*. 55: 66-70.

McIntyre, T. 1993. Behaviorally Disordered Youth in Correctional Settings: Prevalence, Programming, and Teacher Training. *Behavioral Disorders*. 183: 167-176.

Morgan, D. I. 1979. Prevalence and Types of Handicapping Conditions Found in Juvenile Correctional Institutions: A National Survey. *Journal of Special Education*. 13: 283-295.

Murphy, D. M. 1986. The Prevalence of Handicapping Conditions among Juvenile Delinquents. *Remedial and Special Education*. 73: 7-17.

Nelson, C. M. 1987. Handicapped Offenders in the Criminal Justice System. In C. M. Nelson, R. B. Rutherford, and B. I. Wolford, eds. *Special Education in the Criminal Justice System*, pp. 2-17. Columbus, Ohio: Merrill.

Nelson, C. M. and R. B. Rutherford. 1989. September. Impact of the Correctional Special Education Training C/SET Project on Correctional Special Education. Paper presented at the CEC/CCBD National Topical Conference on Behavioral Disorders, Charlotte, North Carolina.

Nelson, C. M., R. B. Rutherford, and B. I. Wolford, eds. 1987. *Special Education in the Criminal Justice System*. Columbus, Ohio: Merrill.

Prescott, M. and E. Van Houten. 1982. The Retarded Juvenile Offender in New Jersey: A Report on Research in Correctional Facilities and Mental Retardation Facilities. In M. B. Santamour and P. S. Watson, eds. *The Retarded Offender*, pp. 166-175. New York: Praeger.

Quinn, M. M., R. B. Rutherford, B. I. Wolford, P. E. Leone, and C. M. Nelson. In press. The Prevalence of Students with Disabilities in Juvenile and Adult Corrections. *ERIC Digest*. Arlington, Virginia: Council for Exceptional Children.

Rutherford, R. B., M. Bullis, C. W. Anderson, and H. M. Griller-Clark. In press. *Youth with Disabilities in the Correctional System: Prevalence Rates and Identification Issues*. Washington, D.C.: American Institutes for Research.

Rutherford, R. B., H. M. Griller-Clark, and C. W. Anderson. Treating Offenders with Educational Disabilities. In J. B. Ashford, B. D. Sales, and W. H. Reid, eds. *Treating Adult and Juvenile Offenders with Special Needs*. pp. 221-245. Washington, D.C.: American Psychological Association.

Rutherford, R. B., C. M. Nelson, and B. I. Wolford. 1985. Special Education in the Most Restrictive Environment: Correctional/Special Education. *Journal of Special Education*. 19: 59-71.

Rutherford, R. B. and B. I. Wolford. 1992. Handicapped Youthful Offenders. In L. M. Bullock, ed. *Exceptionalities in Children and Youth*. pp. 196-219. Needham Heights, Massachusetts: Allyn and Bacon.

Santamour, M. B. 1987. The Criminal Justice System. In C. M. Nelson, R. B. Rutherford, and B. I. Wolford, eds. *The Mentally Retarded Offender*. pp.106-118. Columbus, Ohio: Merrill.

Santamour, M. B. and B. West. 1979. *Retardation and Criminal Justice: A Training Manual for Criminal Justice Personnel*. Washington, D.C.: President's Committee on Mental Retardation and the New Jersey Association for Retarded Citizens.

Sikorski, J. B. 1991. Learning Disorders and the Juvenile Justice System. *Psychiatric Annals*. 2112: 742-747.

U.S. Department of Education. 1994. *16th Annual Report to Congress on the Implementation of the Individuals with Disabilities Education Act*. Washington, D.C.: U.S. Department of Education.

_____. 1997. *To Assure the Free Appropriate Public Education of All Children with Disabilities. 19 th Annual Report to Congress on the Implementation of the Individuals with Disabilities Education Act.* Washington, D.C.: U.S. Department of Education.

_____. 1999. *To Assure the Free Appropriate Public Education of All Children with Disabilities. 21st Annual Report to Congress on the implementation of the Individuals with Disabilities Education Act.* Washington, D.C.: U.S. Department of Education.

Warboys, L. M., S. Burrell, C. Peters, and M. Ramiu. 1994. *California Juvenile Court Special Education Manual.* San Francisco, California: Youth Law Center.

Chapter Four

Civil Rights in Juvenile Correctional Facilities

Steven H. Rosenbaum[1]
Chief, Special Litigation Section, Civil Rights Division
U.S. Department of Justice
Washington, D.C.

Introduction

The Civil Rights Division of the U.S. Department of Justice enforces civil rights laws in juvenile detention and corrections systems. During our enforcement activities, we have identified major, recurring problems in juvenile facilities. This chapter focuses on the recurring problems we have seen in troubled juvenile institutions. These problems concern: 1) crowding; 2) the special needs presented by juveniles who are young or who have a mental illness or mental retardation; 3) the increased use of adult correctional models in juvenile facilities; and 4) the wide range of educational needs among incarcerated youths. Then, we discuss some remedies that have been implemented to address these problems.

Enforcement Authority

Congress has authorized the Department of Justice to protect the federal rights of youths in juvenile detention and correctional facilities. In particular, the Department enforces the Civil Rights of Institutionalized Persons Act (often called "CRIPA" for short), 42 U.S.C. § 1997, a statute Congress has called "the single most effective method for redressing systemic deprivations of institutionalized persons' Constitutional and Federal Statutory rights."[2] The Justice Department also enforces a provision of the 1994 Violent Crime Control and Law Enforcement Act that authorizes the Attorney General to sue to correct a pattern or practice of violations of juveniles' federal rights by juvenile justice administrators. 42 U.S.C. § 14141. The Attorney General has delegated the authority to enforce both provisions to the Special Litigation Section of the Civil Rights Division.[3]

In the twenty-one years since Congress enacted CRIPA, the Special Litigation Section has investigated more than 100 juvenile correctional facilities in 17 states, and the Commonwealths of Puerto Rico and the Northern Mariana Islands. Most of these investigations have taken place in just the last seven years and have been resolved without contested litigation. Kentucky's successful implementation of its settlement covering all of its juvenile facilities resulted in the termination of the settlement and dismissal of the litigation in 2000. We are now monitoring settlements concerning juvenile facilities in Georgia, Louisiana, Puerto Rico, and the Northern Mariana Islands and have ongoing investigations of a handful of juvenile correctional facilities.

In enforcing the federal rights of incarcerated juveniles, we generally focus on three sources of federal rights: the Constitution; the Americans with Disabilities Act, 42 U.S.C. § 12132; and the Individuals with Disabilities Education Act, 20 U.S.C. § 1401 *et seq.*

Under these legal standards, juveniles are entitled to reasonable safety—including protection from juvenile-on-juvenile violence and abuse or excessive force by staff—and adequate medical and mental health care. They are also entitled to reasonable rehabilitative treatment to fulfill the purpose for which they were committed. For certain juveniles with special needs, federal law requires reasonable accommodations in physical plant and programming, including education, to enable those juveniles with disabilities to benefit from school and other programs. To ensure that these rights are realized, juveniles must have adequate access to the courts, their lawyers, and their families.

We do not view ourselves as adversaries of those who administer the facilities and systems we investigate. We recognize that working with troubled adolescents is difficult, even under the best of circumstances, and many systems operate under circumstances that are far from ideal. Some systems are increasingly crowded, stretching resources thin. For many institutions, finding and keeping qualified professional and other staff can be challenging, especially in more remote settings. Juveniles are entering facilities with a multiplicity of problems, including drug and alcohol addiction, mental illness, histories of sexual and physical abuse, deteriorated families, and lifelong exposure to violence and crime. Society asks institutions to maintain order, yet protect juveniles from each other and from excessive force; to treat juveniles fairly; and to provide negative consequences for delinquent behavior while also providing rehabilitative services, all within fiscal austerity.

We are aware of these challenges institutions face. When Special Litigation Section attorneys and experts go into a juvenile facility, we do not go in pointing fingers. We do not go in expecting perfection, looking for problems, or trying to find someone to blame. We go in with an appreciation, built up over the many years we have done this work, for the difficulties of the job, and with a deep respect for those who do it well.

In fact, it has been our experience that quite often administrators view our investigations and subsequent involvement as an opportunity. We regularly encounter administrators who want to run better facilities. However, they require the resources, technical assistance, or the focused attention or commitment of government officials at higher levels of the jurisdiction's government, to do so. Our investigations, findings, and the subsequent dialog are helpful in focusing attention on important issues, helping administrators in making the case for additional resources, and outside expertise and assistance in improving their programs and facilities.

In practice, we attempt to reach an agreement with the jurisdiction about how to correct any problem we find during our investigation before we ever resort to litigation. We view this process as joint problem solving for a common purpose. State authorities often voluntarily comply with the remedies we suggest. When we see steady improvement and genuine effort, we will continue to work with the state. As a result, most CRIPA matters end before contested litigation ever begins.

Recurring Problems

In the past few years, we have investigated and worked with administrators in many juvenile justice facilities and several states. These investigations have ranged from single facilities to statewide systems, from 30-bed detention centers to 700-bed training schools. Each facility is different, but many institutions face similar problems so that we can make a few generalizations about the common challenges we see administrators facing. In particular, major issues we see repeated in troubled institutions concern crowding, special needs populations (especially juveniles who are very young, mentally ill, or mentally retarded), the increased use of adult correctional practices in juvenile facilities, and education.

Crowding

Most systems have increased the number of juveniles they must serve, and many detention facilities have had a dramatic increase in admissions.[4] This is likely due, in part, to an increased recourse to the juvenile justice system in response to the behavior of troubled adolescents. It may also be related to the diminishing capacity of other social service institutions, particularly mental health providers and those who provide services to troubled families in the community. Those systems that have experienced significant population increases have suffered from a variety of problems associated with crowding.

Increased population leads, most obviously, to physical plant capacity problems. As a result, we have been in facilities where three, four, or even five juveniles are sleeping in rooms designed for one or two. This leads not only to sometimes unsanitary conditions, but also to severe problems providing adequate supervision to the juveniles.

An additional effect of crowding results in difficulties in implementing a classification system to separate vulnerable juveniles from those who may harm them. Such failures of classification can, and do, lead to instances of unobserved, preventable physical or sexual abuse. For example, in one detention facility, authorities had housed a youth being held for violation of probation with three youths accused of armed robbery and aggravated assault and the youth was beaten and sexually assaulted without intervention by staff.

Crowding stretches thin all the resources of a facility. Classrooms become crowded, often leading to difficulties in controlling behavior and to teachers facing a wide range of academic abilities and needs within a single class. Frequently, when staffing does not keep pace with population, administrators ask direct care staff to monitor ever-increasing numbers of juveniles. Their job is made more difficult when the density and other effects of crowding lead to increased irritability and conflict among the youths. The pressures of the job often lead to extremely high turnover and additional strain on training and oversight.

Special Needs Juveniles

A second area of concern is the demographics of the populations in juvenile facilities. On the one hand, we ask facilities to serve many juveniles who have committed violent acts. At the same time, a large segment of the population in many facilities is composed of younger juveniles and juveniles with relatively minor offenses. On average, only one-quarter of the juveniles in any system have committed violent offenses.[5]

This diverse population results in a need for adequate classification and a variety of programming. This is especially true for those juveniles with many special needs. Systems experiencing a growth in population are especially likely to see an increase in the number of juveniles with relatively rare conditions and needs. This includes juveniles with serious chronic health conditions (such as diabetes, asthma, and sickle cell disease) or mental illness. It also includes other populations with needs that are simply different from the general population for whom most programs have been developed (such as very young youths and girls). Failing to provide for the special needs of these populations in some cases can result in great harm. For example, failure to identify asthmatics and assess the health risks in a boot camp can lead to life-threatening consequences. Failure to identify and adequately address mental illness often leads to suicide attempts, self-mutilation, and serious behavior problems.

As a result, it is increasingly important for juvenile justice systems to have a systematic intake process. This process should identify the full range of medical, mental health, educational, and other needs and problems of the juveniles placed in its custody. Once authorities identify these needs, juvenile systems must have in place a means to provide adequate care based on the individualized needs of the juvenile. Many problems in juvenile facilities relate to failures to address these special populations adequately. Two, in particular, are worth mentioning.

Young Juveniles. We have found that a growing number of incarcerated juveniles are fourteen years old or younger. We have encountered juveniles as young as nine in secure facilities, often held for minor offenses that would not ordinarily result in secure incarceration. In one investigation, we encountered a very small eleven-year-old boy who was being detained for threatening his fifth grade teacher; a twelve-year-old boy with a seizure disorder incarcerated for making a harassing phone call; a fourteen-year-old girl in secure detention for painting graffiti on a wall; a thirteen-year-old girl who had stolen $127 from her mother's purse; and many children who had run away from troubled homes. Often the decision to place these juveniles in a secure facility reflects the lack of other alternative options, rather than a judgment on the true security risk of the child.

At other times, these very young juveniles have often found their way into secure incarceration because of unusually serious emotional and behavioral problems, frequently after traditional alternative attempts to respond to their behavior have failed. Direct care staff often find these children the most difficult. As a result, all too often these young residents are inappropriately subject to isolation, restraint, use of force, injuries, and exclusion from school.

They are also at increased significant risk for mental health problems and suicide. For example, in one detention facility, we met a thirteen-year-old girl with a history of running away from home because her mother's boyfriend sexually molested her. She was being held after charges were filed against her for breaking a window screen in a group home and attempting to kick a staff member. She had been held in the detention facility for almost a month when our staff met her. The legal justification for holding her was the lack of a suitable parent or other custodian to supervise her pending her hearing. While incarcerated, she suffered from serious depression and had nearly succeeded in committing suicide the morning of the day we met her.

We know that not only do adolescents think and act differently than adults, but very young teenagers think and act differently than older teenagers. The failure to account for those differences, either through the maintenance of appropriate alternative placements, creation of placements specifically for younger children, or through modification of programming and operations, can lead to persistent and serious violations of those juveniles' rights.

Juveniles with Mental Illness or Mental Retardation. Juveniles with mental illness or mental retardation also have special needs. The number of juveniles with mental illness or other significant mental health needs in juvenile facilities nationally is difficult to decide (*see* Rutherford et al., in this volume). One federally funded study found that 60 percent of incarcerated juveniles had a diagnosable mental health disorder, while 20 percent had severe psychological disorders.[6] Whatever the particular numbers, sizable portions of youth in juvenile facilities have significant mental health needs. An adequate mental health system in a juvenile facility must identify youth with mental disabilities, provide treatment to them, keep them from harming themselves or others, and protect them from abuse. The system must ensure that they receive necessary accommodations to enable them to benefit from programs offered at the facility. We frequently find deficiencies in all five areas.

Not every mental disability is immediately identifiable by correctional staff in a juvenile facility. Qualified professionals should systematically evaluate juveniles' mental health needs. This must happen to facilitate appropriate professional treatment, and also to ensure that line staff can become aware of the special needs of individual juveniles and are taught appropriate responses to those needs.

Far too often, inadequately trained staff interpret predictable behavior relating to mental illness or mental retardation as disobedience, defiance, or even threats. Staff respond with anger, discipline, or even force—even though other interventions could have defused the situation.

For example, during one of our investigations, we encountered a youth with a history of psychiatric hospitalizations and self-injury (such as placing staples in his eyes). In one incident, he had been placed in shackles for two and a half hours as punishment for misbehavior in a security unit. When he managed to escape from the cuffs, staff physically subdued him and put the handcuffs back on. He continued to act up, was forcibly restrained, given a shot of Thorazine, then placed back in handcuffs and shackles. When he began to kick the door, staff sprayed him with OC spray. They then showered and put him in the isolation room, where he continued to beat his head against the wall until staff placed him in a straight jacket and helmet. Yet, at no time during or after this incident did a mental health professional visit the youth. Instead, staff who may not have even understood that the youth had a mental health condition treated all of his behavior with correctional responses.

We have seen youths with mental retardation wash out of short-term boot camp programs because they could not comply with staff's compound orders. Staff have interpreted the juveniles' inability to comply with orders as defiance. This staff probably did not understand the needs of youths with mental retardation or, more fundamentally, did not even know that they were working with youths with mental retardation. Youths who fail out of these short-term programs typically end up spending longer sentences in juvenile facilities as a direct result of their disabilities.

Punishing a juvenile for behavior caused by a mental disability is wrong. And expecting correctional officers to supervise juveniles with mental disabilities in appropriate ways is wrong if we have not trained them how to do so.

Moreover, once a mental health need has been identified, it is not enough simply to have a psychiatrist who rarely visits the facility prescribe pyschotropic medications. Professionals must be involved in providing individualized treatment and in considering what reasonable accommodations are necessary to permit the juvenile to benefit from the services offered at the facility. We must provide juveniles with learning disabilities special education services to enable them to benefit from educational services. Juveniles with cognitive disabilities may require special assistance to benefit from substance abuse programming. Youths with severe attention deficit disorder may require accommodations in facility rules to prevent their disability from resulting in disciplinary sanctions.

When we cannot provide adequate mental health care at the facility, the juvenile system should provide alternative placements where it can be provided. Under mounting population pressures, administrators have a significant incentive to reproduce almost identical copies of existing institutions and programs. System planners, however, should recognize the need to provide a continuum of services to respond to the special needs of those who cannot receive adequate services in traditional programs.

Adult Corrections Model

Another recent trend in many juvenile systems concerns the increased use of adult models of operation in juvenile facilities. Both physically and operationally, juvenile facilities are increasingly like adult jails and prisons. From the use of razor wire and jump suits, to the use of restraint chairs and OC spray, authorities run many juvenile facilities in much the same way as prisons, despite the very different needs and legal rights of juveniles. We have found that the wholesale adoption of many adult practices without taking adequate account of the relevant differences between adults and adolescents has often resulted in operational difficulties and violations of juveniles' federal rights.

The use of extended isolation as a method of behavior control, for example, is an import from the adult system that has proven both harmful and counterproductive when applied to juveniles. It too often leads to increased incidents of depression and self-mutilation among isolated juveniles, while also exacerbating their behavior problems.

We also have confronted the use of restraint and physical management techniques designed for use in adult correctional facilities or police departments that have resulted in an increased risk of unnecessary injury to juveniles. These techniques range from tactics that are dangerous and inappropriate in any setting—such as hogtying—to tactics that impose unnecessary risk of injury and infliction of pain in the specific context of a juvenile facility.

Such tactics are especially prone to abuse when staff are not adequately trained in the differences between adult and adolescent behavior. We know that juveniles, more than adults, are prone to temporary bouts of defiance and disobedience that can be addressed through verbal interventions. But we have seen that officers trained in adult prison practices, or who come from a background of adult corrections, are often bewildered by the reactions of juveniles and by the failure of traditional correctional responses to achieve desired results. When staff are trained or allowed to resort too quicky to threats and force in the face of noncompliant adolescent behavior, minor incidents get escalated and the risk of harm increases for both the juvenile and the officer.

Many of the problems we see in juvenile facilities, particularly those running on an adult model, not only violate specific legal rights of juveniles (for example, to be free from excessive force or arbitrary discipline), but also undermine the underlying mission of the facility. Beyond missed opportunities, when security staff do not receive adequate training and supervision, the lessons taught by educators and counselors are easily diluted, if not countermanded, by daily modeling of adult behavior by correctional staff. Lessons on

33

anger management and nonviolence ring hollow when the most significant adults in the juveniles' lives at the time respond to conflict with anger and resolve disputes through force. Lessons in respect for authority can be quickly lost when the correctional staff authority is exercised arbitrarily. Individualized treatment planning by psychiatrists and other mental health professionals is unlikely to be effective when line staff are not involved in its implementation.

Education

We know that the vast majority of juveniles entering facilities have significant educational deficits and that many—from 30 to 60 percent according to most studies[7]—are eligible for special education services. Some of these juveniles have dropped out of school in the community, or attend erratically, while many others were attending school and often receiving special education services directed at helping them overcome learning disabilities or behavior or mental health problems that interfere with their ability to benefit from school. We also know that failure to overcome these deficits will make it particularly difficult for these young people to find employment and successfully reintegrate into their communities when they are released.

An initial, and extremely basic, concern is that the state at least do no harm when it pulls juveniles from their home schools and places them in juvenile justice education programs. That is, too often we find that youths return from a stay in a juvenile facility further behind in school than when they left, having to repeat grades or, faced with the prospect of repeating grades, dropping out of school altogether. This is due in large part to failures to ensure that youths receive credit for the work they performed in the facility schools, but also due to inadequacies in the quality of services provided in the institution.

The basic rehabilitative premise of juvenile institutions requires, however, that facility schools do better than simply doing no harm. Incarceration provides an invaluable opportunity to identify educational needs and respond to them intensively and individually, so that there is a better prospect of the juvenile leaving the facility, returning to school, and graduating. For those students who—because of age, interests, or other reasons—will not return to an academic program, facility schools should provide vocational education opportunities to prepare the students for some form of productive lifestyle when they leave.

We find that facility education programs that are struggling in these areas often do so for common reasons. First, as is true in other areas, appropriate individualized programming requires initial identification of individualized needs, including eligibility for special education services. This requires communication with parents and prior schools, adequate testing, and thorough review of other available documentation. Too often, for example, our education consultants are able to easily identify, from facility records, juveniles who were receiving special education in the community but who have not been identified for special education by the facility.

Second, the information from these assessments must translate into appropriate educational services based on the students' needs. This requires having available a range of services, especially in facilities that house juveniles with a significant range in age and educational level. We have been in institutions where limited resources result in a teacher having to provide instruction to a class ranging in age from eleven to eighteen, with reading levels from kindergarten to high school. Not surprisingly, such teachers are often frustrated and are often unable to provide adequate services to anyone in the class.

Third, adequate education programs must be designed for the special population of students in juvenile facilities. This includes focusing on intensive remedial needs in reading and math. Behavior management programs should strive to maintain order in the classroom without regularly excluding students from receiving educational services based on behavior problems. We know that this is not easy. It requires teachers who are not only dedicated, but qualified through education, certification, and special training to provide services to these youths. But we also know that it is something that is done, and done well, in many facilities.

Fourth, the Individuals with Disabilities Education Act requires that juvenile facilities identify eligible juveniles, whether they have been previously identified or not. Facilities must develop individualized special education programs for such juveniles that are based on their individual needs, which may include mental health counseling, family counseling, and other related services. And for juveniles of appropriate age, special education must include plans and services to aid the student in transitioning to postschool activities, which may require vocational education services or instruction in independent living skills. Importantly, the services to be provided must be based on the individualized needs of the juvenile, not on the resource constraints of the facility.

Unfortunately, we find that services not readily available at the school due to resource limitations are frequently not considered or offered, even when those services have been deemed necessary by independent professionals in the community school systems. To protect against this sort of unwarranted reduction of services, and otherwise protect the rights of disabled juveniles, federal law requires that facilities involve the student's parents in the process and inform them of their rights to challenge the decisions reached by the school for their child, or appoint a surrogate parent when the parent is unavailable.

Remedies

Some jurisdictions have committed to address these problems in the context of agreements resolving our investigations. Of course, no single reform is guaranteed to work and every jurisdiction must consider what is appropriate in the context of its institutions and its particular challenges. Our agreements often have provisions specifically addressed to particular problems we observed, but there are also some more global, institutional changes that jurisdictions have undertaken to improve the quality of services more generally.

Clearly, additional resources are often (although not always) needed to address deficiencies. Our agreements generally require specific commitments to provide the resources necessary to implement the specific reforms agreed to by the parties. On a more operational level, one means of addressing particular problems, such as mental health or education, is to designate highly qualified, state-level staff with focused responsibility for developing policy, securing resources and technical assistance, and monitoring the quality of care in that area.

Similarly, we have asked jurisdictions to develop internal quality assurance mechanisms to improve the quality and quantity of information received by top administrators and to focus attention on specific areas of concern within the institutions. These self-monitoring mechanisms have included processes for ensuring independent, high-quality investigations of allegations of staff misconduct and inquiries into significant, serious events such as attempted suicides and mass disturbances, to evaluate the effectiveness of institutional responses and to identify any potential need for changes in policies or training to minimize the risk of reoccurrence. The idea is to create internal monitoring processes that will outlive the Justice Department's involvement with the institution.

As a part of a program to address crowding or the treatment needs of juveniles (especially special needs populations), jurisdictions have developed a continuum of placements and use risk and needs assessments to assign juveniles to the most appropriate placement. This includes alternatives to secure detention for low-risk youths prior to adjudication; a range of forensic placements for those with serious mental health needs; alternatives to paramilitary boot camps for juveniles who are too young, medically fragile, or mentally ill to benefit from a traditional program; and community placements for juveniles who can receive more effective services in their homes and do not require secure incarceration.

Finally, improved training is generally a component of most reform efforts. Assistance in developing and providing such training is available through several organizations, including the Justice Department's Office of Juvenile Justice and Delinquency Prevention.

Conclusion

Of course, we would prefer not to have to become involved in reform efforts in any jurisdiction, at least not through law enforcement investigations or litigation. The Department of Justice, through the Office of Juvenile Justice and Delinquency Prevention and other resources, seeks to encourage jurisdictions to be proactive, to assess conditions in their own facilities, and to respond to needs without federal law enforcement intervention. But when necessary, the Civil Rights Division does undertake investigations and, when we find serious problems and attempts at a negotiated resolution do not succeed, contested litigation. We hope to minimize these conflicts as much as is possible, consistent with our important law enforcement obligations. But even when we find ourselves in disagreement with administrators, we hope to be able to at least make clear our understanding of the significant challenges faced by all institutions, our appreciation for those who have devoted their lives to improving the lives of young people and their communities, and our desire to find ways to work together in this important endeavor.

Endnotes

[1] Mr. Rosenbaum acknowledges the contributions to this article by Judy Preston and to the speech on which the article is based by Robinsue Frohboese and Kevin Russell.

[2] S. Rep. No. 416 at 27 (1980).

[3] Additional information about the work of the Special Litigation Section can be found on its website, www.usdoj.gov/crt/split.

[4] *See Juvenile Offenders and Victims: 1999 National Report.* Office of Juvenile Justice and Delinquency Prevention, p. 206.

[5] Ibid., p. 190.

[6] Cocozza, J. J. , ed.1992. *Responding to Youth with Mental Disorders in the Juvenile Justice System.* Seattle, Washington: The National Coalition for the Mentally Ill in the Criminal Justice System.

[7] *See* Murphy, D. M. 1986. The Prevalence of Handicapping Conditions among Juvenile Delinquents. *Remedial and Special Education.* 7: 7-17 (analysis of thirteen studies).

Chapter Five

Reentry at the Point of Entry

Kit Glover
Treatment and Education Coordinator
Missouri's Division of Youth Services
Jefferson City, Missouri

Kurt Bumby
Assistant Deputy Director
Missouri Division of Youth Services
Jefferson City, Missouri

A service coordinator ushers a frightened youth into a conference room at the local juvenile detention center. At his dispositional hearing the previous Friday, the court ordered him into the custody of the Missouri Division of Youth Services. "Hi, Jeremy," says the service coordinator. "My name is Tanya and I work for the Division of Youth Services. It is my job to work with you and your family to get you the help you need. To do this, it is important that we talk openly and honestly about the problems that got you to this point and the changes you need to make. That way, you can return home and be successful."

So begins a typical youth's tenure with the Missouri Division of Youth Services—a process guided at the outset with the goal of successful transition back home. The service coordinators at the Division of Youth Services understand the necessity of planning for the eventual release of youths from the very beginning. Such early planning has become an underlying philosophy within the agency. However, like many other juvenile justice agencies across the country, such a notion has not always been present in Missouri. Indeed, too frequently, aftercare and transitional services were an afterthought, leaving such services a neglected component within traditional juvenile justice systems.

Professionals in the field agree that the ultimate measure of success for residential or institutional treatment programs is that youths exiting such facilities maintain positive gains and refrain from reoffending or engaging in otherwise problematic behaviors when they return to the community. The false perception that youths have "completed" treatment or rehabilitation while in residential programs may inadvertently contribute to overconfidence and a subsequent denial of their ongoing risk for recidivism. Herein lies the importance of developing transitional and aftercare programming, where youths receive additional treatment, education, monitoring, and other support services following their release from a residential or institutional treatment program.

In Missouri, the Division of Youth Services is located within the Department of Social Services and manages juvenile offenders. Missouri's approach to juvenile justice includes a balanced focus on rehabilitation and community safety. This is reflected in the mission statement of the Division of Youth Services: "to enable youths to fulfill their needs in a responsible manner within the context of and with respect for the needs of the family and the community." In fulfilling this mission, the Division of Youth Services maintains a commitment to protecting the safety of Missouri's citizens. It accomplishes this by providing individualized and comprehensive needs-based services that ultimately enable youths to successfully return to their families and communities. To accomplish this, the facilities of the Division of Youth Services have evolved during the past two decades from large, statewide training schools that emphasized custodial care into small, regionally based treatment programs designed to serve youths and their families close to home.

Accompanying the movement from large correctional institutions was a dramatic and important shift in philosophies and approaches. More specifically, while maintaining a commitment to public safety, the Division of Youth Services adopted a strong emphasis on providing individualized treatment and educational services within a therapeutic and supportive environment. Each Division of Youth Services facility is small. Most range from ten to thirty beds, with youths placed in groups of ten to ensure more individualized intervention and attention—a thirty-bed facility contains three groups of ten youths housed in cottages or dormitories. There are no cells, no bars on windows, no stark concrete walls, no stale institutional buildings, and no uniforms. Instead, the facilities resemble schools and campuses. Even in secure care programs, surrounded by perimeter fencing, the interiors reflect a natural and homelike atmosphere. The youths display their achievements, educational and treatment projects, artwork and family photos proudly throughout the facilities. Although the division emphasizes safety and security, correctional officers are not present. Facility staff, most of whom have degrees in the social services or juvenile justice, are part of a treatment team.

Overall, the teams strive to provide a consistent, safe, caring, and structured environment. Within this environment, youths have the opportunity to take responsibility for their behaviors. In addition, staff teaches them to recognize the various factors associated with their unhealthy decisions and to identify and practice appropriate and effective ways of meeting their needs while respecting others' rights. While individual and family counseling are significant components of the programming, a group modality is emphasized. The division prohibits shame-based, punitive, highly confrontational and power-based techniques and instead uses invitational, strength-based, respectful and dignified approaches that focus on therapeutic engagement. A versatile blend provides for more individualized approaches that are less rigid and limiting in scope and application. Such approaches allow staff to modify their techniques and behaviors. The services and approaches the Division of Youth Services provides include the following items:

- A continuum of security and programming, ranging from community-based and nonresidential programs, such as alternative living and day treatment, to residential programs, including group homes, and moderate and secure care placements

- Comprehensive, standardized needs and risk assessments that enhance classification and placement decisions and simplify development of individualized treatment plans

- An emphasis on individualized psychosocial, educational, and vocational needs

- Community-based partnerships for job placement and alternative education

- Incorporation of treatment-outcomes exploration, quality assurance, and program reviews to evaluate efficacy and improve service delivery

- Demonstrated investment and commitment including collaboration with local juvenile courts in early intervention and prevention efforts (through the provision of more than $6 million for diversionary programs)

- A singular case management system in which a service coordinator follows each youth throughout his or her tenure with the Division of Youth Services

The development of the case management system has resulted in increased attention to and emphasis on transitional and aftercare services. This has resulted in improvement in assessment, treatment planning, and coordination and monitoring of services for youths and their families. Service coordinators, or case managers, are the primary link between the division, the youths and their families, and the juvenile or family courts. Service coordinators are responsible for ensuring that youths follow court orders, are appropriately supervised, and meet expectations such as attending work, school, treatment, and community service. To that end, service coordinators perform comprehensive risk and needs assessments that lead to the development of individual treatment plans. The plan clearly articulates areas of need, short- and long-term steps toward goals, resources to achieve those goals, and target dates for completion.

Because the ultimate goal for youths is to be successfully reintegrated into the community, a critical element of the service coordinator's role is to identify and deliver comprehensive and appropriate transitional and aftercare services. Thus, comprehensive planning for reentry at the outset is an underlying tenet of the division. Ideally, when service coordinators first meet youths, the court of adjudication provides information, including social histories, that help service coordinators with important contextual information about prior offenses, family composition, medical and educational needs, and possible avenues of support. The hypothetical scenario in the introduction describes meeting first with the youth and then with his parents, because youths are often reluctant to share information in the presence of their parents. Otherwise, anger and resentment may become the focus of the discussion, yielding little useful direction. Service coordinators must establish themselves as advocates for both the youths and their families. Building a foundation of trust and respect is vital to success.

Beyond information-gathering, a primary importance of the interviews with youths and their families is to establish their roles as active partners in the rehabilitation process. The immediate message delivered is that the agency expects the youths and their families to be active collaborators; to engage, invest, and take ownership in the process. Treatment and services are done *with*, rather than *to*, the youths and their families. Interview results, coupled with the risk and needs assessments, serve to guide the service coordinators when developing specific, needs-based and individualized programming. To promote quality and individualized service delivery, the Division of Youth Services maintains a commitment to preserve low caseloads. On average, each service coordinator has fewer than twenty youths assigned. Further, to increase availability to clients and communities, service coordinators are strategically placed in locations that are close to the communities they serve. As such, they make frequent contact, provide resource development, and encourage civic involvement and community interaction.

Aftercare

Missouri's aftercare consists of an indefinite period that youths remain on caseloads after they have transitioned into the community. While transitional and aftercare services occur after residential placement, the service coordinators develop initial individual treatment planning toward reintegration. The division has evolved and broadened its services to maximize the potential for each youth's effective reintegration. Careful and thoughtful consideration of each youth's continued needs has resulted in service delivery that transcends typical work schedules and illustrates the resourcefulness of the staff. The range of services now offered by the Division of Youth Services in the aftercare phase is consistent with the services provided in the residential programming. This includes, for example, family therapy, drug and alcohol counseling, general equivalency diploma (GED) preparation, community service, sex offender groups, mentoring services, and college and vocational programming. The administration of these services inevitably takes on the flavor of the region and locale. Overall, the Division of Youth Services' response to transitional and aftercare programming has been to encourage and expect a "whatever it takes" attitude.

Intensive Care Supervision

The "whatever it takes" approach has resulted in the development of the Intensive Case Supervision Program. In this program, social service aides, known as "trackers," maintain consistent and frequent contact with youths in aftercare or community care. Employed under the direction of the service coordinators, trackers typically are college students majoring in social work or related fields, whose schedules permit them to serve in a variety of capacities, thus enhancing the performance of supervision, monitoring, and support functions. While serving as mentors and role models, trackers also facilitate accountability by ensuring that the youths with whom they work meet program expectations and supervision conditions. This includes curfew restrictions, school attendance, counseling, and community service activities. In addition, trackers provide transportation to therapy and educational meetings, offer tutoring, participate in recreational activities, assist with obtaining and completing employment applications, and provide supportive and paraprofessional counseling services. The trackers are valued complements to case management and intensive supervision components.

Beyond the clear benefits to youths because of frequent and consistent contact and mentoring, trackers are a cost-effective way to enhance supervision of youths while reducing demands on service coordinators' caseloads. This allows the service coordinators to attend to the variety of case management-related issues that arise. Further, trackers enjoy invaluable experience in their fields of study and often become an excellent recruitment source for the Division of Youth Services.

Day Treatment Programs

Further exemplifying the Division of Youth Services' "whatever it takes" approach to transitional and aftercare services has been the establishment of day treatment programs. Although primarily designed to divert lower-risk youths from residential placement, day treatment programs provide an effective transitional service for youths reentering the community following release from residential care.

Day treatment programs give youths community-based, structured, alternative educational programming. Besides academic and vocational instruction, day treatment programs incorporate psychoeducational groups and other treatment interventions. The program includes nontraditional hours of operation, which extend into evenings and weekends to incorporate "day treatment plus" activities. Included among the numerous day treatment plus elements are community service projects, family therapy, individual counseling, GED skills enrichment, substance abuse prevention, life skills, tutoring, and mentoring services. During planned outings, the youths can practice and receive reinforcement in important socialization skills. Typically, the court targets youths committed to the Division of Youth Services for day treatment programs, although local juvenile courts, public schools, and other agencies may refer other at-risk or low-risk youths. Overall, Missouri's day treatment programs and accompanying services allow youths to practice the skills they learned in residential programs. They provide an excellent community resource with sufficient structure to ease a gradual and, consequently, more successful reintegration into a public school or employment setting.

Jobs Program

Treatment and educational services are integral to individual youth development planning, and Missouri continues to refine educational programming. Missouri's Department of Elementary and Secondary Education's School Improvement Plan evaluated the Division of Youth Services and the department received state accreditation. Efforts to provide youths with vocational programming resulted in development of the Division of Youth Services Jobs Program. This program allows youths to gain employment skills and receive minimum wage compensation through a contractual agreement between the Division of Youth Services and the Division of Workforce Development. The Division of Youth Services identifies funding through the state's Workforce Investment Areas.

In some programs, youths train under maintenance staff and have set foundation forms and poured concrete, installed vinyl siding, and landscaped the grounds. The division is developing another approach to providing vital job skills—integrating vocational programming with traditional academics. To that end, the required academic curricula have been structured to focus on career applicability. The intent is to give youths skills beyond those required for entry-level jobs. Thus, upon release from the residential program, youths, whether they obtain a GED or return to public school, are better prepared to seek and maintain employment. Beyond acquiring skills, the wages earned from the Jobs Program have enabled youths to make restitution payments and contributions to the Crime Victims' Compensation Fund.

During the aftercare phase, service coordinators network with government or nonprofit organizations to place transitioning youths in appropriate sites. Here, they may gain a further understanding of the work world and understand the importance of community service. A common collateral effect of these placements is a decrease in the tension in the communities in which the youths committed their crimes.

Health Care

A fundamental service warranting attention from a reentry perspective is the focus on health care needs. Upon commitment to the division, youths receive medical, dental, vision, and mental health screenings, physical examinations, and qualified reviews of any prescribed medications. As youths progress through treatment and approach discharge, a variety of tran sitional health care efforts occur. While residential programming gives youths appropriate health care, challenges often arise during the aftercare phase.

Consequently, service coordinators collaborate with the nursing and treatment staff regarding ongoing and potential health care needs. They assess the ability of the family or guardian to provide for such needs, orient youths and their families to community resources, and when necessary, enroll youths in Missouri's MC+ program, which provides health insurance to qualified persons. Part of the Division of Youth Services' needs-based approach is the recognition that the medical well-being of youths in its care is a primary concern. Left untended, health care needs severely impair the therapeutic value of other services.

Other Services

Additional transitional services for youths in the aftercare phase include sex offender management groups, substance abuse programming, and family therapy services. Juvenile sex offender groups that use cognitive behavioral and relapse prevention models exist in both residential and aftercare settings. Critical aspects of the effective supervision of juvenile sex offenders include involving families and giving them resources and ongoing treatment support. Understanding preoffense patterns and the sex offense cycle, victim empathy, and the creation of a relapse prevention plan are common treatment targets within the groups. The aftercare sex offender groups provide a therapeutic link to the reality of lifetime accountability for behavior and offer the opportunity for juveniles and their families to discuss day-to-day challenges and successes. Similar participation in substance abuse services has become an important transitional and aftercare need for youths.

Family therapy occurs within facilities of the Division of Youth Services and in the families' homes. Ideally, regional family specialists initiate therapy when youths are in residential care, continuing once they reenter the community. Monitoring the youths' reunification process with family allows the possibility of both appropriate intervention and validation of progress that the members might otherwise fail to recognize. Family support groups are designed to provide parents and guardians with an opportunity to share challenges and successes with others in similar positions. These groups attained greater involvement when transportation was offered. When day treatment sites are too remote, service coordinator offices or residential programming sites serve aftercare youths. The emphasis on family involvement reflects an agencywide adherence to a multisystemic approach and recognition that families are critical to successful transition and reentry.

Unfortunately, a common pitfall has been for juvenile justice systems to become solely offender-focused. This means that rehabilitative efforts and services are directed exclusively toward young offenders, while multisystemic needs (in other words, school, peers, family, and community) go unrecognized. Consequently, the juvenile justice system returns those perceived "troubled" but now "rehabilitated" to their families, while other aspects of the system remain status quo, often leading to less than desirable results.

45

Despite the numerous transitional and aftercare services, occasionally youths in the community continue to exhibit difficulties with the reentry process. In those circumstances, the division uses sheltering and sanctioning strategies, depending on the severity of the behaviors and intended outcome of the intervention. Youths involved in the sheltering and/or sanctioning process have reported that the greatest impact on them, beyond removal from the community, is facing many of the youths remaining in the residential program. They discuss and identify lapsing or relapsing behaviors with their peers. Reviewing and critically examining coping strategies and challenges can lead to invaluable insights for all involved.

In an era when a prevailing sentiment is that nothing works for juvenile offenders, Missouri's Division of Youth Services continues to challenge that presumption and demonstrates that with sound transitional planning from the outset and dedication to comprehensive service delivery, a successful reentry can, in fact, be achieved.

Chapter Six

The Ventura Youth Correctional Facility: Providing Needed Treatment Programs to Youthful Female Offenders

Al Palomino
Parole Agent III and Public Information Officer
Ventura Youth Correctional Facility
Camarillo, California

The California Youth Authority emphasizes public protection and offender accountability and believes that the most effective way to protect the public is to ensure that offenders are held accountable for their criminal behavior. The department and its staff are committed to working closely with law enforcement, the courts, district attorneys, and public defenders, probation agencies, and a broad spectrum of public agencies concerned and involved with juvenile offenders.

Operating eleven institutions and four camps, the California Youth Authority offers a variety of housing options and a wide range of quality programs and services to meet the needs of this varied population. At the core of the California Youth Authority programs and services is a dedicated and highly trained staff. The staff provides a safe and healthy environment and the opportunity for youthful offenders to reintegrate into the community and lead law-abiding lives.

Throughout the California Youth Authority, the "treatment and training" notion encompasses all activities, programs, and services in which young people participate. All staff with contact with youthful offenders contribute to their treatment and training program.

The California Youth Authority uses a "treatment team" to deliver services to its population. A core group of staff at each facility carries out program activities. A unit supervisor heads each treatment team, which is composed of an institutional parole agent or social worker, teachers, a supervising youth counselor, and several youth counselors.

Ventura Youth Correctional Facility

The Ventura Youth Correctional Facility (VYCF) in Camarillo, formerly known as the Ventura School for Girls, opened in 1962. Then, the institution was one of two state facilities that housed female offenders. When Los

47

Guilicos (Santa Rosa), the other girls' institution, was closed in 1970, Ventura Youth Correctional Facility became the only state facility housing females committed to the Youth Authority. In 1970, the first males arrived and today, males are more than one-half of the ward population. There are six female living units, five male living units, one detention unit, and one public service/fire camp. We have completely segregated male and female ward programs. Female wards range from age thirteen to twenty-five, and males range from sixteen to twenty-five. Currently, we assign 325 female offenders to Ventura Youth Correctional Facility. The institution is enclosed within a perimeter fence. Security personnel patrol the grounds in vehicles equipped with two-way radios. Staff stationed in a single tower escort and/or monitor single and group ward movements. In addition, a large fence inside the institution separates the male and female offenders.

Specialized Counseling Program

Ventura Youth Correctional Facility's Buenaventura Specialized Counseling Program for violent female offenders is housed in the Buenaventura Cottage at Ventura Youth Correctional Facility. We can lock forty-seven individual wet rooms (rooms with a sink and a toilet) within the facility. The Buenaventura program uses contingency management techniques. In a clinical setting, the results are positive behavioral changes and a decrease in aggressive and other maladaptive behaviors. Buenaventura has developed a system using contingencies for positive programming. This behavioral program is incorporated into the daily activities at the cottage to decrease identified problem behaviors while increasing appropriate interactions. Through this program, the girls learn the natural consequences for their inappropriate behaviors and positive benefits for socially appropriate behaviors. They also learn that they have responsibilities to both themselves and to the community.

The program provides individual psychotherapy for each ward with a staff psychiatrist or psychologist. The youths participate in weekly treatment groups conducted by a youth correctional counselor. The treatment groups include the following: anger management, domestic violence (emotional, verbal, physical, and sexual abuse) counseling, gang awareness, self-image, informal substance abuse counseling, parenting, and commitment offense and changing directions (establishing positive life goals).

Intensive Treatment

Alborada Intensive Treatment Program for females is a forty-seven-bed program with individual wet rooms that they can lock. The program accepts severely emotionally disturbed females who have histories of major mental disorders. These include mood disorders, unipolar and bipolar disorder, suicidal conduct, psychiatric disorders, schizophrenia, organic brain disorder, attention deficit disorder with hyperactivity and seizures, eating disorders, posttraumatic stress disorder, physical and sexual abuse, and personality disorders including borderline, histrionic, and self-mutilation.

The program accepts youths with histories of bizarre offenses, including the murder of one's child, parent, or significant other and those with severe behavioral problems. Most of these wards are first-time commitments from the Juvenile or Superior Court. Personal offenses such as murder, robbery, or assault are most of the commitment offenses of these girls.

The intensive treatment program uses a participatory management decision-making system, which permits participation from staff and wards on decisions affecting cottage life. Five working committees, monitored by a governing board—composed of youth correctional counselors, the supervising correctional officer, and appointed ward representatives—direct all cottage activities. The program uses a sequential system of three treatment phases to organize and deliver services. We link the treatment phases to behavioral accountability and progress on specific goals.

The program provides individual psychotherapy for each ward with two staff psychologists and one psychiatrist. The girls are involved in weekly treatment groups conducted by a youth correctional counselor.

Formalized Drug Program

The Mira Loma Female Drug and Alcohol Abuse Treatment Program (DAATP) operates within a fifty-five-bed, locked living unit at the Ventura Youth Correctional Facility. Mira Loma Drug and Alcohol Abuse Treatment is designed to address the unique problems of the drug-addicted female offender. Research has shown that nearly all female offenders in the program have backgrounds of severe abuse and neglect. The Mira Loma Drug and Alcohol Abuse Treatment Program addresses the dysfunctional behaviorial repertoire of the drug-related offender. This includes severe drug abuse, manipulation and criminal victimization of others, destructive relationships, runaways and escapes, suicide attempts, and self-mutilations.

We transfer wards to Mira Loma Drug and Alcohol Abuse Treatment Program from the Ventura Youth Correctional Facility general population when they have fourteen months or less remaining until their projected parole consideration dates. They are paroled from Mira Loma Drug and Alcohol Abuse Treatment Program without returning to the general population. Besides the fifty-five female offenders currently enrolled, approximately fifty female offenders receive formal drug treatment services within the context of Ventura Youth Correctional Facility's specialized counseling and intensive treatment programs.

Youths enrolled in Mira Loma Drug and Alcohol Abuse Treatment Program are provided with daily opportunities for treatment, education, work, community service, and recreation. We enroll every ward in the living unit in full-time school or work. They attend a minimum of one small group (nine wards per caseload), one special topic small group, and one large group (of approximately twenty-eight wards) each week. Mira Loma Drug and Alcohol

Abuse Treatment Program youths receive advanced treatment services by referral. These services include individual and group psychotherapy, individual psychiatric services, abuse and neglect therapy with a licensed therapist, motivational workshops, and tutoring.

Academic and Vocational Programs

The Ventura Youth Correctional Facility Education Program operates the year around, giving students who have fallen behind academically the opportunity to catch up. We offer students a variety of vocational programs and work assignments that teach relevant skills and are transferable to community employment. These work assignments also provide an emphasis on improvement of attitude and behaviors that have previously impeded employment success.

While in the California Youth Authority, an individual may obtain the following:

- High school credits/requirements for graduation
- A high school diploma
- College course work for an associate of arts degree
- A general equivalency diploma
- Certification in office technology
- Certification in culinary arts
- Certification in animal care

The following special education services also are available:

- Remedial education (Improving America's Schools Act)
- Special education for individuals with exceptional needs
- An English proficiency program (English as a second language)

Work Experience

We offer work experience programs to youths who need a more practical applied program. This includes jobs such as laundry and kitchen work, landscaping, grounds maintenance, painting, carpentry, and electrical work. Currently, approximately 100 wards are employed in work programs.

Additional Services

Religion: Protestant, Catholic, Muslim, and Native American chaplains serve the religious needs of Ventura Youth Correctional Facility wards. They seek to aid all wards in a return to their rightful place in the community with a proper understanding of spiritual and moral responsibilities. The chaplains offer classes in religion, ethics and marriage, as well as individual and small group counseling. There also is an extensive religious volunteer program that gives girls the opportunity to work with people from the community. They contract other religious services, as needed.

Counseling: Besides specialized programs, we require Ventura Youth Correctional Facility wards to participate in counseling programs in the following areas:

- Effect of crime on victims
- Anger management
- Employability skills
- Gang awareness and prevention
- Preparole

Psychiatric/Psychological: Wards receive mental health services of psychiatrists, clinical psychologists, and social workers. Both individual and group therapy focuses on helping youths understand their problems and modify the behaviors that led them to incarceration. In addition, the Ventura Youth Correctional Facility works with universities that provide services to its wards through various intern programs.

Hospital/Clinic: A chief medical officer, a physician, a supervising registered nurse, registered nurses, and hospital aides provide medical services. The seventeen-bed infirmary is equipped to tend to the daily needs of all wards. A dentist and a dental assistant provide dental care. We perform major surgery at a local hospital.

Volunteer Program: There is a long tradition of volunteer work at Ventura Youth Correctional Facility. Many wards do not receive visits and frequently, some of them have special needs. Individuals or groups volunteer to come to Ventura Youth Correctional Facility regularly to provide services to meet many of these needs.

Groups such as the Citizens Advisory Committee, which is composed of local county residents who represent many segments of the community, Volunteers in Parole (a project of the Los Angeles County Bar Association), and religious and social discussion groups contribute thousands of hours each year to supplement programs at the Ventura Youth Correctional Facility.

Included in the California Youth Authority's mission is the protection of the public from criminal activity. Providing treatment, training, and educational opportunities to youthful offenders has accomplished this. The California Youth Authority currently has a ward population of approximately 7,356, with another 4,722 offenders under parole supervision.

Chapter Seven

Juvenile Corrections in Indiana: The Dawning of a New Era

Brent Matthews
Director
Indiana Behavioral Health Choices, Inc.
Indianapolis, Indiana

Ron Leffler
Director, Juvenile Transition Programs
Indiana Department of Correction
Indianapolis, Indiana

On any given day, in any juvenile or family courtroom in America, one can witness the following scene: Once again, even while on probation, Johnny finds himself in front of the juvenile court judge for yet another referral. This is Johnny's last chance, and to be sure he understands the seriousness of the moment, the judge tells him: "I am putting you on suspended commitment."

Historically, authorities hoped that these words would deter youths from corrections. Now, it is the cry of overwhelmed juvenile courts across the country. It is a desperate response to massive probation caseloads, frustration with failed community interventions and services, numb and broken families, and the noncompliance of youthful probationers. The courts' frustration is easy to understand when one considers that many youths entering the correctional system have already received services from many, if not all, of the community's child and family public service systems, such as child welfare, special education, and mental health.

With an increase in the severity and number of crimes committed by youths, public pressure is mounting and directs our concerns toward public protection. In response, youths are removed from the streets and public safety is assured. The commitment to finding new approaches to reach youths and families has been suspended.

Enter juvenile corrections, ready to muster its resources. In most cases, within six to eighteen months, an incarcerated youth is back on the streets. How do we ensure public safety then? Surely, the youth will have made gains that led to his or her release. But is the youth returning to an environment or community that will support those gains? The correctional staff, often isolated from youth-serving systems that previously tried to help, must work diligently to return the youth to his or her family and community. Reconnecting the youth and family with previous support systems can be a discouraging encounter. To find something that "helps," (usually with diminishing funds) correctional staff also must deal with fragmented communications across agencies and with opposing philosophical approaches on how to help.

It is a daunting task, but the Indiana Department of Corrections, Division of Juvenile Services has a vision for how this can be accomplished, which states:

> Our vision is that every child experience successes in caring families and nurturing communities that cherish children and teach them to value family and community. Our vision is guided by the fact that our decisions and actions affecting children today determine the quality of our life tomorrow.

This vision statement reflects an understanding of the children who end up at the door of correctional services. Too many of them have been victims of abuse and neglect. They have lived in households in which alcohol and drugs were abused, or they are substance abusers themselves. They have lived in multiple group homes, foster homes, or treatment centers. They struggle to read and are failing in school. They have few friends or positive role models. They may suffer developmental disabilities or mental health problems. Some are dangerous to others and some are dangerous to themselves.

One's history is not permission to break the law. However, many of today's correctional approaches are designed under the premise that knowing a youth's history may reveal the type of facility, treatment, or support that would be most effective during incarceration. Upon release, we need innovative approaches that protect the community and build the integrity of youths and their families. In Marion County, Indiana, we are attempting such an approach based on a unique partnership between the Department of Corrections' Juvenile Transition Program and a three-year-old community collaboration program in Indianapolis called the Dawn Project.

Juvenile Transition Program

The Juvenile Transition Program resulted from a lawsuit filed against the department of corrections because of conditions at the state's largest juvenile facility for males. The lawsuit alleged that there was crowding, a lack of appropriate programs within the facility, and that youths were simply being housed instead of receiving adequate services. The lawsuit was settled in 1993 and the Juvenile Transition Program was born. A court order mandated a reduction in the number of youths housed at the facility. The settlement outlined a continuum of care and resources were transferred from the facility to the community for the provision of additional services.

This led to a philosophical change for the department. With the help of the National Council on Crime and Delinquency, the department of corrections developed a new classification system in all of the department's juvenile facilities. The National Council on Crime and Delinquency recommended that professionals in the community be hired to deal specifically with juveniles. Then, and now, state parole agents supervised both adults and juveniles and handled their aftercare.

To meet the specific and community-based needs of juveniles, and acting on the recommendations of the National Council on Crime and Delinquency, the department hired seven youth services coordinators (YSC) in 1993, and three others were hired in 1997. These parole agents handle only a juvenile caseload. Analysis showed three out of Indiana's ninety-two counties supplied the department of corrections with most of its juvenile population. Seven of the ten youth services coordinators were placed in Marion County, which includes Indianapolis and is responsible for 40 percent of the department's total population. Ideally, youth services coordinators have a caseload of twenty-five youths, both in and out of the facility.

Day reporting was a key supplement to supervising youth services. Currently, funding resources for day reporting have been reallocated to purchase more beds. At one time, the department of corrections used four day reporting programs, but now it has just one. Other resources were developed and agencies that provided community-based services were contracted through a broad agency announcement. These services cover multiple counties and serve youths referred from either youth services coordinators or state parole agents.

Taking a cue from community policing, the youth services coordinators expanded their collaboration with other agencies in the counties in which they worked. This occurred on a county-by-county basis and each has developed a variety of services in the community for their clients. By sharing these connections and supports with their facilities, they are better able to make positive links with the community in preparing for each youth's release. Youth services coordinators and state parole agents are the eyes and ears of the facilities in the community. They deal with parents and know the neighborhoods to which the youths are returned.

By using youth services coordinators, the department's juvenile division is able to make its mission a reality, as stated here:

> The mission of the Division of Juvenile Services is to provide leadership for change for youths, family units and communities. It operates by creating legitimate, alternative pathways to adulthood through equal access to services that are least intrusive, culturally sensitive and consistent with the highest professional standards.

To accomplish its mission, the juvenile division, already involved in a wide variety of collaborative efforts, reached out to the Dawn Project.

The Dawn Project

In 1995, the state Division of Mental Health received a $75,000 planning grant from the Robert Wood Johnson Foundation. The funds were used to form a consortium in which the state of Indiana and Marion County child and family service agencies agreed to collaborate in a new effort to better serve youths who were placed, or at risk of being placed, in institutional care. The partnering agencies included the Indiana Department of Family and Social Services Administration; Indiana State Division of Mental Health; Indiana State Division of Family and Children; Indiana Department of Education, Division of Special Education; Marion County Office of Family and Children; Marion Superior Court, Juvenile Division; and the Mental Health Association of Marion County. By mid-1996, the consortium had reached out to include parents, other concerned parties, and representatives from other agencies. These members joined with other community representatives to form task forces that worked to build the initial design of the Dawn Project, and on May 1, 1997, the project enrolled the first ten participants.

The mission of the Dawn Project is to provide new and improved levels of assistance to children with serious emotional disturbances and their families. This mission is founded on the belief that children and their families are remarkably resilient and capable of positive development when provided with community-centered support that is defined by the best interests of the children. Services must be child-centered and family-driven, with the needs of children and families the most important factors in deciding the types of services provided. Services must be community-based, building on the strengths, natural supports, and resources of the families and must respect and respond to the unique racial, ethnic, socioeconomic, and religious cultures of each family.

The consortium continues to provide valuable and ongoing guidance, meeting monthly to review progress and outcomes and to support systems reform within each consortium agency. New members are added to the consortium to broaden community representation and help expand community resources for all served.

To manage a community project such as this, a private nonprofit corporation, Indiana Behavioral Health Choices, was formed to coordinate and oversee services for the Dawn Project. Choices provides administrative, financial, clinical, and technical structure to Dawn, and manages the contracts for the provider network that serves the families. Services and care management are funded for clients by a standard monthly case rate that comes with each referral from the referring systems: child welfare, juvenile probation, or special education. Case rates establish a fixed and predictable cost for payers, while streamlining accounting procedures. They also support better care by allowing for more flexibility in using funds for individualized services that traditional systems are unable to access.

While the Dawn Project is unique to Indiana, many similar projects are part of a national movement called "system of care reform." System of care reform supporters seek to implement dynamic care management systems to better serve families with children who have serious emotional disturbances. This is done by adopting an integrated system of care philosophy, applying care management technologies with blended funding principles and using wraparound processes and values that build on the strengths and unique culture of each family.

The values-based approach to serving families guides the Dawn worker, called a service coordinator, in developing outcome-oriented, individualized plans of care called service coordination plans. The service coordinator brings together the family, professionals, and other community members to become part of the Child and Family Team, which develops and implements the service coordination plans. The plans are child-centered, family-driven, culturally competent, community-based, and coordinated across the multiple systems involved with the family, while building upon the strengths and successes of the family.

Forging the Partnership—The Federal Grant

During the course of three years, 31 out of 250 youths served have been sent to the department of corrections juvenile division. Within the last year, a dialog began between the Dawn Project and the department on how to serve the youths who come into contact with both systems. The overwhelming theme of this dialog is that both systems serve the same youths; the only difference is that some youths have been through a correctional facility or program. A partnership was an obvious choice because the youths who are committed to the department of corrections eventually will return to their homes and reside in the communities from which they came.

This dialog has included the chief executive officer and program director of Dawn, the deputy commissioner of juvenile services, the director of juvenile services, the supervisor of the Juvenile Transition Program, and the state director of mental health. This has resulted in some informal agreements on the exchange of information between the two agencies. Much of the discussion has focused on the operations of both systems and how they can work together for the same cause.

The early dialog centered on where the youths that both programs served came from, and what services could be given to them once they returned home. A key component was that Dawn could provide access to twenty-four-hour case management services. This would be a direct way to offset the loss of day reporting and also would lessen the caseload burden for the youth services coordinators. Through information-sharing and discussion of the youths who were in common, authorities discovered that the two agencies were very much alike in their philosophies and goals. As a result of these discussions, the department of corrections was invited to become a member of the Dawn Project Consortium.

Recently, the Dawn Project received a federal grant totaling $7 million over five years. The Indianapolis mayor s office, through a designee, Health and Hospital Corporation, intends to build on Dawn s success through this grant to partner with state agencies not currently involved and bring family-driven, community-based values to new populations.

Those not presently served by Dawn because of financial and system barriers are as follows: youths who become ineligible for Dawn services due to placement in a secure correctional facility; youths in state hospitals who require assistance with transitional care to succeed in the community; and at-risk youths (those not reaching the level of Dawn eligibility). Building on the core values and goals of the Dawn Project, the grant incorporates four key elements:

- Collaboration with child service agencies, government entities, and families
- Blended funding arrangements for Marion County youths at high risk for out-of-home placements and earlier intervention for those at risk
- Strength-based, family-driven, culturally competent approaches to care
- Accessibility to a wide array of services and support

Three primary goals will be addressed through this initiative. Dawn members want full parental involvement incorporated into the design, implementation, and evaluation of the project and its services at each level of the system of care, from the child and family team level to that of city, county, and state governance. A single comprehensive system of care will be provided that allows children and families who experience emotional disturbances to receive culturally competent, coordinated, and uninterrupted care, regardless of whether their primary system of involvement is child welfare, mental health, juvenile justice, corrections, or special education. Finally, a system of care will be developed in which all child service entities achieve positive outcomes through earlier intervention and increased understanding of and adherence to a strength- and values-based approach to care that embraces the unique culture of each child and family.

The federal grant offers a unique opportunity for the Juvenile Transition Program to collaborate with other government youth services agencies to form a seamless continuum of care for the community's most disenfranchised youths. This grant will enable youths who have had services prior to entering the correctional system to continue to have services once they are released, to receive them in the community where the support is needed most, and to do this with their families and communities as full participants.

The kickoff for the new partnership between the Juvenile Transition Program and Dawn was a jointly developed training titled "Breaking the Barriers." The training first allowed staff from each agency to find a common ground by reviewing one another's vision and mission statements and building relations to reach those visions together. The participants then discussed what their work life was really like, both the frustrations and successes. They also shared their nomenclature, acronyms, and processes. In the next phase of development, workers will design the protocols for information exchange and clarify one another's roles and expectations. This will be followed by joint training specifically guiding the workers in the advanced skills of values-based practice in working with families and communities as partners.

Conclusion

The primary goal of correctional agencies is to protect the public. The second goal is to protect their staff from the offenders they serve. The third goal is to rehabilitate the offender and return a better person to the community.

The partnership between the Dawn Project and the Juvenile Transition Program is developing an approach to protecting the community based on the philosophy that the community is safest when its members are supported in achieving their potentials. Success also will depend on collaboration across all youth service agencies and their ability to work with families. It will challenge every professional's ability to support small gains while ensuring that community plans can be designed that offset risk for the community.

Juvenile corrections is needed as a full partner in the youth services system of care movement. It is becoming clear that the zero tolerance approach is overwhelming the system. Perhaps an approach of 100 percent understanding will help us be more effective in reaching our youths and building our communities. The department of corrections can embrace, and even model, the values-based approach of empowering families to be full participants in assessing, planning, implementing, and evaluating their care. Through partnerships that provide better aftercare and by building on the gains youths make while incarcerated, recidivism can be reduced. If adults can reach a new understanding and collaborative approach with today's most disenfranchised youths, these youths may have a chance to become tomorrow's leaders.

Chapter Eight

Watching Grassroots Grow in Louisiana: The Children's Initiatives*

Anne Hasselbrack
Editorial Assistant
American Correctional Association
Lanham, Maryland

Statistics on the overall health and well-being of Louisiana's children are among the worst in the nation. Thirty-two percent of children live in poverty and more than 20 percent of teenage girls give birth before their eighteenth birthday. In addition, Louisiana has the highest incarceration rate per capita of any state. Jannitta Antoine, deputy secretary of the Louisiana Department of Public Safety and Corrections, says the crime trend is both cyclical and generational. Yet, she hopes that the state's current efforts will bring lasting change.

Richard Stalder, secretary of the department of corrections, and Senator Mary Landrieu (D-Louisiana), both members of the state's Children's Cabinet, have the same vision for these children. Stalder says, "It is impossible to overstate the critical importance of programs and services designed to nurture, motivate, and otherwise promote the healthy development of our children. The future reward for such an investment in terms of reduced delinquency and subsequent criminal behavior will far outweigh the short-term costs."

Although the state ranks forty-ninth in computer technology in schools and forty-third in Internet access for adults, the lack of an information superhighway has not deterred a grassroots effort, the Children's Initiatives, to change children's lives. The goal of the Children's Initiatives is to improve the lives of the 70,000 children born in the state each year, and possibly reverse the trend in crime. The vision became a reality in December 1997 with the creation of the Children's Initiatives, programs across the state that provide community outreach focused on parenting skills training, character building, and well-child care. Although the full effect of such an endeavor will not be known for several years, those involved are willing to wait it out. Landrieu, the oldest of nine children and the mother of two adopted children, states, "I envision that, if this is done correctly . . . we could see a 25 percent, 35 percent or 40 percent decline in our prison populations."

---

* Based on an update of Clayton, Susan. "Children's Intiatives: Louisiana Corrections Makes Prevention a Priority." April 1999. *Corrections Today*. 61 (2) 116-119.

She champions the program under the initiatives called Steps to Success, a not-for-profit corporation whose mission is to be a catalyst for networks of comprehensive services for children ages zero to three and their families. The objective is to help insure healthy bodies, educated minds, and promote self-sufficiency.

Initially, the Pfizer Corporation funded the program for $100,000 combined with a $1.2 million grant from the U.S. Department of Education, Early Childhood Development Division. As it expanded into different cities across the state, the program established a volunteer base and public/private partnerships for services that allocated grants in each geographic area. Partners include hospitals, Prevent Child Abuse Louisiana, the Rapides Foundation, The United Way, Entergy (a utilities corporation), the Foundation for the Midsouth, and the state's Department of Social Services. Julia Thornton, the program's executive director, also is pursuing additional federal appropriations. The organization maintains an electronic list of providers in each city served. However, since many of their clients do not have access to the Internet, the organization provides program information through phone mentoring, public service announcements, brochures, newspaper articles, hospitals, churches, and community outreach events.

"Children, particularly from birth to age three, need to have not only their basic needs met, but also the consistent attention and affection of at least one person," says Landrieu. Scientists can now show us what many have suspected all along—that the first few years of a child's life are the most crucial to his or her development. A child's brain is nearly 90 percent developed by age three and 99 percent developed by age six. To illustrate this, recently scientists viewed a scan of two brains. One was small and contained dark spaces as though it were not fully developed. The other looked average in size and was filled in more. When they were asked to identify what it was they were seeing, the scientists agreed that the first brain most likely belonged to an Alzheimer's patient. They said the other was the brain of a healthy adult, but they were wrong. Both brains belonged to three-year-olds. The smaller, less developed brain belonged to an abused child, and the healthy brain to a well cared for child.

However, according to the Rand Corporation, only 10 percent of public spending on children focuses on children in that age bracket, while those age five to eighteen receive 90 percent of public spending on children. In her keynote address at the American Correctional Association's 1999 winter conference, Landrieu stated that the government is "spending money in total reverse proportion to how human beings develop."

Thornton says that, "Essentially, when the mother goes home with the newborn, the child is lost to the system until he or she shows up in kindergarten. The premise of this whole program is to stop that from happening, to do everything possible to ensure that these three to four years are not lost in this child's life."

Steps to Success now operates in seven cities (Alexandria, Baton Rouge, Houma, Lafayette, Lake Charles, Monroe, and Shreveport), with New Orleans to be added in 2002. Each city has its own coordinator to find both public and private sources of funding, and to address and meet the specific needs of that community. For instance, Houma has a high teen pregnancy rate so they offer hands-on parenting classes, and the result has been that when young mothers participate, repeat pregnancy rates decline. Houma received a Teenage Pregnancy Prevention Grant of $73,000 to help fund this effort.

Within correctional facilities, policy dictates that parenting skills be provided to both juveniles and adults. Inmates who are within one year of release may participate, and participation is voluntary. Each institution has discretion in modeling its program to best serve the specific needs of unique populations, and each institution's social services staff provides this training. Therefore, curriculums and program duration will vary.

The Steps to Success program at the Jetson Correctional Center for Youth in Baton Rouge, a coed facility serving approximately 630 youthful offenders, will soon be implementing a program they currently provide in the community: Hands On Parenting. They designed the curriculum of this program to meet the specific needs of parents, such as teen mothers, young dads, new parents, and growing families. Parents who have been in the same circumstances and have persevered are trained to be mentors for this program.

In Baton Rouge, a Children's Book Club in Prisons initiative encourages positive interaction between incarcerated parents and their visiting children. Currently, this program operates in the Dixon Correctional Institute (for males) and the Louisiana Correctional Institute for Women. Scholastic Publications, through the Volunteers of America, donated 5,000 books for preschool through young teens. The Baton Rouge Children's Coalition donated bookmarks, crayons, coloring sheets, and bags in which the children, about 300 a month, may carry home the books of their choosing.

For years, the department has been showing it values the family unit by offering a very open policy for visitation. Called the Program for Caring Parents. Children less than sixteen may visit an incarcerated parent for up to eight hours, one weekend day each week. Antoine explains that because the state is so rural, having the inmate housed close to his or her family is not always geographically possible, although that is the ideal. The department will even rearrange days for a visitation if those set aside are not convenient.

The department has embraced the Children's Initiatives by partnering with Steps to Success and has trained its social workers to implement various programs in juvenile and adult facilities and for probation and parole clients. Besides having the community go into various correctional institutions, the department's staff is heading out into the community. One such endeavor, Character Counts, is an established, nationally recognized program based on the Six Pillars of Character developed by the Josephson Institute of Ethics. These pillars are trustworthiness, respect, responsibility, fairness, caring, and citizenship. The correctional institutions promote one pillar per month using posters and discussions in life skills classes. The probation and parole clients each receive a mailer that discusses that month's character trait. Staff from the department also volunteer at area schools and read books with the children that illustrate particular traits. They introduce younger children to Character Critters. These stories use hand puppets made by inmates in the women's prison to stress the virtues of each trait.

Department staff also volunteer extensively with the Head Start (pre-school) program. Besides reading to the young children, they are hosts for major holiday activities such as a Thanksgiving food drive for the children's families, and a fall festival featuring face-painting and a moonwalk. They also entertain by providing traditional children's activities like musical chairs and the hokey-poky, and some members of the staff serve as clowns and jugglers. For holiday festivities the department's director of purchasing organizes gift donations, which come from the state's chapter of the National Institute of Government Purchasing. The average donation has been two age-appropriate gifts per child.

Department employees also have arranged a "Small-Mart Clothing" closet in the Head Start classroom. So far, they have stocked it entirely with new clothing items that employees have found at good prices. When children arrive at school inappropriately dressed, or soil their clothing during the day, they are escorted to the closet to pick out new clothing items that they may keep. In addition, parenting skills training has been instituted for the parents of the Head Start children. Staff make presentations at the monthly parent-teacher meetings, and to keep things lively, they award door prizes and give the parents information packets to take home.

Antoine found that parental participation in school activities increased greatly since these programs began at Head Start. "We are more role models than anything else," she says. In other words, the parents tend to feel that if the department staff are willing to volunteer their time then they, as parents, can put more effort into finding time, as well. One example of increased participation was during a week of activities that involved every parent and child—such as "muffins with mom" and "donuts with dad." Participation in this program went from two dads one year to twenty dads the next.

Many of these parents already have come in contact with the criminal justice system and recognize the department's volunteers from the various institutions. Far from being negative encounters, the parents are touched that corrections personnel genuinely care about their children. The department, in partnership with Steps to Success, even plans to offer computer training to the parents of the Head Start children. Steps to Success donated twelve computers in need of refurbishing to a juvenile facility for boys. The boys in turn fixed them and provided them to the Head Start class. Parents will be invited to see the interactive programs their children use at school. Ultimately, using software that Steps to Success is soliciting from local vendors, and volunteer department staff, the parents will have the opportunity to learn computer skills and how to use various programs.

At the American Correctional Association's 1999 Winter Conference, Landrieu observed, "For every one inmate you have, there probably are two or three, maybe more, children attached and in some way, family-related. It's a huge population." The cycle is one of poverty, a lack of education, and genera-tion after generation of the same families being incarcerated. So, who better to be at the helm than corrections?

Stalder says that the Children's Initiatives were designed "to help foster a new generation of healthy, nourished, and nurtured children who will be far less likely as they mature to be involved in violence, drop out of school, or use drugs—all high factors for subsequent criminality." But Louisiana—its correc-tions personnel, parents, lawmakers, private corporations, public programs, and volunteers—continues to have faith in an evolving program that is years away from producing measurable results.

Leaders of the various programs are developing new goals and modifying programs as they learn of community needs or changes in the community. The program leaders are always seeking new funding sources. However, they real-ize that the success of each program depends on the caring and dedicated people involved who envision a better Louisiana. The number of such people is growing. Word of mouth is spreading the news and success of the programs. There is even talk of expanding Hands On Parenting to other states. But, as Antoine says, "We want to keep it grassroots. It's so genuine."

Chapter Nine

Turning the Tables: The Safer Foundation's Youth Empowerment Program

Ron Tonn
Associate Vice President for Public Development
Safer Foundation
Chicago, Illinois

D'arcy Collins had been a street-gang member and a narcotics dealer since he was fourteen. He is fortunate to have reached the age of nineteen, having been shot five times in connection with his drug business. After being convicted of drug possession, serving a year and a half in an Illinois Department of Corrections facility, and being released to electronic detention, he has passed the GED high school equivalency test and is now prospering as a student in the DeVry Institute of Technology Electronics Technician certificate program.

Louisa Dent was convicted in the violent assault of her mother in a dispute over the mother's use of money she receives to care for Louisa's two children. Louisa has now completed parole and is employed as a clerk at Malcolm X College. She is enrolled in vocational training and is pursuing the restoration of custody of her children.

Hector Fernandez was adjudicated as a juvenile for armed robbery. He served a month in the Juvenile Detention Center and was sentenced to five years of probation. Like the cases cited above, he entered the Safer Foundation's Youth Empowerment Program and improved his reading and math performance by three grade-level equivalents in just two months. Despite his lack of job experience, he was reluctant to accept a job at a fast-food restaurant. He derided it as a "low-life" job. He took the job anyway, and within a year became a night manager entrusted with bank transactions. He, too, has passed the GED test and, in addition to maintaining his job, he is attending classes to become a certified mechanic.

These names are fictional, but their stories are fact. They are typical of the stories of the 120 or so clients served each year by the Safer Foundation's Youth Empowerment Program on Chicago's near-west side. This classroom program for juvenile and youth parolees and probationers defies every common expectation about young offenders and, for that matter, about classrooms themselves. The first impression is not that of a classroom at all but of a workplace: the continuous hum of people engaged in collective or individual tasks, the apparent absence—at first glance—of a teacher. But these are just the initial surprises.

As the nation's largest private service provider for an exclusively offender clientele, the Safer Foundation has been helping parolees and probationers find jobs, overcome adjustment barriers, and beat recidivism since 1972. The service array has since increased due to the changing needs of the thousands of former offenders who voluntarily seek Safer services each year. Education became part of that array in 1976, beginning an experiment in pedagogy that continues today.

Academic deficiencies are common in offender populations, and the breakdown in social belonging that characterizes the developmental course for many offenders begins with their failure, at a young age, to prosper in school. As children, many were unprepared and overwhelmed by the demands of school. Some were simply the products of teaching failure. Still others, the clever ones, were bored by the tedium and authoritarianism of some classrooms and sought diversion through mischief and rebellious acts. Their estrangement from the mainstream continued in stages from maladjustment through antisocial behavior, to delinquent and criminal acts. By getting off track in school, students acquire gaps in knowledge and skills. An accompanying breakdown in the social integration further compounds these gaps, which are byproducts of the school experience.

Many young offenders, linked in a peer-endorsed value system, proclaim disdain for school culture and academic success. Some conceal their academic talents from peers to gain acceptance. At the same time, most are embarrassed by their deficiencies and apprehensive about their ability to learn. They may resist instruction to avoid the possibility of confronting more failure. They do not lack self-esteem. Instead, they have established different criteria for their self-worth. Educators who ignore these realities and view education as merely a transmission of information miss a crucial point. They must address psychological barriers to learning as an integrated part of any instructional plan. They build these barriers on self-image, and resolving them can have profound implications for the learner. Education is a metamorphic process: not an additive one. All learners must continually relinquish one self-image in exchange for a new one that encompasses the possession of new skills and knowledge. To learn is to become another person, and learning takes many forms.

For young men and women who grew up in homes without a working breadwinner or whose entire peer group is composed of the unemployed or the never-employed, the nature of working is remote and alien. In a subculture where they regard the wage earner as a "chump," a "mark," or a "lunch bucket," the value and necessity of work may be obscured. Incarceration further instills values that contradict those of the workplace. Indifferent to authority, the confinement experience reinforces disdain for productive effort, suspicion of others, and the delinquent and criminal subculture in the free world. Understandably, workplace customs and values are unfamiliar. Employer expectations conflict with the habits that young offenders have acquired during their incarceration or in their immersion in the criminal street culture. Even the relative meanings of the roles of workers and supervisors can be a mystery.

Despite their social isolation and alienation, most young offenders aspire to conventional images of vocational security and domestic comfort. The greatest barrier to these aspirations for many is their pervading sense of pessimism about their reception, both by potential employers and by providers of vocational training and other services. Their anticipation of stigma-based rejection becomes a self-fulfilling prophecy, and they bypass viable opportunities for job training and gainful employment.

Having grandiose fantasies about their future life on the outside is typical of youthful offenders, but their visions are usually short on detail and lacking in specific action steps for their realization. Their lack of a plan undermines their ambitions and their pessimism grows. The reality of a competitive job market is daunting, and accessible wages seem paltry. Resilience, that most valuable of all attributes for job seekers, is not abundant, and discouragement comes easily. Temptation also sabotages good intentions to resume often-lucrative criminal pastimes. Their circumstances virtually define "high risk" in the prospect of their permanent estrangement from working life.

We have designed the Safer Foundation's educational programs for youth and juveniles because of these realities. Inherent in the tactical methods of the Youth Empowerment Program is an awareness of the characteristics typical of an offender clientele: their high need for stimulation, their low tolerance for routine tedium, their hostility toward institutions, their conflicts with self-image, their fears of failure, and their apprehensions about success. Their past failures in school have inclined them to devalue educational goals. Safer's tactics show them how to succeed in learning and revalue education without denying their experiences or resurrecting their embarrassments and fears.

Since the inception of the program, our ground rule has been, "Try everything; keep what works." The result is a coherent methodology that has produced significant outcomes in academic growth, successful transition to employment, and reduced recidivism for adult, youth, and juvenile offender populations in community-based and institutional settings. The Youth Empowerment Program is but one incarnation of this methodology. It is a community-based program for juvenile parolees, aged sixteen through twenty-one, supported by a consortium of public and private funding sources. Clients usually participate in the program voluntarily, without mandates or sanctions.

The Youth Empowerment Program, or YEP, as its clients refer to it, succeeds through active engagement. We strictly avoid instructional approaches that impose a passive, spectator role on learners. "Peer teaching" is an important vehicle. Quite simply, lesser-skilled clients learn from class peers who possess superior skills, or small groups of comparably skilled clients work jointly to devise solutions to new problem material. The client who is proficient at dividing fractions teaches those who are not, while other clients in small groups are similarly engaged in other learning tasks. In this way, clients at a variety of skill levels can be productively engaged, while the instructors (called facilitators) are available to address the individual needs of other clients. Clients seem to be more receptive to assistance rendered by peers than from instructors, whom, being authority figures, they may regard with hostility. This process accommodates the individualization of instruction, permitting clients to focus attention on their own deficiencies. Facilitators become less the focus of group attention, and can function more as resource persons for the client working groups. Lectures and demonstrations become extinct. Consequently, we have transformed the learning environment into a dynamic working space, containing diverse activities and fluid transitions.

Concurrently, the role of facilitators working in this mode more resembles that of a production foreman than that of a conventional classroom teacher. Then, the training environment becomes a model of values and practices common to the workplace. Learners in this simulated work environment unconsciously learn job-related habits and values while they consciously attend to problems in reading, writing, and mathematics. This is a critical step in preemployment training for a clientele that possesses little positive work experience.

The Youth Empowerment Program classroom methodology purposefully cultivates experiences that will enable young offenders to better acclimate themselves to the interpersonal environment of the workplace. Then, we instill basic habits and values associated with working for a living by applying these principles in the academic classroom and in group discussion sessions that focus on these issues. By understanding the motivations, values, and behavioral determinants of its participants, the program staff succeeds in diminishing barriers, anticipating obstacles, and building rationales for success.

This program has pioneered an *inductive* approach to academic skill training. The learning moves from the specific case to the general principle. This means that facilitators are more likely to instruct with questions than with explanations, and clients gain an authentic sense of discovery when they find correct answers. In this process, we hope to stimulate original thinking and to build strong, multiple associations between knowledge and experience for each client. This network of associations is the key to the retention and recall of information and skill in applying that knowledge.

We maintain a lively, improvisational character in the classroom through a process of spontaneous composition. This is an instructional process in which facilitators create learning tasks on the spot in the presence of clients. These tasks could include math computation tasks, contextual math problems, expository writing topics, logic puzzles, or any other task that small groups or individuals can perform in a classroom. As a strategy for mitigating barriers to learning, this process has enormous advantages.

- It encourages greater familiarity between clients and facilitators. The intimacy of the process allows facilitators to develop greater insight into the temperament and learning style of each client. We know our clients better than we otherwise would. It compels facilitator involvement with clients on a close working level. Facilitators cannot pawn clients off on some anonymous task and forget about them. They must stay engaged. It also alleviates the tedium of routine.

- Facilitators create challenges every day, and the opportunity for novelty is always present. Participants are not confronted with the tedium of the same work, class after class.
- It empowers facilitators to control the content of instruction at will. Points that need attention are addressed without interruption or delay. Strategic opportunism becomes possible. Flexibility is infinite.
- It permits portion control. We can easily tailor work tasks to the limits of each client's span of attention and concentration.
- It compels facilitators to invest energy and active thought into client interactions. Facilitators can more easily form a bond of trust with clients when it is apparent that facilitators are invested in their clients' interests.
- It provides facilitators an opportunity to demonstrate their abilities. Their assured command of intellectual domains secures client confidence in the facilitator's ability to help them.
- It casts facilitators in an active role. The process permits facilitators to serve as dynamic, productive role models who are continually engaged in creative endeavors.
- It eliminates client barriers to scrutiny. Provided with workbooks, textbooks, and the like, clients frequently employ these as shields against accountability in an attempt to conceal learning difficulties or lack of effort.
- It permits facilitators to dictate through their action the tempo of the training. Facilitators can stimulate clients to greater levels of concentration and task engagement by setting a brisk working pace themselves.
- Not least, it introduces elements of suspense and unpredictability, alleviating boredom.

Visitors to the Youth Empowerment Program often assume that, in a classroom full of young offenders and school dropouts, discipline and authority would be constant issues. Curiously, the solution to this potential problem is a byproduct of the instructional strategy. The source of most disruptive behavior in classrooms is boredom and distraction. Clients who are engaged in interesting and challenging learning tasks are not behavior problems. The program's capacities for individualization and spontaneity are its most valuable discipline tools.

It is true that our clients are habitually predisposed to evade, resist, or openly challenge any attempts to imposed authority. This is a product of their experience, and we expect it. Facilitators know better than to take these resistive gestures personally, recognizing them as normal defense mechanisms that have become dysfunctional. If facilitators were to present themselves as authority figures, they would only invite challenges and elicit problematic behavior. The resulting struggle over authority issues would take precedence over every other objective. This dynamic takes place in classrooms all around the country, and it is probably the main event in most of them. Learning cannot take place under such conditions. Only by transcending the issue of power can we create an environment where students can attain the learning and acculturation goals of the program.

This transcendence begins only with the recognition that clients and facilitators are equals who have come together by mutual agreement, each to meet certain individual needs. The terms of that agreement must be clearly expressed and communicated. We resolve subsequent behavioral inconsistencies by addressing them as violations of an agreement between equals, not as client transgressions of staff rules. Conflict resolution addressed on this level preserves the dignity of both parties and helps accord. It is the shortest distance between two points; it gets the dispute over with quickly and finally, and gives clients a model of conflict resolution that will serve them well as they make the transition into mainstream life.

Facilitators treat clients as peers whom they respect, not as children over whom they have dominion. Authority comes in handy when leadership fails; when leadership is present, authority is superfluous. By relinquishing the expectation that they should be the lords of the classroom, facilitators usually find the freedom to be more effective, more productive, and more fulfilled in their work.

The temperamental characteristics prevalent in youth offender populations recommend short-term but intense training and motivational interventions. The inability to defer gratification, the need for high stimulation, and the desire for rapid transitions and situational variety are well-documented among lawbreakers. The negative aspects of these characteristics can be moderated and diminished through insightful training, but initially, "playing with their deck" is necessary. Working within these constraints, exposing participants to learning and working experiences that lead them out of criminal subcultures and into mainstream self-sufficiency is possible.

Because of the characteristics of participants in this program, scheduled training is compact by conventional standards. The very high risk of criminal recidivism of our participants has driven us to devise service strategies that permit rapid transitions into mainstream activities. Acknowledging the life circumstances of our clients and their need for rapid transitions into stable situations, we have intentionally compacted the program to an eight-week period. Our clients readily grasp the accelerated intensity of this time scale, and liken it to their image of an athlete in training.

Many of our clients' internal barriers to successful transition are dormant in the training environment. They do not appear until the participant encounters stress in real-world settings. Only then is he or she receptive to the insights that could lead to the resolution of interpersonal difficulties that occur in such settings. Such junctures present opportunistic instructional situations, which previously did not exist.

Recognizing our clients' need for long-term intervention and their incompatibility with long-term training, we have developed an innovative program adjunct of reintervention training. Such training extends far beyond separation from formal training and into the difficult transitional period when barriers surface and are amenable to remedy. It is important that program intervention continue into and through this period of transition and beyond. We preserve the impact of work-acclimation training beyond job or vocational-training placement through a specialized "lifeguard," a kind of *guerrilla case manager*.

As the name implies, the lifeguard will monitor participants as they make the transition into mainstream, post-training placement sites and intervene as problems arise. Conceived as a mobile, quick-response, highly adaptable change agent, the lifeguard shadows participants in transition and intervenes creatively when needed. Examples of such intervention include the following:

- Interpersonal skill training to resolve conflicts resulting from poor relations with coworkers, fellow students, instructors, or supervisors
- Elucidating school or work values and expectations in the context of the participant's placement setting
- Self-control training through opportunities to appropriately vent frustrations and anxieties resulting from the stress of transition and the inevitable conflicts with self-image
- Supplementary academic or job-related skill training to remedy deficiencies in performance
- Debriefing of circumstances that may have led to placement failure
- Retrieval and replacement in the event of initial failure
- Coordination of substance abuse counseling or treatment for the maintenance of sobriety
- Coordination of supplemental training or education

Through frequent contact with participants, their agents of correctional supervision, their families, their trainers, and their employers, the lifeguard diagnoses obstacles to retention or advancement and provides whatever supplemental training or coordination of services are necessary to optimize prospects for successful adjustment.

Often, the lifeguard serves as a sounding board and resource person to debrief, analyze, and strategize around problem situations. The lifeguard maintains a regular schedule of contacts with participants transitioning to employment or training through their successful placement in employment and beyond. These contacts serve to assess the participant's adjustment to employment and to resolve issues before they lead to employment termination. Attention to each participant's domestic environment is vitally important, and coordination of families in support of employment goals is a primary focus for lifeguards. Often forgotten but vitally important is the role that the lifeguard plays in the celebration of successes, as the client progresses through the various milestones on the way to self-sufficiency. Even if no one else cares, clients can brag about their accomplishments to their lifeguard.

These contacts also represent the data collection points for the determination of participant status in employment, police contact, and educational progress. Lifeguard-initiated contact continues for at least one year, and participant-initiated contact with the lifeguard may continue indefinitely.

Increased frequency of contact occurs at the lifeguard's discretion based on need or at the initiation of the participant.

Depending on the participant's status at the time of intervention, the lifeguard revises individual service strategies to address whatever problem the client may face in the preservation of employment, the maintenance of domestic stability, the maintenance of sobriety, and the abstinence from criminal activity. Encouraging successful clients, remotivating failing clients, and retrieving failed clients—these are the lifeguard's objectives. The lifeguard records the subject and contents of each contact in progress notes maintained in each client's database record. Additionally, the lifeguard maintains a status tally chart as a summary of retention, attrition, recidivism, and retrieval. Thus, long-term data collection is a consequence of the delivery of useful and substantive services to clients.

We establish no maximum period for the continuation of lifeguard activities. We have expected that over time the necessity of contact and reintervention will decrease for most participants. Other clients, having greater needs, may continue to require lifeguard contact of longer duration and at more intense levels. At no time, throughout the life of the program, will any participant be considered inaccessible to lifeguard services. Participants may initiate contact anytime following their participation.

Our experience and the best available research indicate that this strategy offers the best hope for populations such as ours, who are extremely alienated from mainstream life. We cannot effect the transition to self-sufficiency for this population in a single training step, whatever its duration. Young trainees poorly internalize the solutions to as-yet-experienced problems. Transition is an incremental process that entails a gradual alteration in self-image from "outlaw" to "citizen." Our clients must grow into this role while they divest themselves of self-destructive and antisocial values. Training can only supplement (and not substitute for) this process.

We have recorded the results of all these activities in multiple parameters. We employ rigorous, objective testing to validate the academic performance improvements that clients experience. We administer official practice versions of the General Educational Development (GED) test to all Youth Empowerment Program participants at the beginning, middle, and conclusion of training. We document mean improvements in GED standard scores of 14 to 16 percent routinely (this corresponds to gains of 2.0 to 2.5 grade-level equivalents on conventional norm-referenced achievement tests). Nearly half of all participants pass the certified high school equivalency test on their first or second attempt after eight weeks of training. The training completion rate for Youth Empowerment Program participants is more than 82 percent.

More than 79 percent of all participants in the last three years were placed in jobs or vocational training through the efforts of another staff member, the transition counselor. Most significant, considering the Safer Foundation's mission of reducing recidivism, is the fact that Youth Empowerment Program participants are 53 percent less likely than the average juvenile parolee in Illinois to be convicted of a new crime within three years after their participation in the program.

The experience of the Youth Empowerment Program demonstrates that many aspects of conventional teaching practice are obstacles to learning and understanding. We avoid the unnecessary abstraction, fragmentation, and isolation of knowledge from meaningful contexts and the total reliance on deductive reasoning that dominate prevalent instructional thinking. Nor is the classroom seen as a place to reinforce the social stratification of its students. Young adult learners should not need to adopt a childlike, subordinate status compared with their teachers simply because they are less skilled. This is especially important for a student population whose prior instructional experience has been characterized by failure and humiliation.

The Basic Skills Training Program is an affirmation of the view that education is more a cultivation of abilities and attitudes than a transmission of information. We distinguish knowledge from information by recognizing that knowledge is information united with self-image through meaningful experience. The interactive, participatory nature of this program is a strategy to enrich the experience of learning. Yet, it is much more than an educational program. It uses education as a catalyst to induce experiences that result in positive changes in the "whole person" to make him or her a more confident, competitive, competent member of the workforce and society. In the end, our staff probably takes its greatest satisfaction from an unsolicited remark that they have heard from hundreds of Youth Empowerment Program clients: "If *real* school had been like this, I would never have dropped out."

Chapter Ten

Writing Our Stories: An Update on the Antiviolence Creative Writing Program for Juveniles*

Anne Hasselbrack
Editorial Assistant
American Correctional Association
Lanham, Maryland

If someone were to overhear Alabama writer Marlin "Bart" Barton say that, "Signing a book with one's writing published in it has to be one of the highlights of a young writer's life," the erroneous conclusion might be that he is referring to a prep school class on poetry. Instead, Barton is referring to youthful offenders chosen to participate in the creative writing program, Writing Our Stories. This program is a cooperative effort between the Alabama Writer's Forum and the Alabama Department of Youth Services.

Now entering its fifth year, the program is the brainchild of Jeannie Thompson, president of the Forum. Several years ago, she accompanied her husband Bill Fuller, then in the Alabama House of Representatives, on a holiday visit to the Mt. Meigs facility for boys. The plan was to have pizza and hand out a few presents, but after telling the boys that she was a writer, several boys approached her to discuss their own writing.

Inspired, Thompson submitted a winning proposal to the Department of Youth Services that included having the Forum supply a part-time creative writing teacher for the boys. Barton, who earned a Master of Fine Arts in creative writing from Wichita State University, won an O'Henry short fiction award. She has taught English and creative writing at the college level, and became the first teacher hired under the Writing Our Stories program. Only a handful of the estimated 250 boys at Mt. Meigs were chosen to participate. Administrators put others on a wait list—a first for any of the academic programs at that facility. As boys were released or dropped out, others rotated into the class. The boys' regular classroom teacher, Queen Barker, says that they "worked beyond normal school hours to create short stories and poems, and to keep a journal. These students were excited!"

Barton is now both a teacher and assistant director of the program, and with the current level of state funding, approximately 130 students a year can participate.

---

* Based on an update of Clayton, Susan. "Writing Our Stories: An Antiviolence Creative Writing Program for Juveniles Changes Lives." February 2000. *Corrections Today*. 62 (1) 26-28.

- The Alabama Council for the Arts funds the Alabama Writer's Forum, which, in part, provides the money for Thompson's and Barton's salaries and the costs of preparing the Department of Youth Services proposal each year.

- The state legislature reviews, and has thus far approved, the contracts between the Forum and the Department of Youth Services.

- The Department of Youth Services pays the writing teachers, funds the anthologies, buys reading material, and covers all other program costs.

In the future, Thompson would like to have a contract that allows each writing teacher to be involved full-time. Meanwhile, she is encouraged by those who believe in the program and those who would like to emulate it in their states. At the American Correctional Association's 1999 Congress of Correction in Denver, Thompson said that she was describing her program to another attendee when he offered to buy the curriculum from her. Yet, no formal curriculum exists. Writing teachers are free to structure their classes as they see fit.

However, that is about to change thanks to the Alabama Children's Trust Fund, which supports community-based child abuse and neglect prevention programs. The Fund recently gave the Forum a grant so they can formalize their curriculum with ideas from all three teachers. Then, with the curriculum in hand, Thompson plans to seek Federal funds to take the program and its message to others. The program has since expanded to include two more Department of Youth Services' campuses, Vacca for boys with writer Danny Gamble, and Chalkville for girls with writer Priscilla Hancock Cooper.

Gamble says that he was apprehensive when approached about teaching creative writing behind what he describes as the "razor wire and magnetic locks" of Vacca. Already an instructor in English at the University of Alabama-Birmingham who earned a Master of Fine Arts in creative writing from the University of Alabama, he says, "I felt I would have little to offer these students. I felt they would have little to offer me."

Hancock Cooper, who earned a Master of Arts degree from the American University in Washington, D.C., is entering her third year of teaching creative writing at Chalkville. She says of the girls there, "They are told that this facility is the 'last stop' before they end up at Tutwiler Women's Prison. Violence, drug use, and sexual abuse have been all too common in their young lives . . . Even as my students write about things that are ugly and brutal, creative writing allows them to share those thoughts with beauty and elegance."

Because she also is a performing artist, she introduces the girls to aspects of self-expression beyond writing. For instance, she added a photography component to her class, in partnership with the Birmingham Museum of Art. Using the camera allows the students to get a different perspective on the world and their own writing. The girls must stay within the Chalkville security perimeter to take their pictures, and for confidentiality reasons cannot directly photograph girls' faces. However, the snapshots that emerged, and particularly the self-portraits, were "both powerful and disturbing" according to Susan Harris, assistant curator of education at the museum. Images included the rough surface of a brick wall, a picture of one manicured hand with someone else's legs in the distance walking away, and the shadow of a torso with the petals of a small flower transposed in the center of a girl's chest. Images included many backs, hair loose, arms wide or crossed, reaching or leading. Hancock Cooper says, "When writing about the photographs, they are working from the emotions/memories evoked not only by the image, but by the process of creating the image."

She also includes a drama segment to share with the girls her love of the spoken word and its power. Writing is very different from interpreting a piece of literature for performance, she says. "For these students who are so often punished or criticized for 'showing off,' the creative dramatics provides an outlet for their oral expression. They get to 'show off' on stage and be applauded for it."

Barton, the Mt. Meigs teacher, speculates that the very act of creating increases his students' ability to move beyond violent images. A student who usually wrote very violent stories one day wrote a story about a boy making a vase on a pottery wheel. When Barton told him how good the story was, the boy said that he was not sure why he used to write such violent things. Barton thought to himself, because you needed to. Perhaps it was the boy's awareness that writing is an act of creation that ultimately changed his attitude and inspired him to write about other forms of creation instead of destruction.

For the few students who are chosen to participate in Writing Our Stories based on maturity levels, interest, and possible benefits, the highlight of the program comes at the end when a perfect-bound, professional anthology edited by each respective teacher is published. Thompson knew that having an anthology would be a great incentive for the students and incorporated the idea in her first proposal, complete with a reading and book signing.

At the first of these events, a standing-room-only crowd of the Department of Youth Services' personnel, family, guests, and local press greeted Barton's students. He says that when his students heard the applause, they were "bursting with pride" and he hopes that can spark something in them that lasts. The program has its share of proponents. Now those who personally know the kids, judges, politicians, and child advocates attend the readings. Thompson says that the students in these facilities "don't have a lot of ways to be praised by the people they respect." Barton describes the students' opportunity to read for the various, distinguished members of the community as a "crowning moment"—when they go from being youthful offenders to proud, published writers.

A Qualitative Study

Sharon McDonough, a student at Auburn University, is doing her dissertation on the Writing Our Stories program. For five months, she attended the classes at the Mt. Meigs facility as both a participant and an observer. The themes that emerged from her observations were "community," "empowerment," and "trust." She says:

[Students] come to view themselves as writers and feel a responsibility for supporting other students in their writing. They tend to see good writing skills as something more than a tool to help [them] pass a test, graduate from high school, or obtain [a] GED. They come to the realization that written expression is a powerful communication tool that can influence what other people think.

However, as interested as McDonough and others would be to track the kids once they are released to study the long-term effects of such a program, privacy laws prevent this. Gamble says he knows for sure that one of his students went on to college. He and others are also highly encouraged that many students who have been released are willing to come back for the anthology readings. If anyone still needs evidence on why the program should be implemented in more schools for youthful offenders, Jeannie Thompson says that one needs to look no further than the nine anthologies.

One perk the students receive by participating is the chance to meet a wide array of adults who are successful writers and positive influences. McDonough says the students are quite surprised that the visitors are so different from each other—different races, educational backgrounds, and writing styles. At first, she says, the kids have an image in their heads of what a writer is. However, when they meet the different visitors over the school year, they dispel their stereotypes.

A favorite visiting writer is Frank X. Walker, a poet from Louisville, Kentucky, whose book of poems is titled *Affrilachia*. Besides having many references in his poetry that the students can relate to, he also gets them involved and thinking with in-class exercises. In one exercise, he draws a single line down the middle of the chalkboard and asks the students to say what they see. They reply: a snake, a skinny tree, a line of cocaine. What he wants them to take away from the varied answers is the value of others' points of view. In another exercise, he has the boys write out their favorite rap lyrics, and then go through the songs, striking out words they feel are not necessary. Then, he has them do the same thing a few more times. The result is that after editing out what Gamble describes as the "violent, profane, gross" language, the students are left with the essence of the song. The lesson for this exercise is that graphic language is superfluous to making one's point, and this helps the students become better communicators in both speaking and writing.

When Gamble's students equate rap music with poetry, he can relate since he was first inspired to write after listening to the Beatles. One book he has his class read is the late Tupac Shakur's poetry, *The Rose That Grew From Concrete*. Because the writing leans toward the literary versus rap, and Shakur is a figurehead who the boys admire, Gamble uses the book to change the boys' perspective on what constitutes good writing. Inevitably, he says he receives fewer copies back of the book than what he handed out.

Writing Our Stories works for these kids, Gamble says, because most have not come from nurturing educational environments. In a small, hands-on writing class, they learn and are eager to share what they know. As one student said, "I used to wonder how to become a writer. Now I wonder what I am going to write next."

In one of Barton's classes at Mt. Meigs, the students rewrote *Romeo and Juliet* to their liking, and then a local group called the Shakespeare Players performed it for them. According to their regular teacher, it was quite a hit. Patricia Foster, an Alabama native and current associate professor of English at the University of Iowa, also visited Mt. Meigs and Chalkville. She did an exercise with the boys at Mt. Meigs called "Straddling Two Worlds: The Visit." The students were to recall a visit they had at the facility, write a list of details about the visit, write out a short conversation they had, and finally, write a narrative about the visit. Foster says, "What was amazing to me was the strength of their writing, the vividness and urgency of their memories. They did not shy away from pain or the disclosure of their own sadness." She also said that they had a good time doing the exercise, laughing, and smiling, and her overall impression was that they loved being in the writing class.

Breakthrough

Typically, prison-based creative writing programs are purely emotional outlets, and instructors do not stress the craft of writing. Writing Our Stories, on the other hand, is part education, part therapy. While learning the craft through both reading and writing, the students, who are typically incarcerated for status crimes, drugs, or theft, are encouraged to write from their own lives. Barton says that usually he does not know why the kids are there, and does not want to know. His experience has been that the boys do not brag, and actually seem embarrassed about what they did to end up at Mt. Meigs. He takes solace in that embarrassment, and when the boys do write about the horrific things they have known in their young lives, like the boy who wrote about molesting his sister, Barton tries not to look or act as taken-aback as he feels, telling them simply, "I'm glad you chose to write about that." He then helps them polish the writing.

When one of his more notorious students, a boy who suffocated his two-year-old sister, wrote about the crime, Barton learned that it was the first time the boy had articulated any aspect of what he did, including in court or with his therapist at the institution. In one poem the boy, J. E. L., writes, "Sister Life wants to make people happy . . . / . . . Brother Death is her enemy." In another, about the day his sister died, he wrote, "Then the moment I dread the most, / that black bag comes out / and in it is a corpse, / the corpse of a person I once loved." His therapist called the writing a breakthrough.

Thompson believes that Writing Our Stories makes "a humanizing connection to children who have been dehumanized." When people ask her what she feels is the purpose of the program she tells them, "The purpose is saving lives."J. Walter Wood, Jr., executive director of the Alabama Department of Youth Services, says that the students' "willingness to take part in the creative writing classes, keep pace with assignments and revise their work" augments the treatment they receive in the facilities. Researcher McDonough agrees, observing that the program is an empowering experience for the youth because as they develop as writers, "they gain more confidence in their abilities and begin to see new possibilities for their own futures."

To do this, many students choose to confront their pasts. In the Chalkville anthology Look Into My Soul, B. N. W.'s poem "A Little Girl" begins: "From patty cake to bakers men, / To trying to remember a date. / Twisting my pigtails, sitting in court, / Trying to remember a rape," and ends: "That one messed-up man / Left a chaotic world in my hands."

W. B. S.'s "I am a Sunrise" is a poem, made more powerful because of its present tense, about a girl discovering herself and the potency of her words. Also, it is a fitting illustration of the program's success.

"I Am a Sunrise"

The early rays everywhere
Are the golden glints of my hair.
Wispy clouds in palest pink
Dance across my creamy cheeks.
Songbirds chirping and twittering high above
Sing out my heart's joy, laughter, and love.
The few morning stars left in the western sky
Are the twinkles in my eyes.
Dark clouds in hues of purple and gray
Are the things I am afraid to say.
But each of them has a silver lining;
These are my hopes and dreams brightly shining.
Like the sun illuminates everything for miles and miles
Nothing can compare to the brightness of my smile.
Just as people can use the sun to find their way,
I use my words and my smile to brighten their day.
But just as the trees block the beautiful horizon,
I can use harsh words to keep you from rising.
I won't even notice if you try to stop me.
The rays of hope shining through are all I see.
Just as the sun can light up the entire world,
I am a bright and shining girl.

Chapter Eleven

Managing Juveniles in Adult Facilities: Identifying Population and Institutional Characterisitics to Determine Staff Training Needs

Salvador A. Godinez
Juvenile Field Services Administrator
Illinois Department of Corrections
Springfield, Illinois

Training modules and/or procedures that relate to the treatment and custody of youthful offenders housed in adult facilities should address the following concerns. Training is the common denominator in determining the success of facility management. The need to develop and maintain an acceptable quality of life for this "high-maintenance" population also underlies the importance of keeping staff prepared and well-trained.

Individualized Approach

Before we can adequately address training needs for staff, we need to address the problems, issues, concerns and/or needs that confront us with this "special population." Clearly, this youthful population is quite different from its adult counterpart. Anyone who has raised children can remark on the differences between a thirteen-year-old and a twenty-one-year-old. The thirteen-year-old obviously will not have matured physically or emotionally as has the twenty-one-year-old. In a correctional setting, the twenty-one-year-old also may not be prepared to deal with a younger and possibly more hyperactive population. Thus, there are several issues to consider when dealing with youthful offenders. Issues related to the offenders themselves include:

- Age. Depending on the state, it could be from age twelve to twenty-six.
- Crime. Most juvenile offenders placed in adult facilities are not violent offenders.
- Culture. Ethnicity, race, and age all heighten anxiety between staff and client.
- Gang involvement. Is the youth being placed in danger to himself/herself or others?

83

- Region/Geography. Is placing the youth far from home an advantage to anyone, including the youth or staff?

Institutional Concerns

Prey or predator. The possibility exists that your program will be "shocked" if you cannot ascertain the issues of prey and predator correctly and respond accordingly. For example, a child who is awaiting charges as an adult in a juvenile facility may be seen as a predator. However, once the child enters an adult facility, he or she quickly can become prey. Thus, childish behavior can present itself in a setting that before may not have experienced problems associated with typical youthful behavior. The best way to respond is to prepare for it and to deal with it consistently, keeping in mind that youthful offenders are kids, not adults.

Leader, Loner, or Follower. Youths tend to be highly impressionable and search, under general circumstances, to be a part of something. Thus, this population can be easily led, used, or manipulated in an adult facility.

Size of Your Population. Do you have one or hundreds? This affects every facet of your facility, especially housing. The size of a particular population will determine whether to house the youthful offenders in a special wing, renovate an existing part of the facility, or build a new housing unit.

Facility Structure. Is your security commensurate with the security needs of the juveniles you house? Juvenile maximum-security facilities have a tendency to have greater external controls to deal with escape risks as opposed to tighter internal controls to deal with aggressive juveniles. The impulsivity of this youthful population requires constant supervision. Clear and extensive sight lines have proved highly effective with a younger population.

Laws. All fifty states have enacted laws that permit the prosecution of juveniles as adults. What does your jurisdiction provide in terms of legal mandates? Do you know which juveniles can be prosecuted as adults? Under what circumstances will this prosecution occur? This knowledge is vital in formulating population projections.

Security Differences. Is a maximum-security thirteen-year-old the same as a maximum- security forty-five-year-old? Do they require the same physical program structure? Given the apparent differences in operational needs, do you have the resources to house the youthful offenders and provide for their particular needs?

Program Differences. Counseling, recreational, educational, work, and dietary programs may need to be tailored for this population.

Jails versus Prisons. Their missions and approaches may be similar, but programming takes into account the lengths of stay, and it is important to remember that much of a jail population is presumed innocent as well. Some jails house inmates sentenced to as many as five years.

Training. Very few jurisdictions, even those with training academies, provide special training modules that deal with youthful offenders. Issues such as the use of force and the use of chemical agents can present problems for administrators. Does your facility/agency have a training plan? Does it encompass the issues surrounding youthful offenders?

The Adultification Process. Several jurisdictions accept the juveniles in their systems as adults but treat them programmatically as juveniles. Other jurisdictions accept the differences between juveniles and adults but treat them the same. This may be confusing for staff.

Reception and Classification. Perhaps the most important issue is classification. It is the beginning of a program for any population and helps determine who goes where and why. Important questions to consider include:

- How do you classify?
- Do you have "special" classifications, such as juvenile felons, sexual predators, or habitual offenders?
- Do you have administrative segregation or disciplinary segregation?
- Are youths put into medical isolation or into any other type of isolation/segregation status as part of classification?
- How do you handle protective custody needs of youthful offenders in adult facilities?
- How do you classify youths with emotional/psychological problems?
- How do you classify youths with gender or sexual orientation issues?

"Kids Being Kids." Disciplinary behavior could range from offenders throwing spitballs at staff to serious weapons-related offenses. This population is a very high-maintenance group in behavior. When addressing classification, you are dealing with unpredictable behavior and the point of maturation cannot be easily foreseen.

Accreditation. Does your system follow adult standards and/or juvenile detention standards? This can influence whether your accreditation or compliance audit is accepted or denied.

Drugs. This popular vice among youths remains constant in correctional facilities. An offender using drugs is more capable and willing to test your structures and programs. Violent, erratic, and aggressive behavior is more likely to occur if an individual is under the influence of drugs and/or alcohol.

Effective Approaches

In addressing these concerns, facilities can take several approaches. They include:

- *Evaluating your classification system.* Consistency, space, and program resources should complement your classification process. If your special needs population's basic requirements can be met, your classification process is validated. Otherwise, you may need to consider whether you can mainstream your juvenile offenders into a similarly classified adult population.

- Taking advantage of technology available in both program areas and in your security/custody approach. Camera surveillance, movement tracking, distance learning, telemedicine, and courtroom conferencing are a few examples of technological approaches that can ease the stress on staff and inmates. Youthful offenders in correctional facilities have traditionally required a higher ratio of staff to inmates. When one considers this requirement with the constant need to monitor the behavior and programs, stress is inevitable. Additionally, the frequent staff shortages many facilities experience increase the probability of stress.
- Evaluating the success or failure of your approach. It will help you draw conclusions about whether the placement of youthful offenders in adult facilities works.
- Developing programs that meet schedules, provide direction, and allow for the productive release of energy. This can be your best security, especially with a youthful and impulsive individual seeking immediate gratification.
- Understanding that the gang-involved youth often is searching for a family. A youth will seek out a gang to fulfill his or her basic needs if we, their custodians, do not meet those needs. If it takes a village to raise a child, then consider the correctional facility the village.
- Making sure that your staff is operating on the same wavelength. Staff must be trained and held accountable. They need to approach their jobs as caring professionals. The best approach will go for naught if this is not consistently reinforced. It also is helpful to identify staff available to you who have degrees in juvenile justice-related fields and/or experience in dealing with juveniles and use them accordingly.

Conclusion

Recently, several states across the country have taken a hard stance on crime committed by juvenile offenders. We do not, however, know if we have been successful in our placement of many of these youths in adult facilities. Currently, we are only measuring our success through programs, and we do not necessarily know if we are successful in changing behavior. Correctional facilities need to focus more on changing behavior in the long run and not just the short run. The question that needs to be asked is: Are these youths more mature and less aggressive when they leave, or do they just go along with the program because they know it will better their situations while they are serving their time?

Depending on factors not necessarily within your control, the issue of juvenile treatment versus adult custody will remain controversial. Political winds can fuel this debate as can situational crises and changes to the law.

In dealing with youthful offenders, the remaining questions include: How has the typical offender changed? What are the attitudes of new and existing staff toward juveniles? These questions will remain, but hopefully not for long, as more research is conducted on juvenile offenders in adult facilities and elements such as exit interviews, aftercare programs, and follow-ups after release become part of our approach. Research will likely spawn literature that will bring corrections professionals closer to the reality and practicality of the issues concerning youthful offenders.

References

Dugan, Bob. 1998. Juveniles in Adult Jails. *American Jails*. October.

Glick, B. and W. Sturgeon. 1998. *No Time to Play: Youthful Offenders in Adult Correctional Systems*. Lanham, Maryland: American Correctional Association.

__2001. *Recess Is Over: A Handbook Managing Youthful Offenders in Adult Systems*. Lanham, Maryland: American Correctional Association.

Howell, James C. et.al., eds. 1995. *Serious Violent and Chronic Juvenile Offenders*. Thousand Oaks, California: Sage Publications.

Riley, Mark. 1998. The Toughest Challenge: Youthful Offenders. *American Jails*. December.

Zedenburg, Jason and Vincent Schiraldi. 1998. The Risks Juveniles Face. *Corrections Today*. August.

Chapter Twelve

Developing a Security Envelope for a Youthful Offender Program

William "Bill" Sturgeon
President
Institute for Adult Education and Training
Pittsfield, Massachusetts,

Coauthor of Recess is Over:
A Handbook for Managing Youthful Offenders in Adult Systems
(available from the American Correctional Association.)

Developing a security plan for a youthful offender program requires thinking through the security requirements for every facet of the program. Over the past years, we have learned a great deal about the security management of youthful offenders in adult facilities. One of the most important things that has been learned is that youthful offenders can be managed, refuting common beliefs of the mid-1990s that youthful offenders were so wild and violent that they could not be managed and that they had to be locked down twenty-three hours per day.

Security in any youthful offender program is, without question, demanding and is truly everyone's responsibility. The involvement of clerical, program, food service, and maintenance personnel in planning the security is mandatory.

Programs also play an important part of the overall security of a youthful offender program. Well-developed programs and the involvement of the program staff can enhance security. Here is a real example that will reinforce this statement. One youthful offender program was averaging eight serious incidents per day. The security staff was worn out from all the incidents and they were willing to try anything. A new group of counselors was selected to work with the youthful offender program. These counselors developed very good programs (that were age specific) and became very involved with the offenders. They spent time in the living areas, recreation areas, and in the dining room. After about thirty days, the serious incidents dropped to one per month.

This example has been shared so that you will understand that a facility cannot just look to the uniformed staff for security in a youthful offender program. Everyone must open his or her security paradigms to embrace a more comprehensive delivery of security. Security and program staff working as a team can create a formidable security plan.

Operations

As the security plan is developed for a youthful offender program, it is crucial that every component of the security plan be able to react quickly and decisively to manage any incident or occurrence. Youthful offenders, because of their immaturity and impulsiveness, often do not understand that there will be consequences for their behavior.

Preparing a security plan for any youthful offender program will require a great amount of detailed work. Developing a comprehensive security plan for a youthful offender program ranks right up there with developing a security plan for a supermax facility. This comparison is made because of the amount of detail that goes into the planning, implementing, and specialized training for both types of facilities. Just as in a supermax facility there is no room for error, so too there is no room for error in a youthful offender program.

As has been stated previously, youthful offenders lack maturity, are impulsive, and do not always think about the consequences of their behavior. These three elements alone can be a test to the program's security plan. One of the best ways to develop a security plan is to prepare it by identifying and implementing security envelopes that take into consideration the following:

- operations
- physical plant (total environment)
- staffing (total staffing)
- technology/material

Security enveloping is the integrating and interfacing of operations, staff, and facilities, augmented by appropriate technology to manage the security operations. Applying basic principles of security enveloping when developing the security plan for the youthful offender program will require a detailed understanding of the daily operations of the program. The best way to do this is to develop a comprehensive daily schedule. Once a daily schedule has been developed, then the individual security envelopes can be developed around the daily operations.

For example: Knowing what time you will wake up the youthful offenders will determine the following:

- When additional staff will be needed to supervise the offenders and perform other tasks.
- When the night security envelope will begin to open to accommodate the daily operations/offender movement of the early part of the day.
- When certain alarms will possibly be shut off and other types of technology will be activated.

When developing the daily schedule, those responsible for designing, implementing, and managing the security plan must carefully examine the following:

- What exactly are the offenders scheduled to do?
- Where exactly are they going to be?
- What will the exact time frames be? (This should include movement to and from activities.)
- How will they get there? (route)
- How will they get to the next activity on the schedule? (route)
- What will be the total staff requirements/responsibilities for every activity on the schedule?
- What will be the exact number of offenders either in movement and/or in activities?

For each event that is on the daily schedule, try to establish a security envelope using all the components: operations, facility, staffing, and technology (where appropriate or available).

Take a look at what the implications are to the security when one awakens the offenders at 4:30 AM. Some of the implications include the following:

- Lack of staff at that hour of the morning.
- The rest of the facility is still in the night security envelope(s).
- How much the night security envelope(s) will have to be opened to accommodate the operations/movements of the youthful offender program?

If you bring in staff to wake the offenders up at 4:30 AM, you need to also consider the following:

- What distance will the staff have to drive to get to work?
- Will there be staff who will want to work those hours?
- What is the normal shift (eight, ten, twelve hours)? Use this example: If the normal shift is eight hours, then the staff that comes in at 4:00-4:15 A.M. will have to leave at 12:00 or 12:15 P.M.. How will that affect the schedule?

It is important to remember that every action that is taken will have some impact on the security envelopes that have been established.

Facility

One of the best ways to develop security envelopes is from the inside (of the facility) to the perimeter fence/walls. The last part of the security envelope, of course, is the perimeter. The best place to start is at the offender living area at midnight. Then, using the daily schedule, develop individual security envelopes for all of the areas and activities listed on the schedule.

When developing security envelopes, it is important to always remember to include inmate movement. Experience has shown that incidents often occur during offender movement from one area to another.

Additional side benefits derived from developing security envelopes include these:

- You really get to know the strengths and weaknesses of your entire facility.
- You develop an understanding about the technology that your facility uses to augment staff.
- You can insure the productivity of the staff.
- You know exactly where every offender is at every minute of the day.

Remember this: If an inmate makes it to your perimeter fence/wall, then all of your internal security envelopes have failed.

When you look at the facility where the youthful offender program will be or is located, insure that the facility has been built to the security levels needed for the program. In most cases, the facilities now being used are for the most part maximum security. But remember, adult facilities were built for adults. Check your facility. In one prison that had a youthful offender program, there was an opening in a corner that a small youth or for that matter an adult inmate, could have squeezed through.

Assess each of the security envelope's strengths and weaknesses that have been identified and develop a plan for taking corrective action. Some things to look for during your assessment process include the following:

- The overall physical condition of areas the youthful offender program will be using. (The living areas should be well maintained and, if possible, freshly painted. By doing this the youthful offenders, as part of their programming, will be required to keep it in the condition that they found it.)
- Replace broken or missing fixtures.
- Replace all lighting and if possible, increase the lighting.
- Identify blind areas and include in your security plan a method for dealing with these blind areas. (Youthful offenders, like adult offenders, will use these blind areas to their best interests, not yours.)
- Use the 360 degrees assessment method when looking at all facilities that the youthful offenders will use. (The 360 degree process is when you assess the ceiling, walls, floor, all openings such as door jambs, windows, vent opening, and so forth.)
- Assess all movement routes using the same 360 degree method.

The facility can be and should be one of the strongest components of your total security envelope only if you know it and use it effectively. Make sure that security assessments are conducted on a regular basis.

Staffing

A basic rule for staffing is to have the correct number correct place, for the correct period of time, with the correct training, doing the correct thing. Without question, staffing is the most important element of the security envelope principle. Knowing that staffing is a crucial element of the security enveloping, the sooner you establish the security envelopes that will be necessary for your program, the sooner you will be able to define the staffing levels.

Four things are unique to a youthful offender program staffing pattern:

1. Do not depend on traditional adult staffing patterns for youthful offender programs.
2. Staff training in how to manage youthful offenders has to be mandatory.
3. Total staffing levels must include interdisciplinary staffing (including security, programs, support, clerical, maintenance, and so forth).
4. Staff should be flexible and move with the operational demands of the program.

Experience has shown that traditional adult staffing patterns do not meet the demands of managing and operating a youthful offender program, and would seriously compromise your security envelopes.

The staffing component of security enveloping has to have the ability to respond to any incidents or events immediately. This can be accomplished by freeing up staff to move with the offenders. Look at fixed posts and assess their purpose, effectiveness, and efficiency. Experience has demonstrated that in many cases fixed posts are not as effective and efficient as fluid posts.

Also, when developing the staffing for your security envelope, include staff other than security. The staff of a youthful offender program must, more than any other group in corrections, work together. For example:

1. When the offenders go to structured recreation, there should be a coach/recreational specialist whose only responsibility is to teach the offenders and to conduct the recreational activity. There should be ample security staff present to provide security.
2. During count times, counselors should be in the living areas to assist the security staff with the count.
3. During meal times, chaplains and counselors should be present to assist security and food service staff and to mill around and talk with the offenders.

Continuous assessment of the staffing requirements, assignments, and deployment is also something that is part of operating a successful youthful offender program. Any change to the daily schedule will have an impact on the staffing component of the security envelopes that have been established.

Technology

In developing security envelopes, the use of technology certainly has its place, but technology should only be used to augment staff, not to replace staff. This population is unique in that, because of their ages, they need to have the physical presence of staff. Also, for the safety of both staff and offenders, it is important to have staff interacting with the offenders on a continuous basis.

Technology should be used in a monitoring capacity that assists in the security, management, and operations of the program. Technology can be used to free staff from mundane monitoring posts so that they can directly supervise offenders. The school of thought here is that if offenders are directly supervised, there will be fewer incidents, better adherence to the daily schedule, and a more effective way to observe the offenders. This direct observation is crucial in a youthful offender program because, as these offenders progress through their adolescent years, they can have mood swings that range from rage to suicide attempts. The ability to have staff in constant and direct contact with them can greatly reduce these moods swings from erupting into serious incidents that will put stress on a security envelope.

It is important to determine what type of technology will be needed to enhance the security envelope(s). A facility must know exactly what is expected from the technology and be able to define how it will enhance the security envelope(s) and augment staff.

Materials

Material can range from smaller handcuffs to uniforms that the offender will wear. Before introducing anything into the program, it must be determined how it might affect the security of the program. Remember, you look at things through your paradigms and that the offenders look at things through their paradigms. For example, an institution was installing a new perimeter fence that was supposed to be impossible to get over. Two groups of people were watching the installation, the staff and the youthful offenders. The staff felt confident that the fence would be virtually impregnable while the offenders were discussing how they could compromise the fence and who would be the first one to escape. One wise person quipped: We see best what we are supposed to see.

Summary

Developing a total security plan for the youthful offender program can be a daunting task but it has to be done. Experience has shown that the best way to accomplish this task is to break the security down into its individual security envelopes. Taking this approach will help you see how each security envelope evolves into the next and how all the individual security envelopes create the total security plan.

References

Glick, B. and W. Sturgeon. 1998. *No Time to Play: Youthful Offenders in Adult Correctional Systems*. Lanham, Maryland: American Correctional Association.

———. 2001. *Recess Is Over: A Handbook for Managing Youthful Offenders in Adult Systems*. Lanham, Maryland: American Correctional Association.

Chapter Thirteen

Increasing Collaboration Between Family Courts and Juvenile Justice

Gina E. Wood
Director
South Carolina Department of Juvenile Justice
Columbia, South Carolina

On July 3, eleven-year-old Henry Campbell's mother hauled him into court. Henry was charged with petty larceny, and the judge sentenced him to live at his grandmother's house. The year was 1899. The location was Cook County, Illinois—the site of America's first juvenile court.

Had Henry been born a few years earlier, before Americans accepted the wisdom of creating separate courts for children, his sentence might have been death. Absurd, but true. To help understand why, this chapter looks at the evolution of both juvenile courts and the juvenile justice system in America.

Evolution of Juvenile Courts

Until the late nineteenth century, society made no formal differentiation between its response to crimes committed by children and its response to crimes committed by adults. Society routinely jailed children with adults, sentenced them to labor, and often brutalized them (Mendel, 2000). In major cities, it was common for jails to hold hundreds of children, some as young as eight. Many came from tenement housing and often were arrested for stealing food or coal. Even children as young as seven could be brought to trial in criminal court and, if found guilty, could be sentenced to prison or even death. The few voices of reason could not be heard above the shouts of the masses: "Toss them in jail and throw away the key."

The late nineteenth century American movement that established a separate court for juveniles has its roots in the sixteenth century European education reform movement. The early reforms changed how society viewed children—from miniature adults to people who are inherently different from adults, less culpable for their actions and more amenable to rehabilitation. The British doctrine of "parens patriae" (the state as parent) became the rationale for the right of the state to intervene in children's lives.

Eventually, society heard the pleas of children's rights advocates and the Illinois Juvenile Court Act of 1899 created the first court system for children in America. Under the unique rules of this new court, we would not try children like adults through a formal, open, and adversarial process. The new court would not punish children for their crimes, but rather, it would serve as a "kind and just parent" to them, using closed and informal hearings to act in their best interests.

Formation of the Juvenile Justice System

Since the day Cain—the symbolic first child—committed murder, people have embraced the abstract idea of juvenile justice. The metamorphosis of this abstract notion into reality, however, is a recent event that parallels the creation of juvenile courts.

Juvenile justice, like juvenile courts, evolved out of the late nineteenth century realization that society should not treat delinquent children the same as adult offenders. Most juvenile justice agencies and departments evolved from both private and public reformatories, as well as almshouses or poorhouses, juvenile training schools, children's centers, and boys' forestry camps that were under the purview of other state agencies such as public welfare.

In South Carolina, we can trace the evolution to 1868, when the state's new constitution called for a reform school. In 1875, the state legislature set aside a wing of the state penitentiary to create a reformatory for delinquent boys. Many years of political wrangling passed before the Lexington Reformatory finally opened in 1901.

Simultaneously, juvenile justice philosophy began to evolve from the idea of punishment to the notion of redemption and education, not only in South Carolina, but throughout the nation. In fact, modern child psychiatry grew out of requests by juvenile court judges for professional assistance in understanding the children who appeared in their courts. This marked the beginning of the now traditional link among juvenile and family courts, juvenile justice, and ancillary state and local services.

In 1909, William Healy, a pioneer in juvenile justice, established the Juvenile Psychopathic Institute, which later became the Institute for Juvenile Research. The purpose of the institute was to evaluate and diagnose children seen by juvenile courts. In his book *The Individual Delinquent*, published in 1915, Healy argued that we could understand children's behavior only by examining their unique individual histories.

During past centuries, the children most likely to come into contact with the American justice system were slaves, orphans, and apprentices involved in civil cases. In 2001, the children most likely to enter the juvenile justice system have not changed much. While today's juvenile offenders are not slaves to other people, far too many are slaves to substance abuse. As many as 70 percent of juvenile offenders may have significant drug and alcohol abuse problems according to a recent study by the National Gains Center for People with Co-occurring Disorders conducted for the National Mental Health Association.

Although today's juveniles may not be orphans or apprentices, many come from single-parent families in which the annual household income is at or below the poverty level, and the children often are left to fend for themselves. According to the latest figures from the Office of Juvenile Justice and Delinquency Prevention, in 1997:

- One-fifth of all juveniles lived below the poverty level.
- Nearly three in ten of these children lived in single-parent homes.
- Nearly one-half of all children living with only their mothers lived in poverty.

Since Healy's landmark research, juvenile justice in America has undergone seesaw-like changes in process and philosophy, fueled by public opinion, and mandated through changes in the law. Especially within the past thirty years, the response to juvenile crime has alternated between community-based delinquency prevention programs to "adult time for adult crime" policies, which have come alarmingly close to nineteenth century attitudes.

During the 1990s, however, the public's understanding of the complex nature of juvenile crime expanded. The public began to see the need to treat juvenile offenders differently from adult offenders and to embrace the importance of a juvenile's social, psychological, and familial condition. Years of research recommended a more balanced, integrated approach to combating youth violence and crime. As a result, comprehensive, community-based initiatives began to emerge as key national strategies for addressing persistent, complex social problems, such as delinquency, substance abuse, and teen pregnancy. Nevertheless, this enlightened attitude of compassion has had to peacefully, if not comfortably, coexist with "compassionate conservatism." The latter advocates adult time for adult crime—a judgment with little or no evidence to support its effectiveness in reducing juvenile crime.

The 1990s marked another phase in the history of the juvenile justice system at the federal, state, and local levels. Policy makers began to embrace a balanced approach, and to incorporate sanctions, offender accountability, and treatment and prevention components into a continuum of youth services.

Because juvenile justice primarily is a state and local responsibility, no single nationwide system exists. Instead, there are fifty-one state systems, including the District of Columbia's. Most of them are divided into local systems. We deliver them through either juvenile or family courts at the county level, at local probation offices, state correctional agencies, and private service providers, each with its own rules and idiosyncrasies. These systems do, however, have a common set of core principles that distinguish them from criminal courts for adult offenders, including:

- limited jurisdiction (up to age seventeen in most states)
- informal proceedings
- a focus on offenders, not their crimes
- indeterminate sentences
- confidentiality

Juvenile justice is a complicated concept. It relates to the multiple facets of children's lives, and it intersects with other equally complex concerns that effect their lives, including mental health, substance abuse, education, and child welfare. For juvenile justice agencies to ensure that they address all aspects of a juvenile's life at the federal, state, and county levels, they must be willing to adopt a holistic approach. This approach embraces collaboration, not only with other state agencies, but also with family court judges.

South Carolina's Collaboration Initiatives

The uniform South Carolina Family Court system was established by statute in 1976. Since then, collaboration between the juvenile justice system and family court judges has been impossible because both are still tied to many other entities. For example, the courts are tied to law enforcement, solicitors, public defenders, and probation officers. Because the law requires that the Department of Juvenile Justice educates the juveniles in its care, juvenile justice in South Carolina is tied to other state and local agencies, such as the departments of education, mental health, and substance abuse. These officials and agencies are also located in many communities. Thus, South Carolina's Department of Juvenile Justice must collaborate with the state's communities, individuals, family courts, and numerous other state agencies.

In South Carolina, and throughout the nation, family and juvenile court judges have only two options when dealing with juvenile delinquents—incarceration or probation. Juvenile justice agencies are working toward changing that, and South Carolina is carrying out effective changes to give judges best-practice alternatives. The following are two examples.

Auxiliary Probation Services. The Department of Juvenile Justice implemented the Auxiliary Probation Services program as a community-based, unique, and successful probation option that judges in twelve of South Carolina's forty-six counties may grant nonviolent juvenile offenders. These offenders usually are in their first term of probation. The program uses volunteers who are sworn in by family court judges as auxiliary probation officers with full probation powers, and are trained by the department's staff. Then, they are assigned to one probationer to supervise for six to twelve months. Supervision includes one home visit each week and a phone call three times per week. However, many auxiliary probation officers, especially retired volunteers, devote more time to their probationers. A judge also may request that a particular juvenile be assigned to a particular auxiliary probation officer.

The primary purpose of this program is to turn juvenile delinquents into law-abiding citizens. The Department of Juvenile Justice began operating the Auxiliary Probation Services program three years ago, and its reputation for helping juveniles change their delinquent lifestyles has prompted family court judges throughout South Carolina to encourage statewide expansion of the program. July 1, 2001 marked the program's third and final year for receiving federal grant funding, but because of its success, a Department of Juvenile Justice Auxiliary Probation Services Sustainment and Expansion Plan is being implemented to allow the program to continue. It is an excellent example of the benefits children can garner when the courts and the juvenile justice system collaborate, and when socially responsible citizens involve themselves in the lives of the community's children.

Juvenile Drug Courts. Administered by justice professionals, juvenile drug courts offer proven alternatives to the traditional court process and to incarceration for first-time, nonviolent juvenile offenders. These nine-to-twelve-month programs strive to help juvenile offenders stop using alcohol and other drugs, end their involvement in crime, and improve their school performance. Most juveniles in drug courts have been adjudicated delinquent; therefore, administrators work closely with a family court judge.

Through the collaborative efforts of judges, many state agencies, and wraparound services, drug courts cover every aspect of children's lives. The youthful offenders are provided counseling, tutoring, and even eyeglasses and similar items when they fall within budget. Drug courts also administer sanctions that run the gamut from writing an essay to incarceration. After successfully completing the program, the court expunges a juvenile's drug charge from his or her record.

Conclusion

The collaboration that takes place between the courts and the juvenile justice system began at their simultaneous births more than a century ago, as communities struggled with how to deal with juvenile crime. Although that struggle continues today, many more dedicated professionals are researching and developing programs to help America's youths get on the right track.

In 1974, the Juvenile Justice and Delinquency Prevention Act created the Office of Juvenile Justice and Delinquency Prevention as a component of the U.S. Department of Justice. The Office of Juvenile Justice and Delinquency Prevention's mandate is to provide national leadership, coordination, and resources in juvenile delinquency, victimization, and juvenile justice. This mandate has led to federal support of the states and local communities through various activities including research and program development; demonstration and evaluation of promising models and programs; training and technical assistance; dissemination of information on effective and promising practices for use by practitioners and policy makers; and broad-based support through formula grants to states wishing to improve their juvenile justice systems. In recent years, authorities have increasingly recognized the connection among mental disorders, substance abuse, and juvenile crime. As a result, the Office of Juvenile Justice and Delinquency Prevention has increased its focus on meeting the mental health needs of youths in the juvenile justice system.

Because of these efforts, and dedicated juvenile justice professionals throughout the United States, the future of balanced and restorative juvenile justice is encouraging. The one thing, above all others, that can propel and encourage advancements in best-practice programs and, thus, lower juvenile crime, is community involvement in the lives of troubled children.

References

Charleston, South Carolina: The Children's Law Office, Juvenile Justice Research Center, University of South Carolina School of Law.

Colonial Williamsburg Foundation. 1996. *Order in the Court: Juvenile Justice in the 18th Century: A Teacher's Guide.* Colonial Williamsburg, Virginia: Public Broadcasting System and Corporation for Public Broadcasting.

Kreisher, Kristen. 2000. The Youngest Inmates: Sentencing Children as Adults. *Children's Voice.* 9(6): 4-7, 30-31. November. Washington, D.C.: Child Welfare League of America.

Mackinem, Mitchell B. and Carson A. Fox. 2001. How to Start a Drug Court. Manual presented at the South Carolina Association of Drug Court Professionals' third annual conference.

Mendel, Richard A. 2000. *Less Hype, More Help: Reducing Juvenile Crime, What Works and What Doesn't.* Washington, D.C.: American Youth Policy Forum.

Snyder, Howard N. and Melissa Sickmund. 1999. *Juvenile Offenders and Victims: 1999 National Report.* Washington, D.C.: Office of Juvenile Justice and Delinquency Prevention.

Trotti, John. 1999. The History of Juvenile Justice in South Carolina: A Juvenile Justice Time Line. Unpublished research paper. Columbia, South Carolina: Department of Juvenile Justice.

Chapter Fourteen

Youth Courts: A National Youth Justice Movement

Scott B. Peterson
Program Manager
Office of Juvenile Justice and Delinquency Prevention
Washington, D.C.

Michael J. Elmendorf, II
Special Assistant to New York Governor George E. Pataki
Albany, New York

Youth courts, also called teen courts, are a rapidly expanding voluntary alternative to the juvenile justice system for young people who have committed their first misdemeanors and/or offenses. Youth courts strive to promote in juveniles feelings of self-esteem and the desire for self-improvement, and to foster a healthy attitude toward rules and authority. Youth courts also offer civic opportunities for young people to become volunteer members of the court. Schools, police departments, probation departments, juvenile and family courts, and nonprofit organizations operate youth courts. Usually, youth courts operate as a joint venture among several agencies. The most successful courts are community-based and include participation from a wide range of organizations and agencies within that community.

Youth court proceedings include juvenile offenders and youths who volunteer to be jurors and members of the court, often in the roles of judge, prosecutor, defender, clerk/bailiff, and jury foreperson. The courts have designed sentencing to hold youths accountable while recognizing that peer pressure exerts a powerful influence on adolescent behavior. Judges, police, probation officials, and schools generally refer cases to adult coordinators who oversee the program. Typical cases that they may hear in a youth court include larceny, criminal mischief, vandalism, minor assault, possession of alcohol, minor drug offenses, and truancy.

Youth courts provide communities with an opportunity to provide immediate consequences for first-time youthful offenders. This occurs while providing a peer-operated sentencing mechanism that allows young people to take responsibility, to be held accountable, and to make restitution for committing crimes. Additionally, while providing constructive consequences for juvenile offenders, youth courts offer a civic opportunity for other young people in the community who want to actively participate in the community decision-making processes for dealing with juvenile delinquency. As a result, they gain hands-on knowledge of the juvenile and criminal justice systems.

A critical aspect of the program is that youth courts allow peers to decide the appropriate sentencing for other youths. If peer pressure contributes to juvenile delinquency, some experts believe that it can be redirected to become a force that leads juveniles into law-abiding behavior (Williamson, Chalk, and Kneeper, 1992). Youth court programs have been in existence for more than twenty-five years, but recently, they have increasingly become a fixture in many communities.

In 1994, only seventy-eight youth court programs operated in the United States. Currently, more than 825 towns and cities operate youth court programs nationwide, and approximately 100 additional youth court programs are in developmental stages. Connecticut, Delaware, New Jersey, and Rhode Island are the only states that do not have youth courts. Most of the youth court programs are grassroots community efforts. This local effort reflects the fact that communities increasingly view youth courts as an effective means for holding youths accountable for delinquent and criminal behavior within the community.

The national youth court movement across America is offering teenagers an opportunity like none other. According to a 2001 survey conducted by the National Youth Court Center, more than 250,000 youths have participated as both offenders and volunteers in youth courts during recent years. By all indications, officials see this number increasing at a rate consistent with the rapid establishment of youth courts.

New York's Colonie Youth Court

One well-known program in the United States is the Colonie Youth Court. Colonie is the largest municipality in the Capital District of New York, in Albany. Nationally, there are four recognized models of youth courts: Adult Judge, Youth Judge, Peer Jury, and Tribunal Model. Established in 1993, the Colonie Youth Court is a nonprofit corporation and operates as the Youth Judge Model, which means youth not only act as members of the jury, but also as the judge, attorneys, and clerk/bailiff.

Since 1995, the Colonie Youth Court has adjudicated more than 650 juvenile cases for disposition and has a 99.5 percent successful completion rate. In 1996, the program, which involves more than 500 youths who volunteer to serve as judges, defenders, prosecutors, clerks, and jurors, was selected to serve as the model for an additional 30 youth court programs in New York. A volunteer board of directors oversees the program. It includes members from the Town of Colonie Police Department and the Albany County Probation Department, local schools, and the U.S. attorney's office for the Northern District of New York.

The program operates on a $60,000 annual budget and includes a full-time program director and a part-time community service coordinator. The state and county bar associations provide the budget through grants from the New York State Division of Criminal Justice Services, the Administration for

Children, Youth and Families, and the local municipality. The Colonie Youth Court was established as a demonstration program with state formula funds from the U.S. Justice Department's Office of Juvenile Justice and Delinquency Prevention.

What Happens in Court?

Colonie Youth Court, Inc., is a voluntary alternative to the criminal justice system for young people who have committed crimes or offenses. The goal of the court is to intervene in early antisocial, delinquent, and criminal behaviors, and to reduce the incidence and prevent the escalation of such behaviors. In youth court, a youth who has admitted guilt to a crime or offense appears for a sentencing hearing before a jury of his or her peers. The jury is presented with evidence relevant to sentencing, and then deliberates and passes sentence. Sentences which stress rehabilitative goals typically include community service and counseling.

Who Participates?

Youth court proceedings often involve youth volunteers who serve as jurors and members of the court. Typically, each volunteer is younger than eighteen, and an adult serves as the coordinator. The offender must complete the sentence imposed by the jury and, in addition, must agree to serve as a juror on the case of another juvenile offender as the final two hours of community service. The remaining jurors are drawn from a pool of young people who wish to volunteer. Jurors do not take a course of instruction. Instead, they often hear and see evidence, listen to the judge's instructions, retire and deliberate in private, and agree on a sentence.

Members of the Colonie Youth Court consist of high school students who have successfully completed eight weeks of a youth court membership training program. Areas of instruction include an overview of the criminal and juvenile justice systems, causes of crime and delinquency, goals of sentencing, penal law, and the operation of youth courts. The training program concludes with mock hearings to prepare members for participation in youth court proceedings. Colonie Youth Court members assume five roles in rotation:

- Judge: Presides over the sentencing hearing, explains criminal charges to the jury, instructs the jury on what evidence and factors to consider in determining a sentence, and sentences the offender according to the jury's verdict.
- Prosecutor: Represents the interests of the community, investigates the circumstances of the offense and background of the offender, presents evidence at the sentencing hearing, and makes a sentencing recommendation to the jury.

105

- Defender: Represents the interests of the offender, investigates the circumstances of the offense and background of the offender, presents evidence at the sentencing hearing to include mitigating circumstances, and makes a sentencing recommendation to the jury.
- Clerk/Bailiff: Maintains accurate records, ensures smooth operation of court proceedings, and administers oaths.
- Jury Foreperson: Leads jury deliberations, ensures participation of all jurors, sees that all appropriate sentencing factors are addressed, mediates disputes among jurors, calls for a vote during deliberations, and announces the verdict.

Volunteer youth members who serve in these youth court roles gain valuable knowledge and skills that strengthen their ability to become responsible citizens. As a result of their participation, these youths often have improved articulation and applied social skills. Educators increasingly see volunteer service in youth court as an opportune area when schools require youths to complete a number of community service hours for high school graduation. As a result of the many benefits youths gain through volunteer participation, some schools provide a half semester of high school social studies credit for two consecutive years of participation.

Juvenile offenders of the Colonie Youth Court must meet certain criteria to be eligible for the program. The criteria is that offenders must be younger than eighteen, admit guilt, and not have committed any prior misdemeanors and/or violations. The final component of their community service—serving as jurors on a subsequent case—allows offenders to participate positively in the criminal justice system. These offenders gain valuable lessons by accepting responsibility for their actions, by participating in community service projects and educational classes, and by having their peers send a strong message that they displayed poor judgment.

Volunteer youth jurors of the Colonie Youth Court are young people in grades seven to twelve who wish to volunteer on a jury and decide the punishment of an offender. Registered jurors are not required to complete the youth court membership training program that members must complete. Instead, each juror is randomly selected from a pool of 400 to 450 jurors to participate in a hearing.

Youth Court Cases

Judges, police, probation officials, and school personnel refer cases appropriate for youth court to the youth court coordinator, who accepts cases meeting established criteria. Youth court programs accept a wide range of cases for disposition. Determining the types of cases a youth court will handle is the decision of the program organizers in collaboration with the local school, court, police, and probation departments. Most cases handled in youth court include violations and misdemeanors, and some nonviolent felonies. Typically, juvenile offenders are younger than eighteen.

Cases the youth court may handle include:

- Shoplifting/theft
- Alcohol possession
- Criminal mischief
- Vandalism/property damage
- Possession of small amounts of marijuana
- Traffic offenses
- Disorderly conduct
- Other offenses deemed appropriate

Cases not traditionally considered for youth court include:

- Sex offenses
- Violent crimes
- Driving under the influence of alcohol
- Distribution and/or felony possession of narcotics

Sentencing

Sentences vary for each youth court. Community resources, program development, the victim, the offender, and the type of crime are several factors that contribute to the sentence that may be imposed. Some youth court programs have a limit on the number of community service hours that they can impose for a particular crime and others, such as the Colonie Youth Court, do not set a limit. Some programs similar to Colonie Youth Court operate their own community service programs during the evenings and on Saturdays, while other programs use existing community service agencies for monitoring the completion of assigned community service hours. Youth courts also must consider the varying ages of the offenders when planning community service sentences.

Typical community service sentences imposed in youth court include:

- Community service hours (typically between twenty and fifty hours)
- Letters of apology
- Essays
- Youth court jury duty
- Restitution
- Educational classes

The jury cannot sentence youths to a detention facility or jail.

Obtained Benefits and Waived Rights

By agreeing to continue in the Colonie Youth Court, offenders obtain certain benefits and waive certain rights that would otherwise apply in the criminal and juvenile justice systems. Benefits include receiving a decision by a jury of their peers aimed at helping end criminal conduct, and the chance to be a positive participant in the criminal and juvenile justice systems rather than being the object of those systems. Rights waived in youth court may include the right to an attorney, the right to a trial for determination of guilt, and the right to request closed proceedings for youths under the age of sixteen.

Operating Budget

Youth court programs are one of the least expensive intervention and prevention programs to operate. Because of the large number of volunteers, including youths and adults, most programs only need to hire one full-time or part-time employee. According to the National Youth Court Center, the various budgets of these courts varies from $10,000 to $75,000. Factors that contribute to the size of a youth court's budget include:

- Jurisdiction size
- Crime rates in the community
- Availability of other diversion programs for first-time offenders
- Whether the youth court operates its own community service program
- Whether a school, a municipality, or a nonprofit organization operates the program
- How often the court will convene and the estimated number of cases to be handled

With support and collaboration from the U.S. Department of Transportation's National Highway and Traffic Safety Administration, the Office of Juvenile Justice and Delinquency Prevention established the National Youth Court Center in 1999. The American Probation and Parole Association operates the National Youth Court Center along with three other agencies: the American Bar Association, the Constitutional Rights Foundation, and Street Law Incorporated. The center's primary goal is to support the national infrastructure of youth courts through the development of technical assistance resources and training to establish or enhance youth court programs.

For more information about the National Youth Court Center, contact Tracy Godwin, Director, c/o American Probation and Parole Association, P.O. Box 11910, Lexington, Kentucky 40578-1910; (859) 244-8215; fax (859) 244-8001; e-mail: nycc@csg.org; Web site: www.youthcourt.net.

References

Godwin, T. M., M. E. Heward, and T. Spina. 2000. *National Youth Court Guidelines*. Lexington, Kentucky: American Probation and Parole Association. National Youth Court Center.

Lockart, P., W. Pericak, and S. Peterson. 1996. Youth Court: The Colonie New York Experience. *Journal for Juvenile Justice and Detention Services*. 11(2): 79-82.

Spina, T. and D. R. Homer. 1994. *Youth Court Training Manual*. Latham, New York: Youth Courts of the Capital District, Inc.

Williamson, Deborah, Michelle Chalk, and Paul Knepper. 1992. Teen Court: Juvenile Justice for the 21st Century? *Federal Probation*. 54 (June): 54-58.

Chapter Fifteen

Workbridge: Employing and Providing Community Service Opportunities for Court-involved Youth

Claudia Thorne
Regional Director
Cornell Abraxas
Washington, D.C.

Dan Zarecky
Program Director
Pittsburgh WorkBridge, Cornell Abraxas
Pittsburgh, Pennsylvania

Earlene Green
Program Director
Philadelphia WorkBridge, Cornell Abraxas
Philadelphia, Pennsylvania

Jennifer M. O'Mara
Evaluation Supervisor
Cornell Companies, Inc.

Kathryn Scott
Evaluation Supervisor
Cornell Companies, Inc.

Introduction

WorkBridge is an employment and community service sentencing alternative for court involved youth that prepares youth for work. The Cornell Abraxas WorkBridge program offers many unique opportunities for supervision and rehabilitation as mandated in Act 33 of Pennsylvania's Juvenile Act, which typically experts call "the balanced approach" or "restorative justice." Act 33 requires the juvenile justice process to recognize all parties in a conflict (the victim, the community, and the offender) through goals that address community protection, offender accountability, and competency development in the offender. Consistent with Act 33, Cornell Abraxas' WorkBridge philosophy is to make youths accountable for their actions. We do this to remove them from a life of crime, while providing the training and support mechanisms for them to become productive and responsible citizens.

This chapter will highlight 1) employment and community service as developmental task of adolescence; 2) the WorkBridge program; 3) work and community service as a rehabilitative tool; 4) statistics; and 5) provide testimony.

Employment and Community Service as Adolescent Developmental Tasks

Adolescence is the period when youths begin to prepare for adult roles and responsibilities. To become a productive adult, it is essential that youths develop academic competencies, prepare to enter the world of work, and engage in positive healthy and mutually supportive relationships with adults and with peers. All these competencies are key for the youths to become contributing members of society and for the continuation of the family and the culture. If no one provides adolescents with these positive constructive outlets, very often they will become involved in an alternative criminal economy. They will develop relationships that are based on exploitation that does not create or sustain healthy communities.

One of the major developmental tasks of adolescence is preparing for economic self-sufficiency in adulthood.[1] In an increasingly complex world, youths must develop many related skills to meet this challenge either as entrepreneurs or as employees. The skills youth must develop include the following: goal setting, devising and carrying out a plan of action to achieve goals, and developing a broad array of academic, and social skills. Outside school, work and community service is the primary avenue for youths to learn these necessary skills. In addition, the practical hands-on experience of working and providing community service gives youths an opportunity to connect to the labor market by permitting them to investigate and plan to pursue career paths.

WorkBridge supports adolescent development by empowering youths to choose careers. When young people are engaged in work and learning through training, shadowing, and mentoring, skilled caring workers can become role models for youth, replacing unhealthy peer and adult attachments. Community service connects young people to the community in a way that lets them know they are resourceful and they have something to give.

The WorkBridge Program

WorkBridge has three major components: employment initiative, community service component, and the work crew project.

The Employment Initiative

The employment initiative component of WorkBridge gives juvenile offenders the competencies needed to secure and maintain paid employment and the opportunity to repay losses to victims through regular restitution payments. Youths are placed with private-sector employers, who give them meaningful paid employment and teach job-related skills. Employers play a key role in reducing long-term dependency on the public welfare system, lowering crime, and recidivism, and enhancing their communities by offering employment opportunities for court-involved youths.

The employment initiative assesses youths for career interest and abilities, and it helps them in securing a work permit, photo identification, and other requirements of the workplace. Before placement, youths participate in job preparation workshops, which prepare them for entry into the workplace. During these workshops, youths build competencies in job-seeking and job-holding skills. The competencies that youths develop include completing job applications, developing interviewing techniques, and becoming oriented to paperwork.

Because court-involved youths have many characteristics and barriers that prevent them from retaining employment once placed, WorkBridge gives them the opportunities to develop job-holding competencies. These job-holding competencies include respecting authority, following rules and procedures, developing positive attitudes, wearing appropriate dress, establishing professional relationships, and engaging in conflict resolution and problem solving. Once youths are placed in employment, staff monitor their on-the-job performance through site visits and telephone calls. If any issues arise with their performance, the staff acts as a mediator with their supervisor to improve their work habits.

Upon employment placement, a restitution contract is signed specifying payment amounts and dates. All youths with restitution court orders make restitution payments by either mailing the payment to the WorkBridge office or by having the employment counselor pick up the money in person.

Community Service Component

The community service component provides an opportunity for a positive diversionary sentence through the performance of community service. Community service holds youths accountable for their actions, provides an opportunity for the losses of victims to be restored, and improves the self-esteem of youths by letting them know that they have something to contribute to the community. In the community service component, youths are placed at more than 100 nonprofit agencies including churches, community centers, hospitals, libraries, and so forth. WorkBridge staff monitors youths to insure they are successful at the site.

The work crew project is an extension of the community service component. In the work crew project, youths are a part of a cooperative team in providing the following community services, including but not limited to: removing graffiti; painting; performing indoor and outdoor janitorial services, general cleaning, grounds maintenance, park clean up, clerical tasks, and/or preparing mailings, and handling other tasks.

Employment and Community Service as a Rehabilitative Tool

Employment and community service are rehabilitative tools for court-involved youths because they are a protective factors to improve the many risk factors in their lives. Employment and community service provide an opportunity for growth and development by supporting the development of positive personal characteristics, positive adult relationships, and healthy beliefs and clear standards.

The WorkBridge Program at Cornell Abraxas believes that clients have the best opportunity for growth and development when youths are involved in meaningful interaction with staff. The purpose of being in a relationship with our clients is to maximize opportunities for staff presence, effective supervision, and to insure that clients achieve service plan goals and have positive outcomes. In WorkBridge, meaningful involvement with staff includes providing back up to employment and community service supervisors and being a liaison to probation officers and court personnel. This occurs by providing either direct supervision, in person or telephone monitoring, and support and guidance to youths addressing issues such as academics and social and life skills.

We structure and design activities to maximize the effort and productivity of the youths. WorkBridge believes that youths need to be engaged in constructive activities while attending the program. We clearly tie participation in constructive activities to attaining treatment goals and general life skills. Work and community service are constructive activities addressing competency development, community protection, and accountability. Constructive use of time, through work and community service, prevents recidivism.

WorkBridge provides opportunities for job searches, employment, volunteer opportunities, and service opportunities that reduce unstructured time for negative behavior. We support youths in academic pursuits and give them access to GED programs, college tours, and admission assistance.

We establish high expectations and hold youth accountable for positive growth and movement toward these expectations. In WorkBridge, there are consequences for every behavior. Cornell Abraxas' work with youths and families is therapeutic and rehabilitative. Our challenge is to promote accountability, responsibility, and high expectations so that youths and families begin to experience the consequences of positive and right action. From a balanced and restorative justice perspective, accountability includes the payment of restitution and community service. Teaching accountability and responsibility and having high expectations involves giving our clients tools to maximize positive behaviors and pointing out and addressing both positive and negative behaviors.

Youths also receive clear expectations for behavior responsibilities, schedules, and consequences for noncompliance. We address negative behaviors immediately and youths learn from the natural consequences of such behaviors. Youths have the opportunity to see how their behavior impacts others at the work site and how it inhibits others from having the opportunity to work. Staff insures that youths are fulfilling court, community, and victim obligations, and they coach them in decision-making skills to encourage their positive contributions to the community.

Staff members, as agents of change, act so that they model the behaviors that we want youths to embrace and carry out. Since staff is always visible, it is imperative that staff model behavior and "walk the talk" that exemplifies "do as I do." The specific behaviors that staff must role model include appropriate professional dress, language, punctuality, good manners, appropriate body language, effort, pride, and self-determination in their jobs. To show the importance of planning, staff must follow a structure and plan of action for youths. Staff must display good communication by being able to give positive constructive criticism to youths. Staff must be responsible for their actions and they must have an excellent follow-through.

Clients and staff work together in a supportive relationship. The program staff, clients, families, referral sources, and the community are all members of a team whose strategic purpose is to achieve positive outcomes for clients. Good communication is key. The major elements of the team must communicate effectively with one another to achieve individual client and program goals. Examples of teamwork and communication include information sharing, staff covering roles and responsibilities other than their own, staff being diplomatic and objective, and giving clients regular feedback on their progress.

We treat youths with dignity and respect. Dignity and respect must be directed to clients and the staff of the work and community service sites in which clients are placed. Dignity and respect include being culturally sensitive and addressing diversity issues such as language barriers, gender, race, and religions. Dignity and respect also mean celebrating client accomplishments through recognition ceremonies.

We create an environment that is conducive to treatment. The environment of care is an important factor in treatment. Youths perform effectively when they are working in a professional setting. A professional setting includes the maintenance of a clean, orderly, and professional environment that is aesthetically pleasing. We must teach youths and staff to maintain orderly work spaces. A clean, comfortable environment promotes productivity.

Statistics

We provide statistics for both the Philadelphia and the Pittsburgh WorkBridge programs. The Pittsburgh program has been operational for only twelve years compared with the Philadelphia program, which has been operational for two years. Thus, the statistics show that the WorkBridge model can be successfully replicated.

From July 2000 to June 2001, Philadelphia WorkBridge served 532 clients with an average of approximately 145 youths daily. WorkBridge has a very high nonrecidivism rate of 92.2 (only 7.8 percent of youths were repeat offenders). The total number of community service hours performed by clients was 3,686. Multiplying those hours by the national minimum wage ($5.15) shows that youths gave back an equivalent of at least $18,983 to the community. The total amount of restitution collected from clients enrolled in the Philadelphia WorkBridge program was $6,463.

From July 2000 to June 2001, Pittsburgh WorkBridge served 2,057 clients with an average of approximately 535 youths daily. Pittsburgh WorkBridge has a very high nonrecidivism rate of 99.5 percent (only .5 percent of youths were repeat offenders). The total number of community service hours performed by clients was 76,324. Multiplying those hours by the national minimum wage ($5.15) indicates that youths gave back an equivalent of at least $393,069 to the community. The total amount of restitution collected from clients enrolled in the Pittsburgh WorkBridge program was $42,231.

Clients report that in 98 percent (Pittsburgh) and 96 percent (Philadelphia) of the time, the program was respectful of racial, ethnic, cultural heritage, and religious beliefs. Ninety-three percent (Pittsburgh) and 88 percent (Philadelphia) of clients stated that the program helped them to understand the impact that their negative behavior had on others. Ninety-six percent (Pittsburgh) and 86 percent (Philadelphia) of clients stated that we held them accountable for their actions. Ninety-five percent (Pittsburgh) and 86 percent (Philadelphia) of clients stated that they felt prepared to leave the program, while 97 percent (Pittsburgh) and 91 percent (Philadelphia) stated that they would recommend the program to others.

Testimony

The following WorkBridge success stories are from several stakeholders in the program: employers, community services site coordinators, youths, and family members. These testimonies support the idea that employment and community service are integral factors in achieving the developmental tasks of adolescence. These tasks are learning accountability and responsibility, and learning to live free of a life of crime.

Recruiter
"(The) Case Manger is very integral in preparing WorkBridge clients for (our) application process. Even though the jobs (we) offer your clients are entry level, our application process is a little more thorough than most organizations. However, the clients come very well prepared in the application process. WorkBridge clients are probably a step ahead of most job training programs, and given the age and lack of job seeking experience most of the youths bring, they do very well."

Juvenile Probation Officer

"The program is very supportive, particularly of the balanced and restorative justice goals, job readiness, payment of restitution, and completion of community service hours. I would use the program again. In fact, I will be referring another client who has to pay over $2,000 in restitution; I know WorkBridge will be successful in the collection and payment process."

Recreation Center

"The WorkBridge youths that have completed community service hours at our recreation center were very nice. They were mannerly, showed up for their assignments on time, and completed their tasks. We would invite other WorkBridge youths to complete their community service hours at our center."

Walid M., age 17

WorkBridge: "What did you learn?"

Walid M: "I learned how to be accountable for my actions and that I am responsible for whatever I do. I also learned what to expect in terms of not always getting what you want out of life; how to roll with the punches."

WorkBridge: "How did WorkBridge prepare you for life, work, etc.?"

Walid M. "I found that I could achieve goals."

WorkBridge: "Have you been rearrested since you completed the Work-Bridge Program?"

Walid M. "I have not had any rearrests."

Germaine S., age 17

WorkBridge: "What did you learn?"

Germaine S. "I learned how to live a crime-free life. I also learned that there are repercussions: I was charged with retail theft; until I participated in the WorkBridge Program, I was clueless as to how my actions impacted on business and the community."

WorkBridge: "How did WorkBridge prepare you for life, work, etc.?"

Germaine S. "I now know that there is a real world out there and that some of the things I took for granted, others may never get to experience."

WorkBridge: "Have you been rearrested since you completed the Work-Bridge Program?"

Germaine S. "I don't have any new arrests; I learned my lesson."

Aimeen H., age 11 (the reporter is the client's maternal grandmother)

WorkBridge: "What did Aimeen learn?"

Lorraine H.: "Aimeen has learned that he should not steal and he is more disciplined."

WorkBridge: "How did WorkBridge prepare Aimeen for life, work, etc.?"

117

Lorraine H.: "Aimeen now cleans up after himself and is not as messy as he used to be."

WorkBridge: "Has Aimeen been rearrested since he completed the Work Bridge Program?"

Lorraine H.: "Aimeen has not been in any trouble and has not been rearrested since he completed the WorkBridge Program. I think the Work-Bridge Program was good for Aimeen. He learned the value of community service as a rehabilitative tool."

Zhilwan R., age 16

WorkBridge: "What did you learn?"

Zhilwan R.: "I committed an Act 26 offense; I got caught carrying a gun to school. My community service hours were completed at my school. I really learned my lesson."

WorkBridge: "How did WorkBridge prepare you for life, work, etc.?"

Zhilwan R.: "I have been working on my job for two years; I was already prepared for work. WorkBridge helped me with my attitude."

WorkBridge: "Have you been rearrested since you completed the Work-Bridge Program?"

Zhilwan R.: "No."

Conclusion

WorkBridge is a successful employment and community-service sentencing alternative for court-involved youths. It is a vehicle to support these youths in achieving major adolescent developmental tasks. These include preparing for economic self-sufficiency in adulthood by hands-on work and community service experiences. The WorkBridge employment initiative supports youths in developing the competencies needed to secure and to maintain employment and gives them the opportunity to repay losses to victims through regular restitution payments. The community service initiative provides an opportunity for a positive diversionary sentence through the performance of community service. The community service initiative holds youths accountable for their actions. We give the youths an opportunity to make amends to the community by giving something back to their community. Sometimes, they restore the losses of crime victims through community service.

We structure the WorkBridge program to be a rehabilitative tool under which youths are involved in meaningful interactions with staff in a program designed to maximize their productivity. The Workbridge program sets high expectations for youths and gives them the support to become successful while simultaneously teaching them responsibility and holding them accountable for their actions. The program relies on staff to be counselors and role models simultaneously, while youths are working with staff in supportive relationships. The "I can do" attitude that permeates the program engenders dignity and respect for all youths in the program and helps them to become contributing members of their community.

Endnote

1. U.S. Department of Labor, Employment and Training Administration and the U.S. Departmentof Justice, Office of Juvenile Justice and Delinquency Prevention. 2000. *Report: Employment and Training for Court Involved Youth*. Washington, D.C.

Chapter Sixteen

Restorative Justice Conferences as an Early Response to Young Offenders

Edmund F. McGarrell
Director, Crime Control Policy Center
Hudson Institute
Indianapolis Indiana

A number of highly publicized and disturbing school shootings and homicides in several communities across the United States have focused the attention of the public and policymakers on the issues of youth violence and school safety. Although important, these issues tend to divert juvenile justice officials' attention from a separate problem: delinquency committed by very young children. In 1999, U.S. police departments reported 218,300 arrests of persons younger than age 13.[1] The most recent juvenile court statistics indicate that offenders under the age of thirteen account for about 16 percent of all individuals referred to juvenile courts (Puzzanchera et al., 2000). Earlier research has shown that children entering juvenile court at such a young age have a very high risk of continued offending. For example, approximately 60 percent of youths ages ten to twelve who are referred to juvenile court subsequently return to court. For youths referred to juvenile court a second time, the odds of returning to court again increase to more than 80 percent (Snyder and Sickmund, 1995).

However, because these youths typically have not committed a particularly serious or violent offense, and because children this young usually have not accumulated a long record, they do not generally receive a great deal of attention from juvenile justice officials (Snyder and Sickmund, 1999). Recently reported findings of the Office of Juvenile Justice and Delinquency Prevention's (OJJDP's) Study Group on Very Young Offenders confirm the seriousness of early offending behavior. Study Group researchers report, for example, that the risk of becoming a more serious offender is two to three times higher for child delinquents (those ages seven to twelve) than for later onset offenders (Loeber, Farrington, and Petechuk, in press).[2] Child delinquents also account for a relatively high proportion of some types of offenses. They represent one in three juvenile arrests for arson, one in five juvenile arrests for vandalism, and one in twelve juvenile arrests for violent crime (Loeber and Farrington, 2000). For some young offenders, early involvement in status offenses and delinquency is a stepping stone in a pathway to serious, violent, and chronic offending. Communities should not ignore the delinquent acts and problem behaviors of young offenders in the hope that they will "grow out of it" (Loeber, Farrington, and Petechuk, in press). Because such young offenders have a high likelihood of reoffending, communities should develop and implement effective early interventions for very young offenders.

One form of early intervention involves the use of restorative justice conferences. Such conferences, sometimes referred to as "family group conferences," have become common in Australia and New Zealand and are being used increasingly throughout the world (Thames Valley Police, 1999). Although some jurisdictions use restorative justice conferences for a variety of offenses, including criminal offenses, restorative justice conferences may be particularly appropriate for very young offenders. Advocates argue that the conferences offer a meaningful response to youthful offending without consuming significant court resources.

In 1996, the Office of Juvenile Justice and Delinquency Prevention provided funds to the Hudson Institute, a public policy research organization in Indianapolis, Indiana, to evaluate the use of restorative justice conferences for young offenders. This funding was awarded through the Office of Juvenile Justice and Delinquency Prevention's Field-Initiated Research and Evaluation Program. This chapter describes the findings of the Hudson Institute's evaluation.

Challenges Posed by Very Young Offenders

More than thirty years ago, a Presidential Commission Report (Lemert, 1967) criticized the nation's juvenile courts for what it labeled the "one-minute hour." According to the report, a heavy volume of cases allowed courts to spend only approximately one minute on juvenile cases and prevented them from taking the time needed to carefully assess cases and link juveniles with necessary services (as the juvenile courts were intended to do). Since that time, the volume of juvenile cases has increased dramatically without a corresponding increase in resources. The rising tide of juvenile arrests that began in the mid-1980s and continued until 1994 (Snyder and Sickmund, 1999) has forced courts into what Lawrence Sherman describes as a "triage" system of conserving scarce resources for the most serious cases.[3] Minor juvenile offenders are often given several "bites of the apple," meaning that juvenile cases may be dismissed or juveniles may be placed on probation supervision with overworked probation officers until the offenders have accumulated a long history of arrests or have committed a particularly heinous offense (Bernard, 1992). Advocates of both system reform and youth warn that the current system fails to hold youths accountable for offenses and sends the message that offenses are "no big deal."

Additional challenges facing the system are the largely passive roles that offenders and their parents often play and the fact that victims are typically excluded from the process. An individual's reasons for committing an offense are regarded as unimportant, and restitution to victims and the community affected by the crime is not typically a primary concern (Van Ness, 1996). Offenders are sometimes required to perform community service as reparation, but often the service is performed for someone not directly affected by the offense (Van Ness, 1996).

Restorative justice conferences attempt to address these shortcomings in the current system. As part of a balanced and restorative justice model (Bazemore and Umbreit, 1994; Office of Juvenile Justice and Delinquency Prevention, 1998), restorative justice conferences are designed to hold youths accountable, involve and meet the needs of victims, and build a community of support around the offending youths.

Restorative Justice Conferencing

In a restorative justice conference, an offending youth, his or her victim, and supporters of both the offender and victim are brought together with a trained facilitator to discuss the incident and the harm it has brought to the victim and the group of supporters. The conference provides an opportunity for victims to explain how they have been harmed and to question offending youths. Supporters also have an opportunity to describe how they have been affected by the incident. At the end of the conference, the participants reach an agreement on how the youth can make amends to the victim and they sign a reparation agreement. The agreement typically includes an apology,[4] and it often includes a requirement that some type of restitution be made to the victim. Sometimes agreements require youth to perform community service or call for other actions such as improving school attendance, completing homework, or performing chores at home or school.

Advocates of restorative justice conferencing point to its many potential benefits. Conferences, for example, are expected to address the emotional needs and tangible losses of victims and hold youths accountable for misdeeds more effectively than the traditional juvenile court system. Conferences also allow youths to learn how their offending has negatively affected others. Finally, conferences create a supportive community for offending youths.

In theory, the effectiveness of restorative justice conferences is based on the principles of control, deterrence, and "reintegrative shaming." From a control perspective, conferences "control" youths' involvement in delinquency by encouraging them through socialization to believe in the moral legitimacy of the law. The control effect depends on youths having strong bonds to family and/or conventional institutions such as school or church (Hirschi, 1969). If, as advocates contend, restorative justice conferences provide a learning opportunity in which the harm caused by offending is directly communicated to youths and their bonds to family members and community institutions are strengthened, conferences become part of the socialization process through which they learn to conform to society's norms. From a deterrence perspective, if conferences hold youths accountable and impose consequences more effectively than the traditional juvenile justice system, then the conferences raise the costs of offending relative to the benefits and therefore may deter youths from committing offenses.

123

The well-known Australian restorative justice writer John Braithwaite's (1989) theory of reintegrative shaming builds on the principles of control and deterrence. Braithwaite argues that people are generally deterred from committing crime by two informal forms of social control: fear of social disapproval and conscience. He contends that punishments or reparation agreements imposed by family members, friends, or other individuals important to an offender are more effective than those imposed by a legal institution. For most people, he argues, fear of being shamed by those they care about is the major deterrent to committing crime because the opinions of family and friends mean more than those of an unknown criminal justice authority.

Braithwaite also predicts that restorative justice conferences may be more effective than traditional courts because conferences include the direct participation of supporters of both victims and youthful offenders. By including supporters, conferences allow youths to be held responsible in the context of a community of care. In such a setting, youths can be held accountable for their acts without being condemned as people (Sherman, 1993). According to reintegrative shaming theorists, this combination of accountability and respect is key to keeping an offender within the community (Braithwaite, 1993). Although too limited to provide definitive answers, research to date supports the positive effects of restorative justice conferences.

The first of two formal experiments that have been conducted involved police-run conferences in Bethlehem, Pennsylvania. That experiment found high levels of victim satisfaction and some evidence of reduced reoffending for person offenses but not property offenses (McCold and Wachtel, 1998). The second, the Reintegrative Shaming Experiments (RISE), also reported high levels of victim satisfaction and showed positive changes in the attitudes of offenders (Strang et al., 1999). The impact of restorative justice conferences on future offending remains under investigation.[5]

The promise of the initial findings from research on restorative justice conferences, coupled with frustration over then-existing interventions for very young offenders, led Indianapolis juvenile justice officials to consider an experimental pilot project.

The Indianapolis Restorative Justice Experiment

In 1996, the Hudson Institute, a public policy research organization in Indianapolis, Indiana, began working with the Indianapolis police department, sheriff's department, juvenile court, prosecutor's office, and mayor on a project involving the use of Australian-style restorative justice conferences as an alternative response to juvenile offending. Encouraged by research from other jurisdictions—yet seeking clearer answers about the effects of conferences— Juvenile Court Judge James Payne and Marion County Prosecutor Scott Newman agreed to work with the Hudson Institute's research team to implement an experimental design. The experiment was initiated in September 1997, and this chapter presents what the research team refers to as the "Stage One" results of the ongoing experiment.

124

Case Study: Clearing Up an Offender's Misunderstanding

David had been arrested for vandalizing a school bathroom and causing considerable damage. During the restorative justice conference, David was quiet and seemed unrepentant. The conference dragged on without much progress. Finally, David spoke up. He explained that the reason he had been so mad on the day of the incident was that his teacher not only had taken away his bag of potato chips but had then eaten the chips in front of the class, which David interpreted as an attempt to humiliate him. One of the conference participants was the teacher who had been involved in the classroom incident. The teacher said that David was wrong—the chips she had eaten were from her own lunch, and David's chips remained unopened in her desk. She explained to David that while it was appropriate for her to take the chips away from a student during class, she would never open the bag and eat them herself. With this information, David's demeanor changed immediately, the atmosphere in the conference shifted significantly, and the group was then able to move forward and reach a successful reparation agreement. The conference ended with David apologizing to the teacher and with David, his mother, and the school officials agreeing that David would attend counseling. As a final condition to the agreement, David agreed to be responsible for carrying notes back and forth between his mother and his teacher to ensure ongoing communication.

Without the active involvement of David's teacher in the conference, it seems unlikely that the reason for his anger would have been discovered. Although a forum other than a restorative justice conference might have held David accountable for his actions, he probably would have remained bitter and continued to feel that he had been treated unfairly—first by the teacher in the classroom and then by those who held him responsible for the damage he had caused. Including David and his teacher in the conference and providing an opportunity for dialog had several benefits: David gained insight into the teacher's actions, the group came to understand David's behavior, and David had the opportunity to make amends to those harmed by his actions.

Method

Program eligibility. Indianapolis justice officials decided to begin using restorative justice conferences with young, first-time offenders. This population was considered the most appropriate both because such youths were not seen as posing an immediate risk to the community and because officials recognized the need to identify more effective early interventions for them. The research team hoped that conferences might provide a more effective tool to prevent young, first-time offenders from becoming deeply entrenched in delinquent behaviors. Consequently, to be eligible for the first phase of the Indianapolis experiment, an offender had to meet the following criteria:

- Be no older than fourteen years of age
- Be a first-time offender (that is, have no prior adjudications)
- Have committed a nonserious, nonviolent offense
- Have no other pending charges
- Admit responsibility for the offense[6]

With the exception of the age criterion, these requirements are essentially the same as those that apply to juvenile court diversion programs. If deemed eligible for such a program, an offender is diverted from court and charges are not filed, pending his or her successful completion of the assigned diversion program.

Random assignment procedure. Formal implementation of the Restorative Justice Conferencing Experiment began on September 1, 1997. Court intake officers screened youths for eligibility. Eligible youths were selected for the program through a random assignment procedure. Specifically, when the intake officer determined that a juvenile offender met the program's eligibility criteria, he or she drew an envelope from a stack prepared by the research team. Each envelope in the stack contained one of two possible responses: "yes" or "no." If the intake officer selected a "yes," the youth was assigned to the restorative justice program and the case was turned over to the county coordinator. A "no" selection indicated normal processing, and the youth was assigned to one of twenty-three other diversion programs.

Sample characteristics. From September 1, 1997, to September 30, 1999, 458 youthful offenders participated in the Indianapolis Restorative Justice Conferencing Experiment. Of these, 232 were assigned to the restorative justice treatment group and the remaining 226 to the "control group." Tables 1 through 3 provide descriptive characteristics of both groups.

Table 1, which reports the racial composition of the two groups, shows that the control group included slightly more nonwhite youth (63 percent) than the restorative justice group (58 percent), though the difference was not statistically significant. These percentages are consistent with the racial composition of the general population of Indianapolis youths adjudicated delinquent in 1998—62 percent of whom were nonwhite (Marion Superior Court Probation Department, 1999).

The percentages of male and female offenders in the two groups also indicate that the sample was representative of the general population of juveniles adjudicated delinquent in Indianapolis. For example, approximately 65 percent of adjudicated juveniles in Marion County in 1998 were male, compared with 63 percent of those in the experimental sample (conference and control group combined) (see Table 2). The restorative justice group, however, included more males (68 percent) than the control group (57 percent). Although in early analyses researchers were concerned about overrepresentation of males in the restorative justice group, the relative distribution became more even between the two groups as the sample size increased, suggesting that the randomization process is "smoothing out" the initially uneven distribution.

The median age of youths in both groups was 13.0 years. The age distributions of youths in the restorative justice and control groups were also quite similar. Approximately 32 percent were age fourteen, just over 26 percent were age thirteen, and approximately 40 percent were age twelve or younger. Previous research has suggested that these young age groups have high rates of reoffending (Snyder and Sickmund, 1995).

Table 3 reports the frequency of primary offenses committed by youths in the restorative justice and control groups. As indicated in the table, conversion (shoplifting) was the most common offense, followed by battery, theft, and criminal mischief. The control group included slightly more youths whose primary offense was conversion, whereas the restorative justice group included more youths charged with theft. Percentages of youths in the two categories combined, however, are almost equivalent for the two groups. Battery (assault) charges accounted for one-quarter of youths in both groups.

Measures. The study had process and outcome measures, including conference observations conducted by trained researchers using an observational checklist; interviews of offending youths, their parents or guardians, and victims; and checks of court records to determine whether participating youths had been rearrested for subsequent offenses.

Table 1: Racial Composition of the Restorative Justice and Control Groups

Race	Restorative Justice Group (n=232)		Control Group (n=226)		Both Groups (n=458)	
	Number	Percent	Number	Percent	Number	Percent
Nonwhite*	135	58	143	63	278	61
White	97	42	83	37	180	39

Note: The chi-square comparison was not significant, meaning that the observed difference between the treatment and control groups was likely produced by chance.
* Because the groups included only three Hispanics and one "other" categorized respondent, these four respondents were grouped in the nonwhite category. The remaining respondents in the nonwhite category are African American.

Table 2: Gender of Youths in the Restorative Justice and Control Groups

Gender	Restorative Justice Group (n=232)		Control Group (n=226)		Both Groups (n=458)	
	Number	Percent	Number	Percent	Number	Percent
Male	159	68	129	57	288	63
Female	73	32	97	43	170	37

Note: Chi-square significant at <0.05, meaning that the difference between the treatment and control groups was greater than that expected to be produced by chance.

Table 3: Primary Offenses Committed by Restorative Justice and Control Group Participants

Primary Offense	Restorative Justice Group (n=232)		Control Group (n=226)		Both Groups (n=458)	
	Number	Percent	Number	Percent	Number	Percent
Conversion (shoplifting)	84	36	105	46	189	41
Battery	59	25	56	25	115	25
Theft	36	16	22	10	58	13
Criminal mischief	26	11	17	8	43	9
Disorderly conduct	14	6	18	8	32	7
Trespass	7	3	5	2	12	3
Other	5	2	3	1	8	2
Intimidation	1	04	0	0	1	0.2

Case Study: A New Approach to Juvenile Offending

An Opportunity To Speak

Thirteen-year-old Jason's face was grim as he looked around at those attending the restorative justice conference and struggled to answer the coordinator's question. "How were you involved in this incident?" Quietly, Jason began his story. He and his friend Michael were on their way to Jason's house that afternoon and cut across the shopping center's parking lot. The car was there. They could see the speakers, and with Michael as lookout, Jason crawled in the car and began pulling out wires. The owner of the car (Rhonda) came out of her office and yelled at them to stop. Jason dropped the speaker, and he and Michael began running. Later that day, Jason heard the sheriff's officer knock on his door and talk to Jason's mother. After the officer questioned Jason and his friend, the boys were handcuffed and taken to the juvenile detention center.

When asked what he was thinking at the time of the incident, Jason replied, "Nothing, just that I saw the speakers and wanted them." Jason struggled when asked who had been affected by his actions, telling the group that he had been affected—by being taken to "juvenile." "What about the owner of the car?" asked the coordinator. "Well, I guess because she got her speakers messed up, she was affected." Pausing for a moment, Jason looked at his mother and whispered that she too had been affected by his behavior.

Jason's friend Michael gave his account of what happened, admitting that he wasn't thinking at the time and now knows he made a big mistake. The person most disappointed in Michael, he explained, was his younger brother, and that was the worst part of all this—losing his brother's trust.

Rhonda next described the incident, explaining that she heard the two boys in the parking lot and ran out to see what was happening. "I saw the one boy in my car holding the speaker. I yelled at him to stop and he dropped it and ran." When asked what she wanted to receive from the conference, Rhonda said she wanted to know why the boys had attempted to steal her speakers. She also wanted the boys to understand how she felt and asked them how they would feel if someone took their possessions.

Moving around the circle, the conference coordinator asked the boys' mothers how the incident had affected them. Jason's mother said that at first she was shocked and had a hard time believing her son would be involved in something like this. Jason, she explained, has money from an allowance and did not need to steal anything. Michael's mother told the group how disappointed she was that her son had participated in the incident. She had always tried to raise her boys to know the difference between right and wrong, and it would take a while to restore her trust in Michael.

Drafting a Contract

After each participant had an opportunity to speak, the contract drafting phase of the conference began. The participants discussed and outlined steps the boys needed to take to make things right. The coordinator asked the boys if they had anything they wanted to say to the victim. Each made a sincere apology for trying to steal Rhonda's speakers. Rhonda said that she believed the boys were remorseful and thought they had learned from their mistake.

When asked if there was anything else she wanted to add to the contract, Rhonda explained that because the speakers were replaced and her car had no permanent damage, restitution was not necessary. She suggested, however, that the boys perform community service work. Following Rhonda's suggestion, the conference participants joined in and traded ideas on what type of work would be appropriate and how many hours would be fair. The boys were asked whether they would agree to community service and whether they knew of any work that was needed around their neighborhood. Finally, the participants agreed that Jason and Michael would perform twenty hours of service at a community center to earn money to pay their court fees. The coordinator wrote up the contract, and all of the participants signed it, putting a formal end to the incident.

Benefits of the Process

As the conference participants rose to leave, Jason and Michael shook hands with everyone in the group. Although the boys had been held accountable for their behavior, they knew that people still cared about them and had worked to help them learn from their mistakes. Having received an apology and having learned why the boys did what they did, Rhonda felt that she could put the incident behind her. The boys' parents had a chance to express how they felt about their sons' actions. They received support from the group, and they helped point their children back in the right direction.

Results

Observations of conferences. In observing restorative justice conferences, researchers examined the length of the proceeding; the role of the conference coordinator; the involvement of the offender, youth supporter(s), victim(s), and victim supporter(s); expressions of shame, apology, and acceptance of responsibility by the offender; and elements included in the reparation agreement. Between September 1, 1997, and September 30, 1999, 182 conferences were conducted. Of these, 157 conferences (86 percent) were observed by one of fifteen trained observers.

Length of proceeding. Restorative justice conferences lasted an average of forty-three minutes. The reintegration ceremony, during which conference participants mingled informally and shared refreshments, averaged ten minutes from the close of the conference.

Role of conference coordinator. Generally, conference coordinators followed the principles of restorative justice conferencing. Observers noted that coordinators maintained a distinction between the offending youth and his or her behavior (that is, treating him or her as a valued member of the community while condemning the act). Coordinators also focused the discussion on the incident and rarely lectured the offending youth. Coordinators were seen as doing an effective job of eliciting the involvement of all conference participants.

Involvement of offender, victim, and supporters. Observers reported that all conference participants tended to display respect toward the offending youth. In a large majority of conferences, the offending youth also was seen as conveying respect toward the victim. In approximately 22 percent of conferences, observers did not believe the offending youth had been respectful of the victim. In nearly all conferences, group participants expressed disapproval of the offense. In more than 80 percent of the conferences, observers reported that the youth had apologized to his or her victim, and in half of the conferences, the youth apologized to his or her own supporters. Observers also noted that most offending youths expressed remorse (76 percent) and understood the injury or harm they had caused (66 percent). Although observers could not tell with certainty whether a victim and other group participants had forgiven an offender, observers reported that more than 80 percent of the conferences appeared to include the victim and the group forgiving the offending youth. In three-quarters of the conferences, the observer reported a strong sense of reintegration at the conference close.

In all of the conferences, every participant signed the reparation agreement. Victims appeared satisfied in more than 80 percent of the conferences, and observers described 77 percent of the conferences as positive. Observers also reported that in more than 80 percent of the conferences, a volunteer was appointed to hold the youth accountable to the terms of the reparation agreement. That is, rather than have a court official monitor the agreement, the group designated someone from the community of support to hold the youth accountable. This person was then contacted by the Marion County Restorative Justice Coordinator to verify the youth's completion of the agreement.

Elements of reparation agreement. Apology was the most common element included in reparation agreements (62 percent). To some extent, however, this percentage underrepresents the frequency of apologies. Because many conferences had already included an apology, it may not have been written into the formal agreement. Other common elements included monetary restitution, personal service, and community service. More than half of the reparation agreements included still other elements (typically activities that the group had tailored to the specific circumstances involved). Examples included imposing a nightly curfew and requiring that the youth improve his or her grades and school attendance or participate in afterschool programs.

Interviews of conference participants. A significant part of the Indianapolis restorative justice study was assessing how victims, offenders, and supporters felt about restorative justice conferencing as an alternative to traditional court-ordered programs. The goal was to collect data on participants' attitudes and beliefs about how their cases were handled and on their sense of justice.

Initially, the Hudson Institute encountered delays in implementing the interview procedures. Consequently, the sample size for the interviews was smaller than that of the total sample of conference and control group cases.[7] Thus, the results from the interviews came principally from cases occurring during late 1998 and 1999. Given the small sample sizes, the researchers report descriptive findings without assessing the statistical significance of the findings. More detailed assessments will be included in the second stage of the project.

Satisfaction. When respondents were asked how satisfied they were with the way their cases were handled, a significant difference emerged between victims in the control group and victims in the conference group. More than 90 percent of victims in the conference group "strongly agreed" or "agreed" that they were satisfied, compared with 68 percent of victims in the control group (*see* Figure 1). Satisfaction levels of youths and parents in both groups were similar. Overall, both groups expressed high levels of satisfaction, but youths and parents in the control group were slightly more likely to express satisfaction. This difference may reflect the extra demands (such as time and accountability) that conferences place on youths and parents.

In measuring participant satisfaction, the study also examined whether participants would recommend the program to a friend involved in a similar situation. Again, the greatest difference between the control and conference groups was for victims. Nearly all victims involved in conferences (98 percent) said that they would recommend the approach, compared with 24 percent of victims in the control group. Offending youths in the conference group were also more likely to recommend the approach (85 percent, compared with 38 percent of youths in the control group). The study found no significant difference between parents in the two groups for this item (*see* Figure 1).

Another indication of participants' satisfaction is whether they would recommend discontinuing the program. Most participants did not recommend stopping the conferences or the control group programs. Conference participants, however, were most likely to endorse continuation of the conferencing program. For example, no victims in the conference group recommended discontinuation. Just over one-fifth of victims in the control group, however, agreed that the program should be stopped. Similarly, 19 percent of youths in the conference group recommended discontinuing the program (compared with 36 percent of those in the control group), and 17 percent of conference parents recommended discontinuation (compared with 25 percent of control group parents) (*see* Figure 1).

The final indicator of participant satisfaction examined was whether participants believed the program was a "good" way to address certain kinds of juvenile crime. Here, both conferences and other court programs received strong endorsements. For victims and parents, the study found little difference between conference and control group participants. Youths in the control group were more likely than those in the conference group (85 percent versus 71 percent) to agree that the program they participated in was a good one (*see* Figure 1).

Perceptions of respect and involvement. Participants in both conference and control group programs felt they had been treated with respect. The study found no significant differences between participants (victims, youths, and parents) in the treatment and control groups in terms of perceptions of respect (*see* Figure 2).

None of the victims in the conference group reported feeling pushed around. However, approximately 20 percent of youths and 15 percent of parents in the conference group felt they had been pushed around. These percentages are lower than those reported by youths and parents in the control group (44 and 38 percent, respectively).[8]

The study found differences in the two groups' feelings of having been involved in the process. Restorative justice conferences are built on the principle that affected parties should participate in the process, and results indicate that this principle is being achieved in the Indianapolis experiment. Nearly all victims in the conference group (97 percent) agreed they had been

Figure 1: Reported Levels of Satisfaction

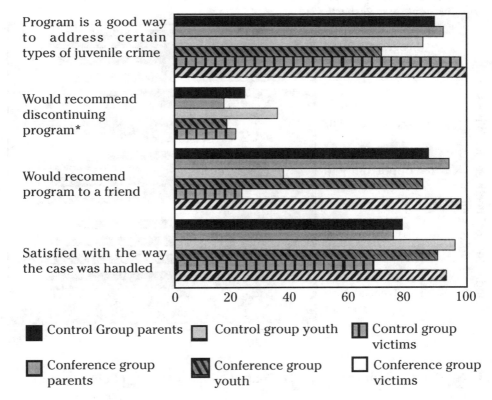

Note: For The first, second, and fourth indicators, the figure reflects the percentage of respondents who "agreed" or "stongly agreed" with the statement. For the third, the figure shows the percentage who responded "yes."
*No conference group victims recommended discontinuing the program

involved, compared with 38 percent of victims in the control group. Offending youths in the conference group were also much more likely than those in the control group to feel they had been involved (84 percent versus 47 percent). Nearly 80 percent of parents in the conference group agreed they had been involved, compared with 40 percent of parents in the control group (*see* Figure 2).

Participants in the conference group were also more likely to report having had an opportunity to express their views. For example, 95 percent of victims in the conference group agreed they had such an opportunity, compared with 56 percent of victims in the control group. Similarly, 86 percent of offending youths and 90 percent of parents in the conference group agreed they had the opportunity to express their views, compared with 55 percent of youths and 68 percent of parents in the control group (*see* Figure 2).

Figure 2: Reported Perceptions of Effectiveness, Fairness, Involvement, and Respect

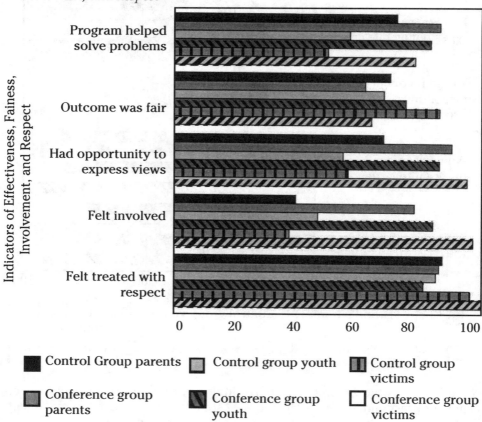

Note: For the third, fourth, and fifth indicators, the figure reflects the percentage of respondents who "agreed" or "strongly agreed" with the statement. For the first, the figure shows the percentage who "definitely" or "somewhat" agreed.

Perception of outcomes. A large majority of participants in both the conference group and the control group believed the outcome of their case was fair (*see* Figure 2). Victims in the conference group were more likely than their control group counterparts to describe the outcome as lenient (36 percent and 14 percent, respectively). Conference group youths were slightly less likely than control group youths to describe the outcome as lenient, whereas conference group parents were somewhat more likely than control group parents to describe the outcome as lenient.

Participants in the conference group were more likely than those in the control group to report that the program had helped to solve problems. More

Case Study: Better Addressing the Needs of Victims

When setting up the restorative justice conference, the coordinator talked with seventeen-year-old Richard about the purpose of the meeting. Richard admitted that he had broken into his neighbor Sue's car and taken her tape player and several other items. Richard agreed to participate in the conference and indicated a willingness to make amends.

On the day of the conference, however, Richard's attitude seemed to walk into the room in front of him, and the other participants sensed that the conference might not go as expected. Sue, the car's owner, nonetheless wanted to proceed.

When the coordinator questioned Richard about the incident, Richard skirted the issue of his responsibility and did not appreciate that so many people had attended the conference to help give him a second chance. When it was Sue's turn to speak, she described how she had felt when she discovered someone had broken into her car and stolen her personal property. Looking directly at Richard, Sue asked him why he had chosen her car. After all, she thought they had been friends.

After Richard and Sue described the incident, other participants had an opportunity to speak. Gary, a friend of Sue's attending the conference as a victim supporter, explained how Richard's behavior had affected Sue. One of Richard's neighbors told the group that she had always trusted Richard, but now her trust in him had been broken and she was not sure how she felt about Richard. Richard's mom told the group that she had not raised her son to steal from others but did not know how to help him change.

Once each participant had spoken, a contract was written. Under the terms of the contract, Richard agreed to pay for damage to Sue's car and replace her personal items. After Richard left the conference, Sue commented that she did not know if she would ever see the restitution payment. She assured her friends and the conference coordinator, however, that the conference had been worth it to her. The most important part, she explained, was the opportunity to tell Richard face-to-face how he had hurt her—that he had destroyed the trust that she had in him, disrupted her sense of safety, and generally made her life miserable for a while.

than three-quarters of victims in the conference group reported this benefit, compared with one-half of those in the control group. More than 80 percent of conference group youths and parents reported that the program had helped to solve problems, compared with 57 percent of control group youths and 72 percent of control group parents (*see* Figure 2).

Analysis of program completion data and rearrest records. The results described thus far indicate that restorative conferences were implemented in a fashion consistent with the philosophy and principles of restorative justice, that they were more effective than many other court programs in addressing victim needs, and that both parents and offending youths felt very much involved in the process. For many policy makers, however, the fundamental issue is the program's impact on future offending. To address this issue, the study compared program completion data and recidivism rates of restorative justice conference participants with those of youths in the control group.[9] (Recidivism was defined as a rearrest after the initial arrest that brought the youth to the juvenile justice system, and recidivism analysis was conducted for both groups at six- and twelve-month intervals.)

Program completion. Youths participating in restorative justice conferences demonstrated a significantly higher completion rate (82.6 percent) than youths in the control group, who were assigned to other diversion programs (57.7 percent). The majority of the twenty-nine youths in the conference group who failed to complete the program were rearrested before attending the conference. In contrast, most of the seventy-one control group youths who failed to complete their assigned programs failed because of juvenile waiver from the program. In such cases, juvenile court staff closed the case without requiring the youths to complete the assigned program.

Six-month rearrest rates. Table 4 shows six-month rearrest rates for all youths who have reached the six-month stage. As the rates for the full sample reflect, the restorative conference group included fewer recidivists than the control group by a margin of 13.5 percent. This statistically significant difference represents a 40 percent reduction in rates of rearrest.[10] The reduction was calculated by dividing the difference between the control and the treatment group rates by the control group rate: (33.9-20.4)/33.9=39.8.

Researchers also conducted an analysis limited to youths who had successfully completed a treatment (either the restorative conference program or one of the control group diversion programs). Because, as noted above, youths in the conference group were significantly more likely to complete their program than youths in the control group (many of whom were waived out of their programs), the portion of high-risk youths remaining among program completers presumably was higher for the conference group than the control group. In other words, the higher dropout rate for youths in the control group likely resulted in a group of lower-risk youths among those who actually completed the program. Thus, limiting the recidivism analysis to program completers provides a conservative estimate of the conference program's effectiveness. This analysis also found a significant difference in rearrest rates for conference and control groups: 12.3 percent and 22.7 percent, respectively. This statistically significant difference represents a 46 percent reduction in rates of rearrest.[11]

Twelve-month rearrest rates. Table 4 shows twelve-month rearrest rates for all youths who have reached the twelve-month stage. Of the full sample of youths participating in the restorative conference program, 30.1 percent had been rearrested within twelve months, compared with 42.3 percent of youths in the control group. This statistically significant difference represents a 29 percent reduction in recidivism.[12]

When researchers examined rearrest rates at twelve months for only those youths who had successfully completed a program, they found a pattern that was consistent with their other results, but the difference in rearrest rates for the conference and control groups did not achieve statistical significance. Specifically, 23.2 percent of youths who successfully completed the restorative conference program had been rearrested at twelve months, compared with 29 percent of youths who successfully completed another diversion program. This represents a 20 percent reduction in rearrest rates, which is not statistically significant.

The lack of statistical significance probably is attributable to two factors: (1) implementation problems in the earliest phase of the experiment, which frequently caused delays in scheduling conferences; and (2) the small number of program completers, particularly in the control group, included in the twelve-month analysis. The Hudson Institute continues to monitor these findings to determine whether twelve-month rearrest differences for program completers reach statistical significance when the sample size is larger.[13]

Rearrest rates by offense, sex, and race. Researchers conducted limited analyses of six-month rearrest rates for selected subgroups of offenders.[14] Youths who committed offenses against property had lower rearrest rates than youths who committed offenses against persons, and this difference was comparable for conference and control group youths. Both males and females in the conference group experienced lower rearrest rates than their counterparts in the control groups; the difference was greater for females than for males. There were no racial differences in rearrest rates for conference and control group youths, and the overall reduction in rearrest rates found for conference group youths was the same for whites and nonwhites. These findings, although preliminary, suggest that the effects of conferences appear consistent for youths across groups based on offense, sex, and race. These results should be considered preliminary, however, until further analyses based on larger sample sizes can verify findings.

Conclusion

Recent years have witnessed considerable interest in restorative justice approaches in general and conferences in particular. The current study and earlier research provide support for continued development of the restorative justice conference approach and experimentation with its use.

One of the basic findings of the experiment described in this chapter is that restorative justice conferences can be successfully implemented in an urban U.S. setting. More than 80 percent of youths who were referred to a conference attended the conference and completed the terms of their reparation agreement. For Indianapolis, this rate compares very favorably with that of other court-related diversion programs.

Trained observers reported that conferences in Indianapolis appeared to incorporate restorative justice principles such as inclusion of affected parties, respect for all participants, and emphasis on problem solving. Victims

Table 4: Rearrest Rates at Six and Twelve Months

Followup Interval	Total Number of Youths in Sample		Youths Who Were Rearrested (%)		
	Restorative Conference	Control	Restorative Conference	Control	*p* Value
Six months					
Full sample*	167	168	20.4	33.9	0.005
Participants who completed program	138	97	12.3	22.7	0.036
Twelve months					
Full sample*	156	156	30.1	42.3	0.025
Participants who completed program	125	93	23.2	29.0	0.330

Note: A p value of < 0.05 indicates that chi-square is statistically significant, meaning that the difference between the treatment and control groups was greater than that expected to be produced by chance.
* The smaller sample sizes reported in this table reflect the fact that at the time of the analysis, not all of the study group youths had reached the six- and twelve-month followup stages. These cases are being tracked in the ongoing study.

received apologies, and reparation agreements included other mutually agreed-upon actions. These characteristics translated into high levels of satisfaction among victims.

Interesting patterns emerge in this study's interview data. Overall, the data indicate reasonably high levels of satisfaction among participants in both conferences and other court-ordered diversion programs (that is, control group programs). Thus, the Indianapolis experiment does not involve a comparison of restorative justice programs and court-ordered programs that are perceived as failing.

The interview data suggest that the conference approach makes a positive difference for victims. When compared with victims participating in other diversion programs, victims in the conference program were more satisfied with how their cases were handled and much more likely to recommend the program to a friend. Victims in the conference program also felt they were treated with respect. Consistent with the principles of restorative justice, victims participating in conferences were much more likely than those participating in other programs to report that they were involved in the process and that they had the opportunity to express their views.

The conference approach also appears to make a difference for parents and youths. Although responses to some interview questions revealed no differences between those who participated in conferences and those who participated in other diversion programs, responses to questions relating to the core principles of restorative justice revealed significant differences. For example, youths and parents who participated in conferences were more likely than control group participants to feel they were involved, had a "say in the matter," and had problems solved.

Study results relating to reoffending are similarly promising. In comparisons for the total sample and for youths who successfully completed their diversion program, youths who attended conferences were significantly less likely than youths who attended other diversion programs to be rearrested during the six months after the incident that initially brought them to the attention of the court. Similar findings were observed at twelve months for the total sample; twelve-month findings for program completers were limited by small sample sizes and were less conclusive.

In subsequent stages of this project, researchers will seek to confirm initial results with larger samples. Larger samples will also allow researchers to address theoretical questions by relating findings from reoffending rates to interviews of youths, parents, and victims. For example, such questions may address whether it is the deterrent effect of increased accountability, the reduced stigmatization, or a combination of the two that is generating decreases in offending (Braithwaite, 1989). In addition, larger samples will allow a more thorough examination of results for various subgroups of offenders (such as those based on sex, race, age, and offense type). Researchers plan to address the issue of the role of police as conference facilitators, including the related question of whether it makes a difference for victims or offenders if the facilitator is a uniformed police officer or a civilian. Finally, the Hudson Institute hopes to extend its experiment to a broader range of offenses and to youths with prior court experience, thereby allowing the Institute to measure the extent to which these promising initial results apply to more serious offenders. The Institute also perceives a clear need to extend the research to the use of conferences with older youths.

Consistent with earlier research, the findings of the Indianapolis study suggest that restorative justice conferences successfully address the needs of many victims of offenses committed by youths. In addition, findings show that conferences are a promising early intervention for young, first-time juvenile offenders. Given the high rate of reoffending among very young children who enter juvenile court, these findings are encouraging and support the need for continued experimentation with and assessment of the restorative justice conference approach.

Endnotes

[1.] H. N. Snyder, personal communication, 2000. Dr. Snyder provided these statistics, based on his analysis of 1999 arrest data from the Federal Bureau of Investigation, to the Office of Juvenile Justice and Delinquency Prevention.

[2.] As used in this chapter, the term "child delinquents" refers to juveniles between the ages of seven and twelve who have committed delinquent acts, as defined by criminal law. This group of juveniles is the focus of the Office of Juvenile Justice and Delinquency Prevention's Study Group on Very Young Offenders.

[3.] L. W. Sherman, personal communication, 1996. The author and Professor Sherman collaborated on a grant proposal in the early stages of this project, and Sherman's thinking is reflected in this chapter.

[4.] A restorative justice program, however, should not force an offender to apologize to his or her victim. Nor should the victim be forced to accept an apology. An offender's apology should be sincere; it should not be viewed as a "quick fix" for the offender.

[5.] Research other than these two formal studies has reported declines in reoffending and high levels of victim satisfaction. This research, however, was not based on rigorous research designs. *See* Thames Valley Police, 1999; Braithwaite, 1999; Moore and O'Connell, 1994.

[6.] Restorative justice conferences are not fact-finding hearings. If a youth challenges the allegations, the matter should proceed to court. This criterion seeks to prevent the "revictimization" of a victim that could occur if the alleged offender failed to take responsibility for the act.

[7.] The sample size for the interviews was as follows: victims in conference group, n=42; victims in control group, n=50; youth in conference group, n=52; youths in control group, n=47; parents in conference group, n=52; and parents in control group, n=47.

[8.] Because control group victims were not asked if they felt they had been pushed around, this measure of perceived involvement and respect is not included in Figure 2.

[9.] At the time of the comparison, program completion data were available for only 167 youths in the restorative conference group and 168 youths in the control group.

[10.] Chi-square statistically significant at <0.01. This level of significance indicates that a difference of the observed magnitude would only be expected to occur in 1 out of 100 samples.

[11.] Chi-square statistically significant at <0.05.

[12.] Chi-square statistically significant at <0.025.

[13.] Additionally, in later stages of the project, researchers will consider issues such as the length of time elapsing between program completion and rearrest and the seriousness of subsequent offending.

[14.] Analyses by subgroup at this stage of the study are limited because sample sizes at this stage become very small when conference and control groups are further divided by characteristics such as offense, sex, and race. In the second stage of the project, when sample sizes are larger, researchers will carefully consider whether the restorative conference approach has different effects on different categories of youths.

References

Bazemore, G. and M. Umbreit. 1994. *Balanced and Restorative Justice*. Summary. Washington, D.C.: U.S. Department of Justice, Office of Justice Programs, Office of Juvenile Justice and Delinquency Prevention.

Bernard, T. J. 1992. *The Cycle of Juvenile Justice*. Cambridge, England: Cambridge University Press.

Braithwaite, J. 1989. *Crime, Shame, and Reintegration*. Cambridge, England: Cambridge University Press.

————. 1993. Juvenile Offending: New Theory and Practice. In L. Atkinson and S. Gerull, eds. National Conference on Juvenile Justice, Conference Proceedings No. 22, pp. 35-42. Canberra, Australia: Australian Institute of Criminology.

————. 1999. Restorative Justice: Assessing Optimistic and Pessimistic Accounts. In M. Tonry, ed. *Crime and Justice: A Review of Research*, pp. 1-127. Chicago: University of Chicago Press.

Hirschi, T. 1969. *Causes of Delinquency*. Berkeley, California: University of California Press.

Lemert, E. M. 1967. The Juvenile Court—Quest and Realities. In Task Force Report: Juvenile Delinquency and Youth Crime, edited by the President's Commission on Law Enforcement and Administration of Justice. Washington, D.C.: U.S. Government Printing Office, pp. 91-106.

Loeber, R. and D. P. Farrington. 2000. *Child Delinquents: Development, Intervention, and Service Needs*. Thousand Oaks, California; Sage Publications.

Loeber, R., D. P. Farrington, and D. Petechuk. In press. *Child Delinquency: Intervention and Prevention*. Bulletin. Washington, D.C.: U.S. Department of Justice, Office of Justice Programs, Office of Juvenile Justice and Delinquency Prevention.

Marion Superior Court Probation Department. 1999. *Marion County Juvenile Probation Annual Report*. Indianapolis, Indiana: Marion Superior Court Probation Department.

McCold, P. and B. Wachtel. 1998. *Restorative Policing Experiment: The Bethlehem Pennsylvania Police Family Group Conferencing Project*. Pipersville, Pennsylvania: Community Service Foundation.

Moore, D. and T. O'Connell. 1994. Family Conferencing in Wagga Wagga: A Communitarian Model of Justice. In C. Alder and J. Wundersitz, eds. *Family Conferencing and Juvenile Justice*. pp. 45-74. Canberra, Australia: Australian Institute of Criminology.

Office of Juvenile Justice and Delinquency Prevention. 1998. *Guide for Implementing the Balanced and Restorative Justice Model*. Report. Washington, D.C.: U.S. Department of Justice, Office of Justice Programs, Office of Juvenile Justice and Delinquency Prevention.

Puzzanchera, C., A. L. Stahl, T. A. Finnegan, H. N. Snyder, R. S. Poole, and N. Tierney. 2000. *Juvenile Court Statistics 1997*. Washington, D.C.: U.S. Department of Justice, Office of Justice Programs, Office of Juvenile Justice and Delinquency Prevention.

Sherman, L.W. 1993. Defiance, Deterrence, and Irrelevance: A Theory of the Criminal Sanction. *Journal of Research in Crime and Delinquency*. 30: 445-473.

Snyder, H. N. and M. Sickmund. 1995. *Juvenile Offenders and Victims: A National Report*. Pittsburgh: National Center for Juvenile Justice.

———. 1999. Juvenile Offenders and Victims: 1999 *National Report*. Report. Washington, D.C.: U.S. Department of Justice, Office of Justice Programs, Office of Juvenile Justice and Delinquency Prevention.

Strang, H., G. C. Barnes, J. Braithwaite, and L. W. Sherman. 1999. *Experiments in Restorative Policing: A Progress Report on the Canberra Reintegrative Shaming Experiments* (RISE). Canberra, Australia: Australian National University.

Thames Valley Police. 1999. Restorative Justice. *Unpublished manuscript*. Thames Valley, Great Britain: Thames Valley Police Department.

Van Ness, D. 1996. Restorative Justice and International Human Rights. In B. Galaway and J. Hudson, eds. *Restorative Justice: International Perspectives*, pp. 17-35. Monsey, New York: Criminal Justice Press.

Chapter Seventeen

Mobilizing Partners: The Kansas Community Experience

Albert Murray
Commissioner
Kansas Juvenile Justice Authority
Topeka, Kansas

Community Planning: Background

We have transformed the juvenile justice system in Kansas into a new and reformed arm of justice. We believe it has the potential of changing dramatically how units of government work together. The Kansas system, led by Commissioner Albert Murray, is nearing its fifth year as a work in progress.

What makes the Kansas system unique is that the design forges a strong partnership among the state, local, and private entities. Under Governor Bill Graves, the Kansas Legislature passed the Juvenile Justice Reform Act (House Bill 2900 passed in 1995 and House Substitute for Senate Bill 69 passed in 1996). It was predicated on the knowledge that the roots of the juvenile crime problems are within families, youths, and their communities. Therefore, the best solutions to local problems are local solutions.

In the past, Kansas, like many states, had a social service structure by which the state assumed the greatest level of ownership and responsibility for juvenile offenders. State workers delivered services to juvenile offenders and their families. The state social and rehabilitation agency bore the primary responsibility for addressing the problems and needs of juveniles who became involved with the system. Local community corrections agencies, which operated under the system of adult corrections, also bore the responsibility of supervising the most serious juvenile offenders who remained in communities. Few community sanctions were available to courts, causing high numbers of admissions and increasingly short lengths of stay at Kansas' juvenile correctional facilities. The state's social and rehabilitation agency managed the programs and facilities for juvenile offenders. They also had the enormous responsibility of providing services for abused and neglected children, the elderly, the disabled, the mentally ill, and adoption and foster care services. The specialized services the social and rehabilitation agency provided to juvenile offenders were buried within the mission of the largest government agency in the state.

The traditional approach to handling juvenile offenders was well ingrained in each region of the state. Communities were often eager to simply remove young "troublemakers" from schools and streets and put them into juvenile correctional facilities because of a lack of placement alternatives. The link between the correctional facilities, community case managers, schools, and families was thin and often nonexistent. Therefore, throughout the community planning initiative discussed in this chapter, the driving philosophy of "local solutions to local problems" became the theme. Kansas shifted its role to that of "steering the boat" and empowering the passengers rather than "rowing the boat." Kansas shifted to providing the following local support:

- Funding for core programs such as juvenile intake and assessment, case management, community sanctions, community supervision, and seed money for prevention

- Guidance about how to properly conduct a community planning process

- Research about prevention and early intervention programs that work nationally

- Technical assistance on what the state expected from community partners and a blueprint on how to get there

Refocusing on the theme of "local solutions" was imperative to the success of teams throughout the planning process, especially when they needed to make tough decisions concerning intricate details of the plans. Community partners, out of frustration and in search of convenience, often wanted to defer to the state for solutions rather than seek out consensus and clarity about what would best serve the community.

The purpose of this chapter is to provide a clear view of the challenges involved with this innovative initiative, which laid the foundation for the system's new approach to prevention and community services. A realistic depiction of the successes and challenges of this system change is important for other jurisdictions that may choose to move in this direction.

The Kansas Juvenile Justice Authority's community planning initiative was completed at a time when the agency was in its infancy. The agency was born out of the Juvenile Justice Reform Act, and its first day of operation was July 1, 1997. The agency was not only in a position of hiring its staff, accruing office space and supplies, and developing a basic infrastructure, but it was focused on the pressing importance of meeting its statutory requirements. Major requirements included the following items:

- Development of an unprecedented $6 million information system connecting courts, intake and assessment centers, local community corrections entities, and juvenile corrections facilities
- Downloading the agency's first community initiatives fund grants to stimulate the immediate growth of graduated sanctions and community service options for juvenile offenders
- Shifting the state's four juvenile correctional facilities and their population of 600 juveniles from a social welfare model to a corrections model
- Assuming responsibility for the supervision and provision of services for 3,500 community-based juvenile offenders
- Preliminary master planning for the upgrade and expansion of existing correctional facilities
- Implementing a new placement matrix to govern the types of juveniles placed in a juvenile correctional facility, and their length of stay
- Beginning an unprecedented statewide community planning process

Stakeholders United: The Power of Partnerships

As outlined in a state statute, a "convener" appointed by the commissioner led each community planning team. Often, the convener was a local administrative, district, or magistrate judge. Other conveners were county commissioners or other respected local leaders. The boundaries for each team, for planning purposes, were the state's thirty-one judicial districts (or a combination of judicial districts in sparsely populated areas). These ranged from a single county to seventeen counties in large rural sections of the state. The statute outlined minimum membership of the teams:

- Courts
- Court services
- Public education
- Juvenile community corrections services
- A county or district attorney
- Juvenile detention
- Health care professionals
- Mental health
- County officials
- Public defenders' office or private defense counsel
- Law enforcement
- Kansas Department of Social and Rehabilitation Services
- Private service providers
- Prevention services
- Business community
- Religious community
- Youth
- Others whom the convener may choose

145

Conveners and all other planning team members—except for the facilitators of each team—were unpaid volunteers. More than 1,000 community planning team members statewide (in a state with a population of 2.5 million) volunteered hundreds of thousands of hours within one year to develop the twenty-nine plans for Kansas. Besides these 1,000 volunteers, each judicial district brought together a group of between 10 and 60 community stakeholders—key leaders whose endorsement of the plans and the process were critical to success. Key leaders included school superintendents, sheriffs, police chiefs, business leaders, county commissioners, city administrators, and many others.

From 1997 to mid-1998, community planning teams collected and analyzed data about their communities according to a specially designed Communities that Care planning model. This popular model, founded by Dr. David Hawkins and Dr. Richard Catalano of the University of Washington at Seattle, helps communities to create strategies for the prevention of adolescent problem behaviors. Communities identified risk factors within schools, communities, families, and individuals that contribute to juvenile crime, and "protective factors" that keep youths on a path toward productive growth. The National Council on Crime and Delinquency teamed with Developmental Research and Programs, an affiliate of the University of Washington, to provide training for the Kansas teams in identifying the graduated sanctions and early intervention programs that are best for each community.

Local planning teams created databases of strategic plans with recommendations and cost projections for prevention, intervention, and graduated community-based sanctions. Communities were asked to develop plans based on needs, not based on available funding, to move away from the common practice of creating services based on the type of funding available.

This was a significant shift in thinking for many stakeholders in the process. Rather than allowing past state funding to decide future solutions, the communities were encouraged to identify what they needed to establish a comprehensive juvenile justice program in their region and to analyze what their regional data identified to be the community's greatest needs for prevention.

Governor Graves and the Kansas legislature appropriated $2 million for the first year of the community planning process, which was fiscal year 1998. During fiscal year 1999, $1.2 million was appropriated, proving a strong commitment to successful grassroots planning. This funding helped communities set up the structure to start the process: acquiring supplies, hiring a facilitator, and budgeting for travel so that teams could attend regional meetings to receive the technical assistance and support needed to make the project a success. The training provided by the Kansas Juvenile Justice Authority was the foundation of the entire process. When it came down to actually writing the plan, the process fell into place because the teams had been well trained. They were ready and able to gather and analyze the data using the risk factor and protective factor models.

What Community Plans Revealed

Community plans revealed the prominent risk factors for adolescent problem behaviors for each community. The leading risk factor identified by twenty-three of the twenty-nine teams was problems within family management. Were parents present? Was there consistent, fair discipline and general order within the home? Were there domestic issues, and did families have healthy ways of resolving difficulties and conflict? The second risk factor, identified by eighteen of the twenty-nine teams, was the presence of early and persistent antisocial behavior within youths. Eighteen of the twenty-nine teams identified community laws and norms that are favorable to problem behaviors. Fourteen of the teams identified a lack of commitment to school as their top priority risk factor, and thirteen of the twenty-nine teams said the availability of drugs was a main problem.

They also identified barriers to efficiency within the juvenile justice system. Things that were lacking included a comprehensive information system, coordination and collaboration among service agencies, and a juvenile offender information system. We currently are addressing the lack of a comprehensive information system, and the Kansas Juvenile Justice Authority is in the process of developing a $6 million juvenile justice information system to link courts, detention centers, correctional facilities, intake centers, and service providers. When complete in 2002, the agency will be able to track juveniles through the state system at all levels, leading to greater accountability and decision making.

The community planning process directly addressed the barrier of coordination and collaboration among stakeholders in local communities. As different stakeholders worked together throughout the year, communities with weak collaboration before the process struggled. Communities with a strong preexisting connection excelled. We cannot emphasize enough the importance of bringing the right stakeholders to the planning table and keeping them motivated. Communities are always better served if the team members resolve philosophical and operational differences at the onset of the planning process, rather than several months into it. Some counties did not easily cooperate with others within their judicial district. Some wanted a guarantee that in the end, they would get "their fair share" of the funding pie. In some cases, specific service providers wanted to control the planning process itself and identify community needs to pursue solutions before the data was even collected.

In such an initiative, we must hear everyone and we must give the strategic planning process a chance to be fully carried out; otherwise, key stakeholders may walk away from the planning table altogether, jeopardizing the process. The plan is a community plan, not a state plan. To achieve the full promise of juvenile justice reform, local leaders must take ownership of the local solutions. This requires patience, trust, few necessary resources, and a visionary who will stand strong and lead.

What the Kansas Juvenile Justice Authority Learned

Among the many lessons that came from this comprehensive initiative, the Kansas Juvenile Justice Authority learned that good research must precede major system change, be based on reliable data, and be properly paced. When conducting the next round of community planning in the coming years, the agency may elect to stagger the process and focus on one region of the state at a time rather than on 105 counties simultaneously. In retrospect, the intent was right, but its practicality may be questionable.

The Kansas Juvenile Justice Authority learned to never underestimate the impact of local politics on such an initiative. The high profile nature of system reform coupled with political risk and culpability makes it essential to secure the full support and buy-in from many elected and appointed officials. A wholesome and regular flow of information to the political infrastructure at each step along the way is important.

We also learned that some communities who had traditionally sought local empowerment really feared such local empowerment when it finally arrived. They asked themselves, "Now that we have it, what do we really do with it?" We noted that some communities were much more open to system change than others, and that setting one "pace" was unrealistic for all communities. Using one community model as a prototype to lead others through the process may be another approach to successful system change. Community stakeholders often understand and buy into the experiences of other communities rather than the promise of a better day by a state agency. Major philosophical differences of opinion exist between urban and rural areas that can impede system change if not handled properly.

Finally, the Kansas Juvenile Justice Authority learned that a major initiative such as this will go much smoother if we walk each community through the entire process as a "dry run" before their discontinuing the existing system. This is most desirable but understandably not always practical. System leaders must be gutsy change agents. They must surround themselves with strong professionals who can make things happen, and be willing to endure enormous amounts of political pressure while they are carrying out change.

Challenges

Some of the greatest challenges to the community planning process had little to do with the process itself, but concerned the power and impact of past and current local politics. We had to overcome preexisting turf battles. Although community planning was an overarching statewide initiative, it did not usurp historical political issues.

Local officials acknowledged that the planning process in some communities allowed citizens to mend fences and set aside differences they had on past issues. By giving communities an opportunity to collaborate and focus on their most important resource, their children, most communities could move beyond past disputes. Some communities still struggle. We advise states attempting this process to strengthen the collaboration at the planning table, and to involve people in the process who are effective mediators and community peacemakers. Finding local allies who share the vision of what community planning will eventually bring to the community is another important role.

How Community Plans Are Being Implemented

Communities submitted the plans to the Kansas Juvenile Justice Authority in November of 1998, after which communities, through administrative counties within each judicial district, submitted grant requests that identified their priorities. During the legislative session of 1999 (January-May), the Kansas Juvenile Justice Authority advocated for increased funds to carry out these programs. The legislature appropriated money for new community programs, and allocated some prevention dollars to each community based on an agency-developed funding formula. That formula is largely based on each judicial district's percentage of the high school graduation failures, a readily available statistic tied into one top predictor of juvenile crime.

They allocated funding for community intervention and sanctions programs using a formula that puts funding where it is most needed. Each community received some state funds in proportion to their region's percentage of juvenile offender convictions. In developing the formulas, the Kansas Juvenile Justice Authority looked for a common database of information and an equitable formula that would ensure funding is appropriated in proportion to the need.

The new programs include a variety of mentoring initiatives, youth courts for low-level infractions, parent education, early childhood interventions including home visitations for new parents, a variety of school-based interventions, funding for school resource officers, truancy tracking and reporting, and after-school recreation and tutoring. Local communities received 53 percent of the Kansas Juvenile Justice Authority's Fiscal Year 2001 budget to fund community programs. Another 3 percent of the budget was used for staff to provide technical assistance and additional support on accessing federal funding, and providing guidance on effective prevention and early intervention strategies.

Community plans are critical working documents. Juvenile Corrections Advisory Boards in each judicial district meet routinely to review progress on carrying out plans, and each funding cycle the board revisits priorities. Juvenile Corrections Advisory Boards have representatives from all counties within each judicial district. Outlined in the Juvenile Justice Reform Act, they typically have members who were part of the original planning teams. They also include key leaders in the planning process such as chiefs of police, sheriffs, county or district attorneys, district court judges, court services officers, executive directors of community mental health centers, four appointees from counties, and three appointees from cities. Juvenile Corrections Advisory Boards advise the administrative counties in assessing the judicial district's juvenile justice priorities. They are responsible for the juvenile justice block grants that come from the Kansas Juvenile Justice Authority to fund community programs identified in the community plans.

In sharing state and local responsibilities and resources, this initiative is consistent with the balanced approach toward working with juvenile offenders. Communities have taken a greater level of responsibility for youths in their communities and are continuing to benefit from additional resources, flexibility in spending, creativity, and guidance provided by the Kansas Juvenile Justice Authority. While not a flawless system, it has greatly improved the delivery of services to juvenile offenders and has earned the respect of many stakeholders across the state.

Kansas Juvenile Justice Authority FY 2001 Expenditures

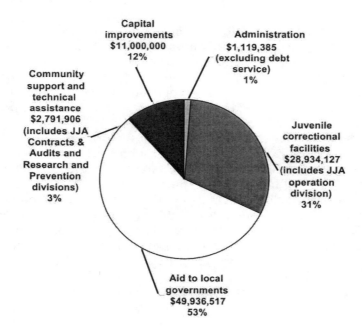

Chapter Eighteen

The Oregon Youth Authority's Gangbusters Program and Office of Minority Services

Lonnie Jackson
Manager, Office of Minority Services
Oregon Youth Authority
Salem Oregon and

author of
Gangbusters: Strategies for Prevention and Intervention
(available from the American Correctional Association)

We are pleased to share the Oregon Youth Authority's Statewide Office of Minority Services and other efforts Oregon is making in addressing cultural competency/diversity, disproportionate minority confinement, minority over-representation, gang issues, and reintegration efforts (especially, intensive aftercare programs and transition).[1]

The Oregon Youth Authority was established January 1, 1996 when it assumed responsibility for services to youthful offenders previously provided by the Children's Services Division of the Oregon's Department of Human Resources (now known as the Department of Human Services). The Oregon Youth Authority provides a continuum of services to protect the public, hold youthful offenders accountable, and reduce juvenile crime through programs and partnerships with local communities and counties. We emphasizedecisive intervention in delinquent behavior, restitution to victims, and effective and innovative rehabilitation for youthful offenders. The Oregon Youth Authority is evaluating its methodologies against best practices research emphasizing youth skill acquisition. These approaches assist us in focusing on individual needs and strengths allowing us to develop focused and meaningful intervention encompassing the youth, his or her family, community, and culture.

The mission of the Oregon Youth Authority is to protect the public by holding youth offenders accountable and providing opportunities for reformation. To achieve this, we

- emphasize public safety
- provide certain, consistent sanctions for youth offenders
- support the concerns of crime victims

- provide comprehensive youth reformation programs
- promote and support juvenile crime prevention activities
- encourage family involvement and responsibility
- select, train, support, and empower a competent and diverse workforce

To the author's knowledge, the Oregon Youth Authority is the only juvenile correctional agency in the country to have a statewide Office of Minority Services.[2]

Treatment services, policies, and training in juvenile facilities often have been a "one-size-fits-all" approach. Not only is this unfair to Caucasian youths who come from diverse backgrounds themselves, but also it is almost certain to fall short in meeting the needs of minority youths.

The mission of the Office of Minority Services is to provide leadership, advocacy, and guiding principles to assist the Oregon Youth Authority in its ongoing efforts to become a culturally competent organization and address the complex issues of a culturally and ethnically diverse agency. The Office of Minority Services supports the Oregon Youth Authority in embracing the values and strengths of all cultures and the implementation of culturally relevant, gender-specific and language-appropriate treatment services that empower youths to make positive changes.

The goals of the Office of Minority Services are to do the following things:

- To design and implement programs that strive to instill accountability and responsibility to help youth develop skills necessary to lead a crime-free life
- To continue development of positive relationships with colleagues, stakeholders, and community partners concerned with issues of juvenile crime and violence prevention and intervention efforts, which deter youth from involvement in the juvenile justice system
- To decrease minority overrepresentation in the juvenile justice system
- To continue to assist the Oregon Youth Authority in becoming a culturally competent organization

Organizational Cultural Competency Principles of the Oregon Youth Authority

The Office of Minority Services developed the following cultural competency principles that were formally adopted in May 2000, by the Oregon Youth Authority Juvenile Policy Committee. These principles lay the foundation and direction for integrating cultural competency/diversity into all aspects of the Oregon Youth Authority and its partnerships:

152

The Oregon Youth Authority mission, policies, and cultural competency principles provide the framework that supports a culturally competent organization. All Oregon Youth Authority employees, contractors, and partners understand these principles and the value of culturally competent efforts. The Oregon Youth Authority values a culturally diverse work force, which reflects the diversity in our youth offender population. Support from Oregon Youth Authority administration and management continues and is a key ingredient in implementing our competency goals and plans.

Resources and funding are made available to support Oregon Youth Authority cultural competency goals and plans. The Oregon Youth Authority strives to create an environment and work site that is welcoming, safe, free of discrimination, and is supportive of all cultures, race, ethnic groups, religious affiliations, sexual orientations, and persons with disabilities. The Oregon Youth Authority implements and reinforces civil rights mandates in all aspects of the organization. Equal access and equal services benefit all Oregon Youth Authority youth and staff.

Changes in population and new trends are evaluated and incorporated into the way Oregon Youth Authority does business. Best practices in cultural competency and treatment services are adopted to benefit youths in the Oregon Youth Authority system.

Potential Problems of Gangs in Detention and Juvenile Correctional Facilities/Training Schools

During the past two decades, the youth gang problem has grown at an alarming rate. According to the National Youth Gang Center, the number of cities with youth gang problems has increased from an estimated 286 with more than 2,000 gangs and nearly 100,000 gang members in 1980 to about 2,000 cities with more than 25,000 gangs and 650,000 members in 1995. Youth gangs are present and active in nearly every state, and in Puerto Rico, and the other territories. Few large cities are gang-free and even many cities and towns with populations of less than 25,000 are reporting gang problems. Thus, the issue of youth gangs is now affecting new localities, such as small towns and rural areas.

Clearly, youth gangs present a serious threat to juvenile correctional facilities. James C. Howell, a juvenile justice consultant with the National Gangs Research Project and David W. Roucsh, director of the National Juvenile Detention Association Center for Research and Professional Development at Eastern Kentucky University, have noted that concerns about the negative influences of youth gang members in these facilities include violent behaviors that threaten resident and staff safety, undermine programs, compromise institutional security, and jeopardize public safety. Juvenile correctional facilities should develop suppression strategies for youth gang members and have a "zero-tolerance" approach to gang behavior and activity.

153

Early on, the Oregon Youth Authority realized that these facilities need to create committees or task forces to assess the nature and extent of their youth gang problem. Then, these facilities had to develop policies, procedures, and criteria to identify gang members and to gather intelligence on gang activity. Flowing from this information, we developed plans for implementing systemic change by providing training and understanding the value and role of cultural awareness and diversity in reforming gang mentality.

For many years, juvenile correctional facilities have had a number of good and generally effective treatment programs for sex offenders, violent offenders, youths with drug and alcohol abuse issues, and youths with anger management problems. Although these programs have merit, they were not geared to help urban youths with hard core street life and gang mentality. Existing programs failed to pierce the particular mind-set such youths were bringing to juvenile correctional facilities in increasing numbers.

To get to the root of the problem, we had to address minority recidivism as a treatment issue. This included identifying factors unique to the experience of most minority youths, factors that led to their involvement with criminal behavior. Then, we had to address these issues in a way to reduce the likelihood of a young person's return to criminal behavior after incarceration. We realized that such a program would have to do more than instruct. It would have to convey an authentic understanding of how the youths came to be the way they are and to instill in them a sincere concern about their own future if they did not make appropriate changes.

We had to develop a comprehensive strategy of treatment and intervention. These young people contend with multiple issues. Like the sex offender, the addict, or the alcoholic in denial, these young people are intensely resistant to reform. Their gang and their gang lifestyle are their life.

We learned that we cannot overcome their passionate devotion to their gang lifestyle with minimal or token effort. The challenge requires a comprehensive approach that makes them check their thinking, their value system, their actions, and their way of living. We believe that treatment providers must view the gang mentality as a treatment issue and address it in an extensive, systemic, and personal manner using a culturally aware and culturally sensitive, well-trained staff.

We have a golden opportunity to work with these young men and women when they come to our facilities for a set period of time. We may have some for six months, others for a year or more. Regardless of the length of time they are incarcerated, they are in a structured environment and we know where they are. Their minds are not clouded by drugs and alcohol. We can expose them to information and education to show them alternatives to gangs. We can deal with the mind-set that makes gang activities not only acceptable but also appealing.

Cultural sensitivity increases the youths' receptivity to the information we want to share with them. It also helps the youths see their connection to a greater cultural history—not how they currently live through a series of isolated, insignificant chance occurrences. This cultural identity increases their feeling of self-worth and helps them see the need to change.

Additionally, these streetwise youths are more likely to reject or ignore generic or neutral instruction. Unless something relates directly to them, their situation, and their lives, many will not be open and listen. Thus, all superintendents who know they have a significant gang population are encouraged to develop a culturally specific program to address the issues that have led youths to join gangs.

Individuals working in institutions housing gang-involved youths must proactively develop and refine programs that address gang involvement as a treatment issue and tailor treatment to get through the mind-set and defenses of urbanized, hard-core, streetwise youths. Otherwise, we will have perpetual aimlessness and recidivism among the gang-affiliated population.

The Oregon Youth Authority has recognized gang mentality as a treatment issue, which requires serious intervention to elicit positive changes in attitudes and behaviors from gang members. Youths in secure custody receive gang intervention/youth empowerment treatment services.

Gang Intervention/Youth Empowerment Treatment Services

Gang Intervention/Youth Empowerment Treatment Services have a three-fold purpose:

Prevention – Prevent youths who are infatuated "wannabe's" from joining gangs.
Intervention – Help youths who are already involved get out.
Youth Empowerment – Empower youths to take responsibility for life and become constructive and positive in the community.

Intervention tools that have been useful in the groups include guest speakers, video presentations, role plays, rap music (addressing lyrics that are destructive, gang related, violent, negative portrayal of females), written assignments, problem solving groups, individual counseling, using forensic information, and straight talk mixed with frightening reality.

Some of the topics and issues we address are the development of pro-social behaviors and attitudes. We instill a sense of hope that they can be something other than a gangster or drug dealer. We counter racism and prejudice by developing cultural and ethnic pride through a "knowledge of self." We help them deal with their frustration and anger appropriately by learning and using coping skills. We teach them to understand family issues, consider self-determination and goal setting; and deal with negative peer pressure. We help them learn to find rebuttals for being called "squares" and "suckers." We also address ethnic on ethnic crime/violence and alternatives such as jobs, education, and vocational skill training. For more information on gang intervention/prevention, *see Gangbusters: Strategies for Prevention and Intervention* published by the American Correctional Association.

Other Office of Minority Services Key Focus Areas

The Office of Minority Services has identified the following as key focus areas to support the Oregon Youth Authority, the State of Oregon, and national efforts:

Culturally Relevant Support/Treatment Services and Programs within Secure Facilities

Hillcrest and MacLaren Youth Correctional Facilities have comprehensive multicultural programs on campus. Ron Weaver, Multicultural Facilities Coordinator, coordinates services with all of Minority Services facility staff. Some of the services that are provided in these facilities include:

Culturally Specific Treatment Groups

Culturally specific treatment groups provide youths the opportunity to interact and learn about their own and other racial, cultural, and ethnic backgrounds. It also provides youths the opportunity to learn the history of different ethnic groups and their contribution to society while working on their treatment issues.

Rolando Ramirez, Minority Services Hispanic Services Coordinator at MacLaren Youth Correctional Facility provides Sex Offender Treatment in Spanish to youths with Limited English Proficiency.

Gang Tattoo Removal Program

The Oregon Psychiatric Association and the Oregon Youth Authority/Office of Minority Services have collaborated to study the effects of removing gang-related tattoos from gang-affected youths. Youths under the custody of the Oregon Youth Authority may apply for inclusion in the Gang Tattoo Removal Program.

The program began in the early 1990s and is coordinated by Griselda Solano, Minority Services Hispanic Services Coordinator at Hillcrest Youth Correctional Facility in Salem, Oregon with assistance from Lily Caceres, Statewide Minority Services Hispanic Coordinator. The purpose of the program is to remove gang-related tattoos. The decision to admit the youths in the program is based on their overall treatment plan and expected results. The facility treatment managers and the Office of Minority Services staff must approve and confirm participation of the youth based on how he or she is responding to the treatment plan. Each tattoo takes an average of five to six treatments, but depending on the size and extent, it may take more. To date,

186 youths have received 609 treatments and approximately 350 youths are on the waiting list for treatments.

This program has been so successful that Portland Oregon's Emmanuel Hospital has modeled the program and is now doing gang tattoo removal treatments in the community in collaboration with the Oregon Psychiatric Association.

Culturally Specific Spiritual Services

John Fraser, Native American Services Coordinator, and Matt Poteet coordinate Native American Services at Hillcrest and MacLaren Youth Correctional Facilities with the assistance of Jack Lawson, Statewide Minority Services Native American Coordinator. These include a sweatlodge, pipe ceremonies, and pow-wows.

All five Oregon Youth Authority Regional Youth Correctional Facilities have built sweatlodges and sweats are facilitated by community volunteers such as the Southern Oregon Indian Center. The Office of Minority Services contracts with Gloria Brooks from the Confederated Tribes of Siletz to provide Native American Services to the young women at Hillcrest Youth Correctional Facility.

Cultural Events and Activities

Oregon Youth Authority/Office of Minority Services Staff coordinate with youths and Oregon Youth Authority staff on special cultural events and activities such as Black History Month, Cinco de Mayo, Women's Symposium, Gospel Festival, Juneteenth, Native American Heritage Month, Hispanic Heritage Month, Pow-wows, and other cultural events.

Minority Youth Transition Program

The Minority Youth Transition Program is coordinated by Christina Puentes, the Minority Youth Transition Program Coordinator, Faith Love, Transition Specialist, Kara Song, Transition Specialist, and Shawna Hill, Office of Minority Services Technical Services Coordinator.

The Transition Program is designed to assist minority youths in transition from juvenile correctional facilities back into their communities. The program creates a support system that provides culturally specific, language-appropriate services tailored to fit the individual needs of minority youths. The primary objective of the Transition Program is to reduce recidivism and address the overrepresentation of minorities in the juvenile justice system.

The program relies on effective collaboration with Oregon Youth Authority Juvenile Parole/Probation Supervisors and Officers, the Department of Education, the Department of Corrections, community providers, Native American tribes, youths and their families, and others intricately involved with issues of juvenile crime.

The Transition Program began in 1996 with a grant from the Office of Juvenile Justice and Delinquency Prevention, a Federal Byrne Grant through the Oregon State Police, Criminal Justice Services Division. In 1996 African-American males represented 12 percent of the Oregon Youth Authority secure custody population. By 2001 the total African-American juvenile offender population had decreased to 7 percent. In 1997 the Transition Program was expanded to include Hispanic males (through the Byrne Grant). In 1999 the the Office of Minority Services received a grant from the Commission on Children and Families to expand the program to include Native American males and minority females. Because of the program's effectiveness, the Oregon Youth Authority received funds to continue the Transition Program.

The Transition Program has received both statewide and national recognition and was featured at the 2000 Office of Juvenile Justice and Delinquency Prevention national conference in Washington D.C. "I haven't come in contact with another program that's as comprehensive as this one is," Emily Martin, Director of Training and Technical Assistance for the Office of Juvenile Justice and Delinquency Prevention, said in *The Oregonian* newspaper, October 2001.

Each youth on the Transition Program has an individualized transition plan developed prior to the youth leaving the facility. The transition plan is developed in collaboration with the transition specialist, the parole officer, the treatment manager, other facility staff, community providers, the youths, and their families. Culturally specific and language appropriate program services include: mentorship, drug and alcohol treatment, mental health services, family support, anger management, grief counseling, conflict resolution, gang intervention/mediation, prosocial development, bus passes, clothing vouchers, employment/job readiness, education assistance, and twenty-four-hour crisis response.[3]

One of the "intangibles" that contribute to the program's success is the flexibility of the transition specialist, especially their nontraditional work hours. Family involvement is a critical element in a youth's transition plan. Often youths come from single-parent families where the parent works during the days and taking off work to meet with a transition specialist, although beneficial for the youth, would be a hardship for the family. Because of the transition specialists' nontraditional work hours, they are able to meet with family members in the evening. This flexibility also enhances the relationship and builds trust between the family members and the transition specialist. Because of the relationship that is built, families are more likely to support the transition plan and contact transition specialists as issues arise, allowing the transition specialist to intervene and possibly keep the youth from lapsing into past behaviors.

Other intangibles that contribute to the success of the program are the commitment and dedication of the staff; the staffs ability to develop constructive, positive relationships with youths, their families, and other key stakeholders and partners. They achieve this through consistency, accountability, and a belief that youths can be empowered and make positive changes in their lives. As previously indicated, the twenty-four-hour crisis response to youths and their families is critical.

Another key element that contributes to the success of the Transition Program is the use of incentives and graduated sanctions. Incentives are given on an individual (case by case basis) and may include: school supplies; personal grooming supplies; opportunities for community involvement, such as speaking at conferences; speaking to other youths about the dangers of drugs, gangs, and violence; growth-enhancing opportunities such as out-of-town trips, fishing trips, participation in youth summits; learning etiquette and manners while dining at various restaurants; midnight basketball with community mentors—which includes guest speakers on topics such as drug and alcohol, gangs, family, goal setting, and responsibilities.

Each youth who participates in the Transition Program has a transition specialist who is an advocate to employers, the education system, the parole officer, the family, and provides community support. The youth and his or her family have access to the transition specialist twenty-four hours a day. When youth successfully complete the program, they are awarded a graduation certificate (they often come back to the facility for a special cultural event and the certificate is awarded at the event). Often the youth's relationship continues with the transition program after completion of the program and linkages are established with other resources and support networks within the community for ongoing support.

Youths who participate in the program also may receive graduated sanctions. These are listed on the Transition Plan, which is developed and signed by the youths before leaving the facility. (The youths know what the expectations and consequences are prior to leaving the facility). Some of the graduated sanctions used include the following:

More frequent meeting (check in's) with transition specialist
Journal activities
Phone call to the probation officer
Structured meeting with the probation officer, transition specialist, family, and youths
Technical violation
Detention time and or revocation

Since the program became a general funded program in July 1999, 107 youths have participated in the program.

A recent letter received from one of the youth on the Transition Program conveys its value from the youth's perspective:

Dear Faith,

I thought that I would e-mail you and tell you thank you for all of the help that you and your people have been giving me. I want you to know that all of your help is greatly appreciated and that I see how much I am benefiting. I am pretty sure that if I did not have the support that I have

159

been receiving then I would not have made it this far in my reentry to society. I know that I still have a little ways further to go but the important thing to me is that I am getting there. If I were to have had to do this transition thing alone I would not have made it this far. Sadly enough I would have given up and would have been running the streets or back in jail if it was not for your help and support. Working gives me a great sense of pride and accomplishment and it is really good for my self-esteem (I feel like a good young black man instead of unredeemable convict). I feel as if I am actually doing something worthwhile. I want you to know Faith, that you were the one who had found me in MacLaren and who had just tracked me until I got out. To be honest, I did not think that you would have gone the distance for me like you have already shown you would. I don't think I can ever repay that kind of loyalty and honesty. Well if there is anything I can do for your program all you have to do is ask. If you need me to guest speak for any of your employers or write letters, etc. I am more then willing to do that. (No documentaries or film crews please.) In a way you guys have saved my life and I am learning even when I thought there was nothing left to learn. You have a good day and once again thank you for all your support!! Lepri

Oregon Youth Authority Juvenile Justice Training Academy (OJJTA)/The Office of Minority Services Partnership

The Oregon Youth Authority Juvenile Justice Training Academy under the direction of Joe VanMeter coordinates with the Office of Minority Services to provide cultural competency training to all Oregon Youth Authority staff at the Annual Staff Update Training and Basic Facilities Training. The Office of Minority Services also assists with reviewing cultural competency training for residential providers and other training upon request and provides technical assistance relating to cultural competency to many juvenile justice workers.

The theme for the 2002 Annual Staff Update Training provided by the Office of Minority Services is "Cross-cultural Communication which Enhances Positive Cross-cultural Relationships." The training focuses on misunderstandings resulting from nonverbal and verbal cross-cultural communication, comparing and contrasting typical social customs in other cultures with those of your own, developing an awareness of the cultural lenses through which any society may perceive and evaluate others, recognizing the importance of cross-cultural communication in the treatment and reformation efforts of the Oregon Youth Authority, and identifying tips for better cross-cultural communication in treatment and reformation.

Oregon Youth Authority Employee Services/Office of Minority Services Partnership

The Office of Minority Services partners with Oregon Youth Authority Employee Services to assist the Oregon Youth Authority in aggressive strategies to recruit and retain a diverse workforce. The Office of Minority Services reviews and provides technical assistance upon request on personnel issues, personnel reviews, and the Equal Employment Opportunity (EEO)/Affirmative Action Plan (AAP).

Oregon Youth Authority Community Resources Unit/Office of Minority Services Partnership

The Office of Minority Services coordinates with the Oregon Youth Authority's Community Resources Unit to develop cultural competency guidelines for service providers and participates in residential program evaluations relating to program cultural competency.

Regional Diversity Workplans

The Office of Minority Services works with regional liaisons in each of the five Oregon Youth Authority regions to develop regional diversity workplans. The Office of Minority Services meets with staff regularly to develop key focus areas in each of the regions. Some of the goals of the regional workplans are as follows:

Enhance communication
Enhance cultural awareness
Address Minority Issues – Assess need level and provide education on cultural issues, conduct gap analysis to determine needs and current service levels, prioritze unmet needs for services.
Create linkages with the Oregon Youth Authority and the community
Provide education services
Facilitate culturally appropriate services delivery
Reduce recidivism
Develop/provide mentorship (programs)
Provide cultural competency/diversity training

The Office of Minority Services continues to meet with regional liaisons to identify key focus areas.

Ethnic Advisory Committees

The Office of Minority Services coordinates the Native American and Hispanic Advisory Committees. These committees assist the Oregon Youth Authority in maintaining a level of cultural competency and sensitivity in pro-

161

grams and services. Each committee has identified a representative to participate on the Oregon Youth Authority Advisory Committee. The Office of Minority Services also participates in the NorthEast Rescue Plan Action Committee (NERPAC) to address issues relating to African-American youths.

The mission of the Hispanic Advisory Committee is to support the vision and mission of the Office of Minority Services. The Hispanic Advisory Committee will advocate for the best culturally specific, gender-specific, and language-appropriate services for Hispanic/Latino youths and their families in the following ways:

Assist in implementing the Hispanic work plan and/or area work plan in Oregon Youth Authority regions.

Assist in building links between the Oregon Youth Authority and the Hispanic/Latino communities in Oregon.

Assist the Oregon Youth Authority in maintaining a level of cultural competency in programs, services, and policies regarding Hispanic/Latino youths in the system.

Assist in recruiting volunteers, mentors, and guest speakers to support the Oregon Youth Authority's services to the Hispanic/Latino youths.

Assist Oregon Youth Authority in recruiting Hispanic/Latino staff.

Assist the Oregon Youth Authority in supporting transition services for Hispanic/Latino youths.

Assist in establishing community resources for foster homes, residential treatment, sex offenders, and transition services.

The Purpose and Goals of the Native American Advisory Committee are as follows:

Establish community links between the Oregon Youth Authority and Native American communities.

Consult to assist in the cultural competency of programs, services, and policies regarding Native American youths within the Oregon Youth Authority.

Recruit volunteers to support services offered by the Oregon Youth Authority for Native American youths in close custody.

Recruit and retain Native American staff. Oregon Youth Authority is expanding as an agency and is committed to having an employee work force that reflects the diversity of the youth population we serve.

Consult on transition services for Native American youths.

Provide staff training on Native American culture and tribal structure.

Establish resources for foster homes.

Address key issues of youths.

Ensure safety in the community and in the Oregon Youth Authority facilities.

Advocate for the best interest of youth and families.

Develop communication and trust between the Oregon Youth Authority and the tribes.

Governor's Executive Order 96–30

In 1996 Governor John Kitzhaber mandated that all state agencies formalize relationships with Oregon's nine federally recognized tribes. Governor Kitzhaber's Executive Order 96-30 states:

> There are nine federally recognized Indian tribal governments located in the State of Oregon. These Indian tribes were in existence prior to the formation of the Untied States of America, and thus retain a unique legal statue. The importance of recognizing the relationship that exists between the tribes and state government cannot be underestimated.
>
> As sovereigns the tribes and the State of Oregon must work together to develop mutual respect for the sovereign interest of both parties. The relationships between our governmental structures can only be built through trust and mutual respect.
>
> The purpose of formalizing the government-to-government relationships that exists between Oregon's Indian tribes and the State is to establish a process which can assist in resolving potential conflicts, maximize key intergovernmental relations and enhance an exchange of ideas and resources for the greater good of all of Oregon's citizens, whether tribal members or not.

The Oregon Youth Authority currently has signed memorandums of understanding with the Burns Paiute Tribe, Confederated Tribe of Siletz, Cow Creek Band of Umpqua Indians, Coquille Indian Tribe, and the Klamath Tribes. Some of the common themes in the memorandums of understanding include the following: a statement of purpose, description of areas of mutual concern, establishment of a Native American advisory committee, development of a notification process, development of an Indian Child Welfare Act (ICWA) statement, listing of the Oregon Youth Authority and the tribal supportive services, key contacts, and process of communication.

State of Oregon Efforts

Governor's Summit on Overrepresentation of Minorities in the Juvenile Justice System

For the past five years, the Oregon Youth Authority has provided leadership and support in the coordination of the Governor's Summit on the Overrepresentation of Minorities in the Juvenile Justice System. Disproportionate minority confinement or minority overrepresentation is a national problem that each state must address. Governor Kitzhaber may be the only Governor who has made this issue a priority for his administration. According to the *Building Blocks for Youth Report and Justice for Some* (by Youth Law Center):

The overrepresentation of minorities, particularly African Americans, in the nation's prison has received much attention in recent years. However, the disproportionate representation of racial/ethnic groups is not limited to adult prisons and jails. It is also found among youth confined in secure juvenile facilities.

While public attention has tended to focus on the disproportionate number of minorities in confinement, minority over-representation is often a product of actions that occur at earlier points in the juvenile justice system, such as the decision to make the initial arrest, the decision to hold a youth in detention pending investigation, the decision to refer a case to juvenile court, the prosecutor's decision to petition a case, and the judicial decision and subsequent sanction.

Some have argued that this overrepresentation of minority youth in the justice system simply is a result of minority youth committing more crimes than white youth. However, a fair analysis is much more complicated. Thus it is not clear whether this overrepresentation is the result of differential police policies and practices (e.g. targeting patrols in certain low-income neighborhood, policies requiring immediate release to biological parents, group arrest procedures); location of offenses (minority youth using or selling drugs on street corners, white youth using or selling drugs in homes); different behavior by minority youth (e.g., whether minority youth commit more crimes than white youth); differential reactions of victims to offenses committed by white and minority youth (e.g., whether white victims of crimes disproportionately perceive the offenders to be minority youth); or racial bias within the justice system.

It is clear that minority youth are more likely than others to come into contact with the juvenile justice system. Research suggests that this disparity is most pronounced at the beginning stages of involvement with the juvenile justice system. When racial/ethnic differences are found, they tend to accumulate as youth are processed through the system.

Processing decisions in many states and local juvenile justice systems are not racially neutral. Minority youth are more likely than white youth to become involved in the system with their disproportionate involvement increasing at each stage of the process. The first Governor's Summit on Overrepresentation of Minorities in the Juvenile Justice System was in 1997 with keynote speaker Michael Lindsey, a national consultant. We have been fortunate to have other outstanding speakers—Emily Martin, Director of the Training and Technical Assistance Division, U.S. Department of Justices (1999); James Bell from the Youth Law Center (2000); and Senator Avel Gordly (2001). Special thanks go to Senator Avel Gordly for her commitment, vision, and leadership in addressing minority overrepresentation and moderating the Summit for the past five years.

The 2001 Governor's Summit featured all three branches of government. Senator Avel Gordly (legislature), Governor John Kitzhaber (executive), and Chief Justice Wallace P. Carson (judicial) hosted approximately 500 participants from all decision points in the juvenile justice system.

Governor Kitzhaber said in his 1999 speech at the Summit:

If a chain of events leads minority youth to cross the line of the law, then we must form a chain of our own—a chain of prevention. But as long as there are disconnected links in that chain, too many children, especially too many minority children, will surely slip through the cracks. And I say that's not acceptable. . . . That's why we must seek ways to collaborate—ways for the various parts of the system to work together to help these kids either from getting involved in the first place of from penetrating the system any further.

Of course, such an event takes months of planning from highly committed individuals.[4] Participants in the Summit include:

Defense and district attorneys
The Oregon Youth Authority
The Department of Corrections
Judges
Education representatives
Local juvenile departments
Tribal governments
Social services
Advocacy organizations
Law enforcement
Business
Boards and commissions
Faith representatives
Community representatives
Families and youths

Each year at the summit, agencies and disciplines are asked to submit commitments to the governor's office. Prior to each summit, each agency/discipline is asked to submit a report of their accomplishments relating to the commitments that were made at the previous Summit. Some of the accomplishments that were submitted for the 2000 Summit Report are:

Local Juvenile Justice Agencies

They incorporated specific language into the Association's vision and mission statements to address the issues of enhancing cultural competency and reducing the overrepresentation of minorities in the juvenile justice system.

They also developed a strategic plan in 2001 that identified enhancing cultural competency and reducing minority overrepresentation as one of six primary work areas.

Education

The school system promoted multicultural education activities through-out the state.They promoted cultural competency training at the district, regional, and state level.They developed a countywide database to desegre-gate data for minority students as an assessment/evaluation tool for program design.

Oregon Youth Authority

They continue to coordinate and provide mentorship services for youths through the Minority Youth Transition Program. They provide mentorship pro-grams for youths in both the youth correctional facilities and the community. Hillcrest and MacLaren have comprehensive multicultural programs on cam-pus including the following:

Gang intervention/youth empowerment treatment
Culturally specific treatment groups
Multicultural support groups
Gang tattoo removal program
Special events and cultural celebrations

Regional diversity plans have been developed and implemented within all five regions. Additionally the Oregon Youth Authority/Office of Minority Services has signed and formalized memorandums of understanding with the Klamath Tribe, the Coquille Tribe, the Cow Creek Tribe, the Burns Paiute Tribe, and with the Siletz Tribe.

The Theme for the 2001 Summit was "Effective Solutions for Reducing the Overrepresentation of Minorities in the Juvenile Justice System." Not only were agencies and disciplines asked to make commitments, but each individ-ual was asked to make a personal commitment to reduce minority overrepre-sentation. The Oregon Youth Authority has received two consecutive awards from the Governor for "Outstanding Efforts in Preventing the Overrepresenta-tion of Minorities in the Juvenile Justice System."

Juvenile Crime Prevention Advisory Committee/SB555 Cultural Competency and Gender Specific Subcommittee

In the 1999–2001 Oregon Legislative Session, the legislature allocated $20 million to the thirty-six Oregon counties to develop and implement juvenile crime prevention plans focusing on early prevention. The governor's office established the Juvenile Crime Prevention Advisory Committee with members from state agency administrators/directors, county commissioners and local/county public officials.

The purpose of the Juvenile Crime Prevention Advisory Committee is to monitor, coordinate, and provide leadership to counties regarding their juvenile crime prevention plans and to review and approve the juvenile crime prevention plans. When juvenile crime prevention plans were submitted to the Juvenile Crime Prevention Advisory Committee, the plans were appropriate in a number of areas. The Juvenile Crime Prevention Advisory Committee felt many of the plans were not addressing how they would address cultural competency and gender-specific issues in their counties. The Juvenile Crime Prevention Advisory Committee mandated the counties to address these issues.

To assist the counties in incorporating cultural competency and gender-specific services in their plans, the Juvenile Crime Prevention Advisory Committee commissioned the Oregon Youth Authority/Office of Minority Services to develop an interagency subcommittee to design and facilitate cultural competency and gender-specific training for the counties. Training in "Culture as a Conceptual Tool for Juvenile Crime Prevention" was provided throughout the state with key individuals, organizations, and stakeholders attending.

The development and facilitation of this training was a collaborative effort between the Oregon Youth Authority, the Department of Human Services–Office of Alcohol and Drug Abuse Programs, the Judicial Department, the Multnomah County Juvenile Justice Division, the Criminal Justice Commission, the Oregon Commission on Children and Families, and private gender-specific consultants.

Topics of the training included:
Cultural Competency – Creating a Common Language
At Risk Female Youth – Gender Specific: Moving from Words to Action
Race and Ethnicity – Specific Issues Asian
Race and Ethnicity – Specific Issues Hispanic
Race and Ethnicity – Specific Issues African American
Race and Ethnicity – Specific Issues Native American

On completion of the training, the Juvenile Crime Prevention Advisory Committee formally adopted the Juvenile Crime Prevention Advisory Committee Cultural Competency and Gender Specific Subcommittee to provide technical assistance/consultation, training, review juvenile crime prevention plans for cultural competency and gender-specific services, make recommendations to the Juvenile Crime Prevention Advisory Committee for approval of counties juvenile crime prevention plans relating to cultural competency and gender-specific services, develop statewide training of trainers, develop cultural competency and gender- specific resource guide, and develop cultural competency and gender-specific self-assessment tools. The Juvenile Crime Prevention Advisory Committee/Cultural Competency and Gender Specific Subcommittee has merged with the Senate Bill (SB) 555 Committee and the

Oregon Commission on Children and Families Cultural Competency committee to coordinate efforts.

Cultural Competency Coordinator

Stacy Johnson, the Cultural Competency Coordinator, has a unique position that is shared among three state agencies: the Oregon Youth Authority, the Criminal Justice Commission, and the Oregon Commission on Children and Families. The Cultural Competency Coordinator is a broker to counties for technical assistance and training on cultural competency and gender-specific services relating to the counties' juvenile crime prevention plans.

Statewide Structure Committee

The Statewide Structure Committee was developed as a result of the State of Oregon Cultural Gathering that met to work on cultural diversity issues, to foster a network, and discuss common needs and resources. Jack Lawson, Minority Services Native American Coordinator is chair of the Statewide Structure Committee. Focus areas of the Statewide Structure Committee include: creation of a formal network; development of common standards, terminology, and language; development of resource lists of individuals with expertise, measurement of the progress of state agencies; recruitment and retention of a diverse workforce; definition of critical elements of organizational cultural competency; and provision of technical assistance/resources to state agencies regarding cultural competency/diversity.

The Statewide Structure Committee has developed recommendations to present to Mike Greenfield, Director of the Department of Administrative Services to create a statewide structure to coordinate and develop a strategy for the implementation of policy, action plans, guidelines, and practice for cultural competency. The overall goal of the committee is to raise the standard in providing services to the ethnic, cultural, and racial minority citizens of Oregon. This goal would be obtained by developing common language, leveraging and maximizing existing resources, developing an avenue of communication among state agencies, and identifying effective training and managerial competencies.

National Efforts

Juvenile Reintegration and Aftercare Center, Intensive Aftercare Programs Mission

The mission of the Intensive Aftercare Programs of the Juvenile Reintegration and Aftercare Center is to help agencies, both public and private, develop and implement programming for successful transition and reentry of juvenile offenders into the community from out-of-home placement. The

Center's primary goal is to promote best practices in juvenile transition and aftercare systems through training, technical assistance, ongoing research, and linkage with other technical assistance and service providers. The Intensive Community Based Aftercare model provides for increased public safety and normalization of offenders in the community by providing intensified treatment services and higher levels of community surveillance.

Purpose

Each year tens of thousands of juveniles enter juvenile detention, correctional, and treatment programs. Many youths spend significant time in one or more public and private residential placements. All but a few of these youths will eventually return to their home community.

The Intensive Aftercare Programs of the Reintegration and Aftercare Center promotes best practices in juvenile transition and community aftercare services and provides training and technical assistance to state and local juvenile justice organizations and service providers. It conducts and reviews ongoing research and links with other juvenile justice technical assistance and program providers to share information and resources.

Project

The Intensive Aftercare Programs is a research-based approach to transitioning youths from confinement into the community. The research and development of this project began in 1988 under the direction of Dr. David Altschuler, Johns Hopkins University, and Dr. Troy Armstrong, California State University, Sacramento. Funding has been provided by the Office of Juvenile Justice and Delinquency Prevention. Intensive Aftercare Programs stress that both surveillance and treatment services are critical to the successful reintegration of youths into the community. Planning for reintegration begins when a youth first enters residential placement and involves the cooperative assistance of institutional staff, community aftercare staff, and community service providers. The success of the Intensive Aftercare Programs model depends on close collaborations involving juvenile justice professionals, the youth's family, and his or her home community.

Intensive Aftercare Programs Principles

The Intensive Aftercare Programs model is grounded in five underlying principles for reintegration:

- Preparing youths for progressively increased responsibility and freedom in the community
- Facilitating youth-community interaction and involvement
- Working with both the offender and community support systems on qualities needed for the constructive interaction and the youths' successful return to the community

169

- Developing new resources and supports where needed
- Monitoring and testing the youth's and the community's ability to work productively together.

(There are many Intensive Aftercare Programs publications online at: ojjdp.ncjrs.org/pubs/pubs.html)

Juvenile Reintegration and Aftercare Center Services

The Juvenile Reintegration and Aftercare Center is designed to provide state, county, and local community agencies with assistance on developing and implementing effective transition and community aftercare services. The Center provides training and technical assistance, information dissemination, and linkage to aftercare resources.

Training and Technical Assistance. The Center maintains a pool of consultants with special knowledge and experience in the design and implementation of intensive juvenile aftercare services using the Intensive Aftercare Programs model. The Center functions as a clearinghouse for requests for training and technical assistance, including requests for information (education) sessions, skills training and development, system assessment, strategic planning, organizational development, program development and implementation, and program evaluation.

Information Dissemination. The Center maintains a library of Intensive Aftercare Programs documents and a database of available resources that is provided to anyone requesting information about the Intensive Aftercare Programs model or other aftercare/reintegration projects. The Center's website (www.csus.edu/ssis/cdcps/) provides an overview of the Intensive Aftercare Programs project, downloadable Intensive Aftercare Programs documents, links to aftercare documents from the Office of Juvenile Justice and Delinquency Prevention, training and technical assistance information and applications forms, consultant information, and links to other aftercare initiatives.

Linkage to Aftercare Resources

The Center has established both formal and informal links with other aftercare initiatives and technical assistance resources to provide states and communities with the latest information and available services. Examples of existing initiatives and resources include:

Performance-based Standards for Juvenile Correction and Detention Facilities—Council of Juvenile Correctional Administrators (www.performance-standards.org)

Demonstration Projects for Youth Offenders—U.S. Department of Labor (wdsc.doleta.gov/sga)

Transition Planning and Services—National Center on Education, Disability, and Juvenile Justice (www.edjj.org)

Critical Elements of Successful Aftercare Services Training—National Institute of Corrections (www.nicic.org)
American Corrections Association (www.corrections.com/aca/)
American Probation and Parole Association—Annual Training Institute (www.appa-net.org)
JAIBG Funding for Intensive Aftercare Programs Program Development—Development Services Group (www.dsgonline.com)
The National Council of Juvenile and Family Court Judges (www.ncjfc.unr.edu)[5]

The Oregon Youth Authority/Office of Minority Services has recently developed the curriculum for the Intensive Aftercare Programs Special Populations (Minority Populations) Training for the Office of Juvenile Justice and Delinquency Prevention Intensive Aftercare Programs Training Manual. This training module discusses the need for and development of culturally specific Intensive Aftercare Programs. It reviews the national problem of disproportionate minority confinement and discusses how the Intensive Aftercare Programs model can contribute to the reduction of overrepresentation of minority youth in secure facilities and recidivism rates among juvenile offenders. The programmatic benefits of cultural sensitivity are discussed and key principles of the Intensive Aftercare Programs model, which complement and augment the basic principles of culturally specific programming, are outlined.

Traditionally, treatment in juvenile facilities has been a "one-size-fits-all" approach. Minority youths experience unique issues related to culture, life experiences, and identity. To enhance positive outcomes for minority youths, these cultural issues must be addressed and incorporated into the treatment process.

Culturally specific services are especially necessary in aftercare planning because they help to ensure that we meet the needs and issues of each youth. They enhance treatment services and provide minority youths with avenues for successful treatment from within their cultural values. They provide another level for holding youths accountable for their behaviors and attitudes within their cultural values.

Sensitivity, knowledge, skills, and awareness of addressing cultural issues such as dress, language, values, beliefs, history, and life experiences enhance relationship building. Youths need assistance to develop prosocial skills to become productive members of their community.

The Intensive Aftercare Programs model is an effective framework because it requires the development of productive collaborations, individualized services, language-appropriate services, culturally specific treatment services, family involvement, effective monitoring/supervision, and graduated sanctions. Research and best practices indicate that youths who are released from close custody facilities are more likely to succeed when community, culturally specific treatment programs, and family are involved in the development and implementation of the youths' individualized transition plans.

Furthermore, key elements of the Intensive Aftercare Programs model, such as effective monitoring, supervision, and graduated sanctions, are critical in ensuring public safety, accountability, and compliance with the transition plan.

A primary objective of a culturally specific Intensive Aftercare Programs model is to increase treatment success of minority youths, reduce recidivism, and address the issue of overrepresentation of minorities in the juvenile justice system. A culturally specific Intensive Aftercare Programs model can assist in creating a support system that provides culturally specific, language-appropriate services, tailored to fit the individual needs of minority youths. A culturally specific Intensive Aftercare Programs model provides guidelines for positive reintegration for minority youths into their community by addressing cultural issues and concerns across a continuum of prerelease, transition, and community follow-up.

Closing Remarks

As someone who is employed by the Oregon Youth Authority, this author has been extremely impressed with the vision and understanding needed for the balance of public safety issues, accountability of the juvenile offenders, and the reformation/rehabilitation of juvenile offenders. The agency's willingness to develop partnerships and take risks to accomplish these objectives is impressive. The staff has worked unselfishly and shows consistent commitment to making a difference in the lives of Oregon's youths.

While only five years old, the Oregon Youth Authority's innovative programs and approaches to administering juvenile corrections is a model for other states, and this author is proud to be part of such an outstanding organization.

Endnotes

[1.] The author would like to express his appreciation to Oregon Youth Authority's administration including Karen Brazeau, director; Bob Jester, deputy director; Karen Andall, executive assistant to the director; Theresa Mattis, executive support to the director; assistant directors Brian Florip and Karen Olson, area coordinators, Faye Fagel, Debbie Rios, Bob Amela, Robyn Cole, and Brad Mulvihill, all of the superintendents, managers, and staff for their commitment in making organizational cultural competency a high priority for our agency.

[2.] The author would like to commend former Oregon Youth Authority director Rick Hill for having the vision to establish and empower such an office, a branch of the Director's Office, to provide leadership and ensure that Oregon Youth Authority's funded programs, services, training, and policies are culturally competent and sensitive to the needs of all youths in its custody.

[3.]The contractors who provide culturally specific and language-appropriate services for youths in the Transition Program include Marcus Branch, Services for Humanity; Leonard Clark, Reaching In Serving Kids (RISK); David Jones, Siloam International; Nora Farwell, Native American Youth Association; Native American Rehabilitation Association; Oregon Council for Hispanic Advancement; and Robert Richardson. Because of their commitment and dedication to youths, the Transition Program is a success.

[4.]The Summit Planning Committee is a collaborative effort. This author is cochair with Pam Curtis, Policy Advisor for Public Safety from the Governor's Office. Summit Planning participants include the Governor's Office, the Oregon Youth Authority, the Criminal Justice Commission, the Oregon Commission on Children and Families, the Department of Education, the Oregon State Police, Community Partners and Advocates, local juvenile departments, the Oregon Juvenile Department Directors Association (OJDDA), and the Department of Human Services.

[5.]The author would like to thank Drs. Armstrong and Altschuler for the opportunity to be a consultant for the Juvenile Reintegration and Aftercare Center, Intensive Aftercare Programs. He also acknowledges the other consultants on this project with whom he has had the fortune to work: David Bennett, Regional Director, Colorado Division of Youth Corrections; Valerie Boykin, Deputy Administrator, Court and Community Services; Michael Guilfoyle; Julieann Myers, President, Comprehensive Human Services, Inc.; Mark Randleson, Director, Aftercare Services, South Alabama Boys and Girls Clubs; Robert Salisbury, Juvenile Parole Services Administrator; Randy Thomas, Ed Necco and Associates; William Lane; and Barbara Mendenhall, Assistant Director, Center for Delinquency and Crime Policy Studies.

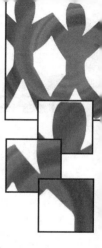

Chapter Nineteen

Identifying Juvenile Offenders with Mental Health Disorders

Lisa Melanie Boesky, Ph.D.
Clinical Psychologist

Author of Juvenile Offenders with Mental Health Disorder:
Who Are They and What Do We Do with Them?
(available from the American Correctional Association)

A significant number of juveniles with mental health disorders are entering and remaining in the juvenile justice system. The exact number of juvenile offenders with mental health disorders is currently unknown; however, it is clear that the prevalence of mental health disorders is higher among youth in juvenile justice than among their peers in the general population (Edens and Otto, 1997). Sadly, juvenile correctional facilities often have become the default placement for youth with mental health disorders who are not receiving appropriate mental health care in the community.

The identification of mental health disorders among juvenile offenders can be challenging. Because most correctional workers have not been trained regarding mental health disorders, it is easy for them to overlook subtle signs and symptoms of a youth's mental illness. Further, many staff members misinterpret a young offender's mental health symptoms as an attempt by the youth to avoid unpleasant tasks, be intentionally resistant toward adult requests, or to manipulate others into getting whatever it is the juvenile wants. When mentally ill juvenile offenders are not correctly identified, they are often viewed as "troublemakers" or "bad" kids in need of sanctions instead of "sick" kids in need of assistance or treatment.

To run safe and secure living units within a correctional facility, and effectively supervise youth on probation/parole (which typically translates into public safety), correctional workers need to be able to identify young offenders with mental health disorders. Correctional officers, in particular, are in a key position to make referrals to appropriate mental health professionals when mental illness is suspected among youths under their supervision. Correctional personnel within residential facilities are often the first to notice a change in a young offender's behavior and can provide critical information to the clinicians who evaluate these youths. The likelihood of developing positive interpersonal relationships and using effective management strategies with youths is significantly increased when juvenile justice professionals increase their ability to recognize a young offender's mental health symptoms as signs of a psychiatric disorder versus oppositional or manipulative behavior.

Common Mental Disorders Found Among Juvenile Offenders

The following are brief descriptions of some of the most common mental health disorders seen among youths involved with the justice system. All of the symptoms listed are from the *Diagnostic and Statistical Manual for Mental Disorders, Fourth Edition*, Text Revision (DSM-IV-TR, American Psychiatric Association, 2000), the most commonly used source for providing psychiatric diagnoses.

Oppositional Defiant Disorder

Juvenile offenders diagnosed with Oppositional Defiant Disorder exhibit a pattern of negative, hostile, and defiant behavior that lasts at least six months. These youths typically argue repeatedly with adults, defy or refuse to comply with rules or adult requests, frequently lose their temper, regularly annoy others in a deliberate fashion, are often spiteful and vindictive, are frequently and easily annoyed by those around them, and are often angry and resentful. Although many adolescents (offenders and nonoffenders alike) engage in these behaviors, they do not all have Oppositional Defiant Disorder. Youths who receive this diagnosis engage in these behaviors more often than peers of the same age and developmental level, and these behaviors significantly interfere with their ability to function (for example, in relationships, at school or work, and so forth).

Conduct Disorder

Conduct Disorder is one of the most commonly diagnosed mental health disorders among youths involved with the juvenile justice system. These youths display a recurring and enduring pattern of behavior in which the basic rights of others or major age-appropriate societal norms and rules are violated. Juveniles with Conduct Disorder typically are aggressive toward others (for example, physical fights, intimidation, robbery, rape, weapon use, physical cruelty toward people and/or animals), are destructive with property (for example, deliberate fire-setting, property defacing), engage in theft or deceitfulness (such as lies, forgery, shoplifting, car/house/building break-ins), and violate important rules (including school truancy, curfew violations, running away from home).

The diagnosis of Conduct Disorder is given to youths who are under the age of eighteen when these behaviors significantly interfere with the juvenile's ability to function in school, work, or interpersonal relationships. Although many juveniles experiment with these behaviors during their pre-adolescent and/or adolescent years, youths with Conduct Disorder engage in these behaviors on a repetitive basis. In comparison to the general population of teenagers, the negative and problematic behaviors of juveniles with Conduct Disorder tend to be more intense, frequent, and chronic. Youths diagnosed

176

with Conduct Disorder usually exhibit a multitude of these behaviors and their symptoms are typically not a reaction to a short-term stressor (such as a breakup of a romantic relationship, moving to a new school), but instead reflect a persistent pattern of behavior.

Attention Deficit/Hyperactivity Disorder (ADHD)

Juvenile offenders with Attention-Deficit/Hyperactivity Disorder display a continual pattern of difficulties related to inattention and/or hyperactivity-impulsivity that causes them significant problems. Their symptoms of inattention and/or hyperactivity-impulsivity are more frequent and severe than other youths who are the same age or at the same level of development.

Youths who have difficulty with *inattention* tend to be easily distracted, have difficulty with organization, lose things, find it difficult to pay attention to one task or activity for a significant period of time, forget things, appear as if they are not listening, avoid tasks requiring sustained mental effort, often do not follow through on instructions, and make careless mistakes. These juveniles frequently have a hard time completing chores or responsibilities. Although it may appear that they are behaving in an intentionally disobedient manner, this is often not the case. It is common for these youths literally to forget what it is they have been instructed to do. In addition, juveniles with Attention-Deficit Hyperactivity Disorder may attempt to avoid written assignments in a classroom or on a living unit because it is too difficult for them to pay attention long enough to complete it. These youths frequently misplace their belongings including trivial objects and items that are important to them.

Youths who primarily have difficulty with *hyperactivity-impulsivity* tend to move around excessively, fidget with their hands or feet, find it difficult to remain seated for long periods of time, have difficulty quietly engaging in play activities, talk constantly, appear "revved up" and full of energy, interrupt others, call out answers before a question is finished, and have difficulty waiting for their turn. These youths often touch and take things that do not belong to them and they often damage items or knock things over because they move around so quickly. They are often disruptive in school and/or on a living unit within a correctional facility because they can be noisy, overly energetic, and have difficulty sitting still.

Major Depression

Juvenile offenders with Major Depression experience several of the following symptoms for a period of at least two weeks, and the symptoms usually represent a change from a youth's typical functioning. Not surprisingly, juvenile offenders experiencing Major Depression often display a depressed and/or irritable mood and typically lose interest or pleasure in most activities. Depressed youths also frequently display a significant change in appetite and/or sleep patterns, noticeable restlessness or slowed body movements, loss of energy/feelings of fatigue, feelings of worthlessness/excessive or inappropriate feelings of guilt, indecisiveness/difficulties with thinking and concentration, and repeated thoughts of death and/or a suicide attempt.

Major Depression is one of the most misunderstood mental health disorders among youths involved with the justice system, and it is often challenging to diagnose among this population. For example, most adults associate depression with sadness, crying, and social withdrawal. Many adolescents (particularly males) manifest Major Depression in an irritable mood instead of a sad, gloomy mood. Juvenile offenders suffering from Major Depression often appear agitated, angry, and aggressive. Because many adults do not recognize these symptoms as signs of Major Depression, these irritable youth can be misdiagnosed with Oppositional Defiant Disorder or Conduct Disorder. This can result in a depressed youth receiving numerous sanctions within a correctional facility in relation to their aggressive behavior and they may never be identified as in need of mental health services and referred for treatment. If correctional staff notice a change in a juvenile's functioning that includes extreme irritability or aggression, and a lack of interest and pleasure in things the youth used to enjoy (such as basketball, watching videos, family visits) depression is a possibility and should be further explored.

Depressed youths with a predominantly irritable mood are also at high risk for serious suicide attempts. Because corrections staff does not always recognize the symptoms of aggressive juveniles suffering from Major Depression, they often do not take this type of threat of suicide as seriously as a youth who is crying and visibly upset. Room confinement/seclusion is often used as a management strategy for aggressive youths. However, room confinement/seclusion offers one of the most high-risk periods for depressed offenders to engage in suicidal behavior, as they often have little to occupy their mind other than all of the things about which they are depressed.

Dysthymic Disorder

Juvenile offenders diagnosed with Dysthymic Disorder also suffer from a depressed or irritable mood. These mood states are typically less intense than those found among individuals suffering from Major Depression, but they last for a significantly longer period of time (at least one year). There is also the presence of fatigue/low energy, feelings of hopelessness, indecisiveness/concentration difficulties, lack of appetite or overeating, sleeping too little or too much, and/or low self-esteem.

Rather than being a *change* from how a youth usually appears (as in Major Depression), the irritability and sadness typical of a youth with Dysthymic Disorder are how a youth *usually* appears. Dysthymic youths with a predominantly irritable mood seem to be easily annoyed by everyone and everything around them. Those with a predominantly sad mood usually walk around looking mildly depressed all of the time, rarely getting excited about anything.

Bipolar Disorder

Juvenile offenders diagnosed with Bipolar Disorder suffer from severe changes in mood that cause them significant distress and/or interfere with their ability to function. This disorder has been referred to as "Manic-Depressive Disorder" in the past because individuals tend to experience episodes of *mania* and episodes of *depression*. The typical features of depression are listed above under the Major Depression section of this chapter.

Juveniles suffering from an episode of mania experience a discrete period of time (at least one week) when their mood is abnormally and consistently overly joyous, extroverted, or irritable. Their manic mood state is so extreme and excessive that these youths sometimes require psychiatric hospitalization. During their intense mood state, juveniles with mania also suffer from some of the following symptoms: being more talkative than usual, using rapid and pressured speech, showing an increase in activity/physical agitation, displaying grandiosity or inflated self-esteem, racing thoughts and accelerated speech with abrupt topic changes, being easily distracted, having excessive involvement in pleasurable activities that have a high potential for painful consequences, and a decreased need for sleep (for example, being able to go several nights without sleep, feeling rested after only three or four hours of sleep).

The pattern of mood changes among youths with Bipolar Disorder is very individualized. Some juveniles may experience a manic episode that is immediately followed by an episode of depression. Others may experience a significant time period between episodes of mania and depression (such as weeks, months, or years) where their mood state is fairly stable. Intense emotions and a wide variation of moods are common among youths during their adolescent years; these should not be confused with Bipolar Disorder. Bipolar Disorder is a serious, often disabling disorder that interferes with a juvenile's ability to function in important daily activities.

Mental Retardation

Juvenile offenders with Mental Retardation have significantly subaverage general intellectual functioning (IQ of approximately 70 or less) *and* deficits in their ability to cope with the everyday demands of life and ability to function independently. Mentally retarded youths are typically unable to function in a manner expected for their age or developmental level in areas related to taking care of themselves, interacting with others, communicating, and/or keeping themselves safe, and so forth. The onset of this disorder must occur prior to the age of eighteen, and the severity of mental retardation is based on the level of a youth's intellectual impairment (in other words, mild, moderate, severe, profound).

The majority of mentally retarded juvenile offenders fall into the mild range of Mental Retardation and typically function at about a sixth-grade level. These youths tend to need additional guidance and supervision in comparison

179

to their peers. Juveniles whose IQ and level of adaptive functioning place them into the moderate range of Mental Retardation function close to a second-grade level and need a tremendous amount of adult supervision and support. Even with additional support and structure, moderately mentally retarded youths often have an extremely difficult time adjusting to a correctional environment. The majority of youths in the severe and profound range of Mental Retardation reside with their families or in specialized residential facilities.

Juvenile offenders with Mental Retardation comprise a heterogeneous group of youngsters. Some juveniles with Mental Retardation are gentle, compliant, and dependent on adults; others are aggressive, impulsive and oppositional; and some youths will display a combination of these behaviors. It is common to see juvenile offenders with Mental Retardation become hostile or aggressive when they are having difficulty communicating their wants and needs to those around them. These youths may not always understand the rules of a correctional facility or how certain consequences are related to specific behaviors. Supervising juveniles with Mental Retardation can be frustrating for correctional staff, particularly when they do not understand the motivation underlying a youth's behavior. It is often difficult to determine if a juvenile's negative behavior is purposefully oppositional or if it is associated with the youth's cognitive limitations.

Learning Disorders

Juvenile offenders with a Learning Disorder demonstrate a significant discrepancy between how they *should* perform on standardized academic tests (given their intellectual ability and education) and how they *actually* perform on these types of tests. For example, if a youth's IQ is in the above average range and they have received adequate schooling, one would expect them to perform fairly well on a test of reading, written expression, or mathematics. It would be unexpected for this youth to perform poorly, given his or her above-average intellectual ability and educational experience. A Learning Disorder is typically diagnosed when this discrepancy is substantial. Juveniles with an average, above-average, or below-average IQ can be diagnosed with a Learning Disorder as long as a major discrepancy exists between their intellectual ability (IQ) and scores on individually administered standardized school-based tests. The difficulties also must interfere with academic achievement or everyday activities that require reading, writing, or using mathematical skills. A juvenile offender can have a Learning Disorder in reading, mathematics, or written expression, and many youth involved with the justice system suffer from more than one Learning Disorder simultaneously.

Problems related to information processing are common among juveniles with Learning Disorders. These juveniles are often bright, and many are of at least average intelligence. However, transferring what is in their brain onto a piece of paper can be difficult, especially when under time constraints. Some youths have difficulty learning information solely by hearing it aloud and need to see information in written form. Others know what they want to say, but may have difficulty translating their thoughts into words when they are speaking aloud. Some juveniles with learning disorders do not comprehend what someone is saying in the way the speaker intended it. Not surprisingly, incidents of miscommunication are commonplace when interacting with these youths.

Information processing difficulties can interfere with a youth's ability to be successful within interpersonal relationships, and many juvenile offenders with Learning Disorders have poor social skills. Many of these youths do not understand the "give and take" of relationships, can be slow to pick up on subtle social cues, and may misinterpret what peers or adults are saying to them. Because of this, their interpersonal style can inadvertently irritate or offend others.

Posttraumatic Stress Disorder (PTSD)

Posttraumatic Stress Disorder is an anxiety disorder. To receive the diagnosis of Posttraumatic Stress Disorder, youths must be exposed to a *traumatic* event in which they witnessed or experienced an event involving threatened or actual serious injury or death. At the time of the trauma, the youth's response typically involves intense fear, horror, or helplessness.

Youths with Posttraumatic Stress Disorder repeatedly *re-experience* the traumatic event with frequent intrusive and upsetting thoughts and memories of the event and/or repeated nightmares about the event. They may actually experience flashbacks, feeling as though the traumatic event is happening all over again. Juvenile offenders with Posttraumatic Stress Disorder tend to avoid things that remind them of the trauma and become less responsive in general. They typically avoid places, people, or activities associated with the traumatic event and often do not want to talk about what happened to them. They may lose interest in activities they used to enjoy and often display a restricted range of emotions (such as being unable to feel joy). It is common for youths with Posttraumatic Stress Disorder to describe feeling "different" and separate from others because of the negative event(s) that have happened to them and many have a sense of a foreshortened future (for example, they do not expect to live past age twenty-one).

Because Posttraumatic Stress Disorder is an anxiety disorder, juveniles suffering from this disorder typically experience symptoms of increased arousal including an exaggerated startle response, problems falling or remaining asleep, concentration difficulties, irritability or outbursts of anger, and/or a need to be excessively attentive or watchful regarding what is going on around them.

A significant number of juvenile offenders have witnessed or directly experienced one or more traumatic events in their lives (Steiner, Garcia, and Matthews, 1997). Physical abuse, sexual abuse, parental abandonment and neglect are common among youths involved with the juvenile justice system. Some juvenile offenders have been sold into pornography or prostitution at very early ages; some have been raped numerous times. Sadly, witnessing the

181

death of a parent, relative, or close friend is not an infrequent occurrence in the lives of these youths. Some of these young people have been shot or severely beaten. Because the rate of traumatic experiences is so high among this population of youths, it is not surprising that many juvenile offenders suffer from Posttraumatic Stress Disorder. However, just because a youth experienced a traumatic event does not automatically imply that he or she is suffering from Posttraumatic Stress Disorder. This diagnosis is only given when a youth is experiencing several of the symptoms of Posttraumatic Stress Disorder and the symptoms must be present for more than a month and cause significant distress or impairment in the youth's ability to function in the important areas of his or her life (such as school, work, or relationships).

Many juvenile offenders with Posttraumatic Stress Disorder have significant difficulty regulating their emotions. They may experience severe mood swings (for example, becoming angry and hostile with minimal provocation), impulsivity, and the perception that they are constantly being threatened in some way. Once emotionally upset, juvenile offenders with Posttraumatic Stress Disorder often find it difficult to calm themselves. Stomachaches, headaches, and vague muscle or joint pain are common among youth with anxiety disorders, including Posttraumatic Stress Disorder. Juvenile offenders, particularly male offenders who are concerned about looking tough and in control, may be reluctant to report feelings of anxiety or fear related to a traumatic incident. For some of these youths, anxiety manifests itself in more physical, health-related symptoms.

Self-injury/self-mutilation is a behavior frequently associated with youths suffering from Posttraumatic Stress Disorder. These youths are often very anxious and self-injury can serve as a way to release built-up tension. When these youths are anxious, they often cut themselves or burn themselves as an attempt to help them relax.

Psychotic Disorders

The term *psychosis* typically refers to an impairment in reality testing. Individuals who are psychotic tend to have difficulty differentiating what is real from what is not real. Psychotic individuals typically experience and exhibit hallucinations, delusions, disorganized speech, disorganized behavior, and "negative" symptoms.

Hallucinations are false sensory perceptions that are not associated with real external stimuli. Although youths can experience hallucinations with any of the five senses, the type of hallucination most commonly reported among juveniles is auditory—hearing voices that other people cannot hear. Psychotic youths may report that these voices are coming from inside or outside of their head; regardless, they do not perceive these voices as their own thoughts, but as someone else talking to them or about them. The voices may tell a juvenile to behave in certain ways, such as kill himself or herself or kill a staff member, or the voices may comment on the youth or the youth's behavior (such as telling them they are stupid or ugly, ridiculing them for something they have done, and so forth). Although less common, some psychotic juveniles will see things that others cannot see, such as people or animals in their room.

Delusions are personal beliefs that an individual rigidly holds onto despite obvious proof that the belief is false and/or irrational. Examples of delusional beliefs held by psychotic juveniles include thinking that other people are plotting against them, are talking negatively about them, are trying to steal or control their thoughts, or are trying to read their mind. Psychotic juveniles may believe that correctional staff is trying to poison them, certain people/agencies are in a conspiracy against them, parts of their body are diseased, decayed or rotting away even though all medical tests are normal, or that they have special/magical gifts or talents.

Disorganized thinking and speech are also common among youths suffering from a psychotic disorder. Psychotic youths may speak in sentences that do not make sense or are only loosely related. They may use words that do not make sense, talk in rhymes or with a singsong tune, or repeatedly parrot back what others have said. What comes out of their mouth may sound strange and confusing, or the youth's words may make no sense at all. Psychotic youths may repeat certain words over and over, or they may completely stop talking in the middle of a sentence for no apparent reason. Some psychotic youths will take a very long time to answer questions asked of them or they may have little to no speech at all. Even when asked to elaborate, some psychotic juveniles may only provide one or two-word answers or sentences.

Youths with *disorganized behavior* usually exhibit a messy appearance, restless or agitated behavior, bizarre movements or posturing, pacing, and rocking. Poor hygiene is also common. Psychotic youths may appear odd or strange to correctional staff. They may repeatedly engage in unusual and stereotypical movements with specific parts of their body, or they may sit on their bed or in a corner of a room and rock back and forth for hours. Within juvenile justice facilities, some psychotic youths like to crawl into tight spaces when in their room, such as under their bed or in-between their toilet and the wall. These juveniles may appear extremely tense and nervous, wringing their hands and walking back and forth in the small space of their dorm room or in one particular segment of the living unit. Whereas some psychotic youths may be unable to remain still and feel like they have to constantly keep moving, others will remain still, without any movement, for extended periods of time.

Symptoms of psychoses can be associated with a variety of different mental health disorders. Youths with Schizophrenia commonly exhibit psychotic symptoms, but youths suffering from Major Depression or Bipolar Disorder can experience symptoms of the psychosis as well. In addition, juveniles who use large quantities of drugs (for example, methamphetamine, LSD, PCP) may also experience symptoms of psychoses.

Comorbidity

Most mentally ill juvenile offenders suffer from more than one of these mental health disorders simultaneously. In fact, it is common for a youth involved with the juvenile justice system to be diagnosed with three or four mental health disorders at the same time. For example, juveniles may have Attention-Deficit/Hyperactivity Disorder, a Learning Disorder, and Conduct Disorder. They may then develop Major Depression while incarcerated. If they have been raped or severely beaten in the community or in a correctional facility, they may also develop Posttraumatic Stress Disorder. As one can imagine, the assessment and treatment of mentally ill youths become more clinically complex with each additional diagnosis.

Conclusion

The role of correctional staff should never be overlooked in the continuum of care for juvenile offenders with mental health disorders. Although identifying mental illness among this clinically complex group of youths can be challenging, juvenile justice staff are in an ideal position to observe youth behavior and refer juveniles in possible need of treatment to mental health/medical professionals. When unidentified or misclassified, juvenile offenders with mental health disorders often receive a significant number of sanctions and are not referred for appropriate mental health treatment. Because some symptoms of mental illness appear similar to youth behavior that is defiant and intentionally oppositional (for example, disruptions during treatment groups, repeated conflict with staff, not following adult directives, irritability, aggression), it is common for correctional staff to misinterpret much of this type of behavior and respond by becoming more restrictive or punitive with a youth. Although mentally ill juveniles should be held accountable for negative behavior, they also should receive treatment and services for their mental health disorder. Providing juvenile justice staff with education and training on the identification and management of juvenile offenders with mental health disorders increases the likelihood of more strategic and effective referral and intervention decisions.

For more detailed information on the identification and management of mentally ill juvenile offenders, please refer to Dr. Boesky's book, *Juvenile Offenders with Mental Health Disorders: Who Are They and What Do We Do With Them?* (available from the American Correctional Association, Lanham, Maryland). The book expands on the disorders addressed here and also discusses issues related to suicide, self-injury/self-mutilation, cultural factors, gender, mental health screening and assessment, mental health treatment, and juveniles who have cooccurring mental health and substance abuse disorders. The book is appropriate for any professional who comes into contact with juvenile offenders, whether working in a correctional facility or in the community.

References

American Psychiatric Association. 2000. *Diagnostic Statistical Manual of Mental Disorders, Fourth Edition*, Text Revision. Washington, D.C.: American Psychiatric Association.

Edens, J. F. and R. K. Otto. 1997. Prevalence of Mental Disorders among Youth in the Juvenile Justice System. *Focal Point*. 11: 1-8.

Steiner, H., I. G. Garcia, and Z. Matthews. 1997. Posttraumatic Stress Disorder in Incarcerated Juvenile Delinquents. *Journal of the American Academy of Child and Adolescent Psychiatry*. 36: 357-365.

Index

A

abuse
    civil rights protection from, 28, 29, 33
    of physical management techniques, 33
    by staff, 16
academic/vocational programs (institutional)
    Character Counts program (Louisiana), 63
    civil rights requirements for, 28, 32, 34,35
    funding competition, 1-2
    GED programs, 43, 74
    trends affecting needs, 1-2
    Ventura Youth Correctional Facility (VYCF), 50
    for violent offenders, 6
    Writing Our Stories, creative writing program (Alabama), 77,82
academic/vocational programs (postrelease)
    authority/power relationships in, 69, 71,72, 75
    day treatment programs (Missouri), 43,44
    GED programs, 114
    individualized, 69,70
    inductive/improvisational approach in, 70,72, 75
    Jobs Program (Missouri), 44
    peer teaching concept, 69,70
    Safer Foundation's Youth Empowerment Program, 67,75

WorkBridge program (Pennsylvania), 114
    workplace modeling, 70
accountability (offender), 126
    community service in, 113,14
    early offenders and, 122,24
    restorative justice conferences, 122-24, 130-31
    WorkBridge program (Pennsylvania), 111, 113-16, 118
    youth courts in, 103, 105
accreditation standards for facility design, 8, 85
ADA (Americans with Disabilities Act), 19, 28
ADD (attention deficit disorder), 32
ADHD (attention deficit /hyperactivity disorder), 177
Administration for Children, Youth and Families (New York), 104
adolescent development competencies, 112
adult corrections model and juvenile rights, 33-34
Affrilachia (Walker), 80
African-Americans. See also cultural specificity in treatment programs
    ethnic advisory committees, 162
    minority confinement overrepresentation, 1, 164
    Minority Youth Transition Program, 157-60
aftercare. See also transition to the community
Character Counts program (Louisiana), 63
    day treatment programs, 43-44
    facility design in successful, 9

family therapy in, 45
health care services, 44-45
individualized, needs-based, 42
Intensive Aftercare Program
(Oregon), 168-72
intensive care supervision, 43,
168-72
Missouri Division of Youth
Services, 42-46
resources/website, 170-71
sheltering/sanctioning strategies,
46
substance abuse programs, 45
aging population effect on corrections,
1-2
Alabama, Antiviolence Creative Writing
Program, 77?82
Alabama Children's Trust Fund, 78
Alabama Council for the Arts, 78
Alabama Department of Youth Services,
77-82
Alabama Writer's Forum, 77-82
Alborada Intensive Treatment Program
(California), 48-49
alcohol abuse, offender treatment, 49-50,
100
Altschuler, David, 169
American Bar Association, 108
Americans with Disabilities Act (ADA),
19, 28
Antiviolence Creative Writing Program,
77-82
Antoine, Jannitta, 61, 64
anxiety disorder identification, 182
Armstrong, Troy, 169
assessment/intake systems
early offenders, 30-31
for educational needs, 34-35
for mental illness/mental
retardation, 31?33
violent offenders, 4-5
attention deficit disorder (ADD), 32
attention deficit /hyperactivity disorder
(ADHD), 177
Australia, restorative justice
conferences, 122
auxiliary probation, 100?101

B

balanced justice model. See restorative
justice conferences; WorkBridge
program at Cornell Abraxas
Barber, Margaret (contact information),
102
Barker, Queen, 77
Barton, Marlin "Bart," 77?82
Basic Skills Training Program, 75
Baton Rouge Children's Coalition, 63
behavior management
juvenile versus adult needs, 33
for staff safety, 14?15
violent offender treatment
programs, 48?49
Bell, James, 164
Bethlehem, Pennsylvania restorative
justice experiment, 124
biological impairment in violent
offenders, 5
bipolar disorder identification, 179
Birmingham Museum of Art, 78
boot camps, 32
boundary/limit setting by staff, 16
Braithwaite, John, 123?24
Brooks, Gloria, 157
Buenaventua Specialized Counseling
Program (California), 48
Building Blocks for Youth Report and
Justice for Some (Youth Law Center),
164
Burch, Jim (contact information), 102
Bush, Elizabeth Catherine, 3, 10

C

Caceres, Lily, 156
California Youth Authority, 6, 47-51.
See also Ventura Youth Correctional
Facility (VYCF)
Campbell, Henry, 97
Carson, Wallace P., 165
case management system of transition,
41-42
Catalano, Richard, 146
Chalkville youth facility (Alabama), 78-79
Character Counts program (Louisiana),
63
child-centered care plans, 56-57

child delinquents. *See also* delinquent youth; restorative justice conferences
 arrest statistics, 121
 challenges of, 122-23
 civil rights issues of, 30-31
 juvenile court/justice system history, 97-100
 recidivism statistics, 121, 124
child psychiatry, history, 98
child services
 Children's Book Club in Prisons (Louisiana), 63
 Head Start, 63
 Louisiana: The Children's Initiatives, 61-65
Small-Mart Clothing closet (Louisiana), 63
children, birth to three, 61?65
children with disabilities, 19
Children's Book Club in Prisons (Louisiana), 63
children's court formation, 97?98
The Children's Initiatives (Louisiana), 61-65
Civil Rights Division of U.S., Special Litigation Section, 27?29
civil rights (in correctional facilities)
 adult practices as violations of, 33-34
 crowding issues, 29-30, 36
 educational requirements, 28, 32, 34-35
 enforcement authority, 27-29
 legal standards, 28
 solutions suggested, 35-36
 special needs populations, 31-35
 summary, 36-37
Civil Rights of Institutionalized Persons Act (CRIPA), 27-29
classification system
 juvenile versus adult needs, 85
 for separation of vulnerable juveniles, 29
 for special needs juveniles, 30
cognitive disabilities. *See* learning disabilities
Collins, D'arcy, 67
Colonie Youth Court, New York, 104?108
Communities that Care model, 146
community-based programs. *See also* restorative justice conferences

auxiliary probation, 100-101
The Children's Initiatives (Louisiana), 61-65
Dawn Project (Indiana), 56-57
day treatment programs, 43-44
history, 99
Intensive Aftercare Program (Oregon), 168-72
Kansas, community planning initiative, 143-50
parenting skills classes, 61, 62-63
Safer Foundation's Youth Empowerment Program, 67-75
youth courts, 103-9
community service
 early offenders and, 122-24
 in rehabilitation, 112-13
 restorative justice conferences, 122-24, 131
 as sentencing alternative, 113-14
 WorkBridge program (Pennsylvania), 111-16, 118
 youth courts and, 103?9
compassionate conservatism, 99
conditional release. See aftercare; transition to the community
conduct disorder identification, 176-77
Confederated Tribes of Siletz, 157
Connecticut, youth courts system, 104
Constitutional Rights Foundation, 108
Cornell Abraxas WorkBridge program (Pennsylvania). *See* WorkBridge program (Pennsylvania)
Corrections Technology Advisory Committee, 9
creative writing program, antiviolence, 77-82
crime prevention
 compassionate conservatism, 99
 Louisiana: The Children's Initiatives, 61-65
 Oregon programs, 166-68
 WorkBridge program (Pennsylvania), 111-19
CRIPA (Civil Rights of Institutionalized Persons Act), 27-29
crowding, 29?30, 36
cultural specificity in treatment programs
Gang Intervention/Youth Empowerment Treatment Services, 155-56

Gang Tattoo Removal Program
(Oregon), 156-57
Intensive Aftercare Program
(Oregon), 171
non-English speaking educational
programs, 156
Oregon (State) programs
overview, 166-68
Oregon Youth Authority
Community Resources Unit, 161
spiritual services, 157
Transition Program (Oregon),
157-60
Culture as a Conceptual Tool for Juvenile
Crime Prevention, 167-68

D

Davidson, William, 5
Dawn Project, Indiana Division of Mental
Health, 55?58
day treatment programs, 43?44
Delaware, youth courts system, 104
delinquent youth. See also child
delinquents; restorative justice
conferences
emotional disturbance and, 21
peer sentencing in youth courts,
103-109
probation/parole options,
100-101
progressive stages of, 68
Dent, Louisa, 67
depression (major) identification, 177?78
deterrence, 146?47, 155?56. See also
recidivism prevention
Developmental Research and Programs,
University of Washington, 146
disabled offenders, 28. See also specific
disabilities, such as learning disabilities
Dixon Correctional Institute (Louisiana),
63
drug abuse, offender treatment,
49-50, 100
drug courts, probation options, 101
dysthmic disorder identification, 178

E

early offenders. See also restorative
justice conferences

arrest statistics, 121
challenges of, 122-23
civil rights issues of, 30-31
juvenile court/justice system
history, 97-100
recidivism statistics, 121, 124
Education for All Handicapped Children
Act, 19
educational programs. See academic/
vocational programs
Emmanuel Hospital, Portland, Oregon,
157
emotionally disturbed youth. See also
mental illness
characteristics correlated in delinquent
youth, 21
Dawn Project (Indiana), 55-58
funding of care for, 56
in general population versus
justice system, 19, 20, 21
system of care reform, 56-57, 59
transition to the community, 58
employment
Jobs Program (Missouri), 44
modeling work behaviors, 68
preemployment training, 70,
112-13
realities postincarceration, 69
in rehabilitation, 114-15
as sentencing alternative, 112-13
WorkBridge program
(Pennsylvania), 112-15, 118
Entergy, 62
environment of care, 115

F

facility design
for aftercare success, 9
for individualized treatment, 40
juvenile versus adult differences,
8-9, 84-85, 86, 91-92
Missouri Division of Youth
Services, 40-41
perimeter barriers, 14
rooms/doors/locks, 14
security systems, 14, 84, 86,
91-92
for staff safety, 13-14
trends affecting, 1-2
violent offender needs, 8-9

youthful offender programs, 84,
86, 91-92
family-centered care plans
aftercare family therapy, 45
Dawn Project (Indiana), 56-57, 58
for emotionally disturbed youth,
56-57
Minority Youth Transition
Program (Oregon), 158-59
Missouri Division of Youth
Services, 42, 45
in rehabilitation, 42, 45
transition to the community, 58
family courts collaboration with juvenile
justice, 97-102
family group conferences. *See*
restorative justice conferences
Family Services Research Center, 6
female offenders. See also violent
offenders (female)
Chalkville youth facility
(Alabama), 78-79
civil rights issues, 30
dramatics/performance
programs, 79
mental illness treatment
programs, 48-49
photography programs, 78-79
substance abuse treatment
programs, 49-50
Ventura Youth Correctional
Facility, 47-51
Writing Our Stories, creative
writing program, 77-82
Fernandez, Hector, 67
fixed versus fluid posts for security
enveloping, 93
Foster, Patricia, 81
Foundation for the Mid-south, 62
Fourteenth Amendment to the U.S.
Constitution, 19
Fraser, John, 157
Fuller, Bill, 77

G

Gamble, Danny, 78, 80-81
Gang Intervention/Youth Empowerment
Treatment Services, 155-56
gang issues
growth statistics, 153

youthful offenders in adult
facilities, 86
gang member treatment programs
Gang Intervention/Youth
Empowerment Treatment
Services, 155-56
Gang Tattoo Removal Program,
156-57
Gang Tattoo Removal Program (Oregon),
156-57
Gangbusters: Strategies for Prevention
and Intervention (ACA), 156
Georgia, civil rights litigation, 28
Globus, Albert, 5
Goodwin, Tracy (contact information),
108
Gordly, Avel, 164, 165
Graves, Bill, 143
Greenfield, Mike, 168

H

Hancock Cooper, Priscilla, 78-79
Hands On Parenting (Louisiana), 63, 64
Harris, Susan, 79
Hawkins, David, 146
Head Start, 63
Healey, William, 98
health care services. *See* medical/health
care issues
Hill, Shawna, 157?60
Hillcrest Youth Correctional Facility
(Oregon), 156
Hispanic Advisory Committee, 161?62
Hispanic increases in minority
confinement, 1
Hispanic treatment programs, 157. *See*
also cultural specificity in treatment
programs
Howell, James C., 153
Hudson Institute, 122, 124?39

I

"I Am a Sunrise" (W.B.S.), 81
IDEA (Individuals with Disabilities
Education Act), 19, 20, 28, 35
Illinois Juvenile Court Act of 1899, 97
Illinois, Safer Foundation's Youth
Empowerment Program, 67-75
impulsivity identification, 177

incarceration options, 100-101. *See* also sentencing alternative programs
Indiana Behavioral Health Choices, 56
Indiana Department of Education, Special Education Division, 56
Indiana Department of Family and Social Services Administration, 56
Indiana Division of Juvenile Services
  Dawn Project (Indiana), 55-58
  Juvenile Transition Program, 54-55, 57-58
  mission statement, 55
  vision statement, 54
Indiana Division of Mental Health, 55-58
Indiana, Indianapolis Restorative Justice Experiment, 124-37
Indiana State Division of Family and Children, 56
Indiana State Division of Mental Health, 56
Indianapolis Restorative Justice Experiment, 124?39
  case studies
  Better Addressing the Needs of Victims, 135
  Clearing Up an Offender's Misunderstanding, 125
  New Approach to Juvenile Offending, 128-30
  method
  eligibility criteria, 125?27
  measures, 127
  primary offense data, 128
  race/gender/age data, 127
  observation measures
  coordinator role, 130
  length of proceeding, 130
  participant involvement, 130-31
  reparation agreement, 131
  outcome measures
  completion rates, 135-36
  outcomes perceptions, 134-35, 134
  participant involvement, 132-33, 134
  participant satisfaction, 131-32
  recidivism data, 136-37, 138
  respect perceptions, 132-33, 134
  satisfaction data, 133
  summary, 137-39
The Individual Delinquent (Healey), 98

Individuals with Disabilities Education Act (IDEA), 19, 20, 28, 35
Institute for Juvenile Research, 98
intake/assessment systems
  early offenders, 30-31
  for educational needs, 34-35
  for mental illness/mental retardation, 31-33
  violent offenders, 4-5
Intensive Aftercare Program (Oregon), 168-72
Intensive Case Supervision Program, 43
intergenerational transmission of violent offending, 6
isolation for behavior control
  juvenile versus adult needs, 33
  suicide and, 178

J

jails versus prisons for youthful offenders, 84
Jetson Correctional Center for Youth (Louisiana), 62-63
job skills. See academic/vocational programs; employment
Johnson, Stacy, 168
Josephson Institute of Ethics, 4, 63
juvenile courts. *See* also restorative justice conferences
  drug courts, 101
  early offender challenges, 122-23
  family courts collaboration, South Carolina, 100-102
  history and evolution, 97-100
  youth courts, 103-109
Juvenile Crime Prevention Advisory Committee, 166-68
juvenile drug courts, 101
Juvenile Justice and Delinquency Prevention Act, 101
Juvenile Justice Reform Act (Kansas), 143, 144
juvenile justice system
  early offender challenges, 122-23
  family courts collaboration, South Carolina, 100-102
  history and evolution, 97-100
  incarceration options, 100-101
  minority confinement overrepresentation, 1-2, 163-68

reform, Kansas community
planning initiative, 143-50
youth courts, 103-9
Juvenile Offenders with Mental Health
Disorders (Boesky), 183
Juvenile Psychopathic Institute, 98
Juvenile Reintegration and Aftercare
Center (Oregon), 168-72
Juvenile Transition Program (Indiana),
54-55, 57-58
juvenile versus adult offenders, differing
needs. See also youthful offenders in
adult facilities
adult corrections model and
juvenile rights, 33-34
aids to support a safe
environment, 15
classification system, 85
court system commonalities, 99
in facility design, 8-9, 84, 86,
91-92
isolation for behavior control, 33
laws regarding, 84
physical management/restraints,
33, 85
predator/prey concerns, 84
security/custody approach,
84, 86
staff training techniques, 33
transfer effects, 8-9
treatment programs, 84, 86

K

Kansas, community planning initiative,
143-50
background, 143-45
challenges, 148
funding/expenses, 146, 149-50
planning teams, 145?46
recommendations, 148
results, 147
solutions/implementation, 147,
149-50
Kansas Juvenile Justice Authority, 143-50
Kentucky
civil rights litigation, 27-28
National Juvenile Detention
Association Center for Research
and Professional Development,
153

Kitzhaber, John, 163, 165

L

Landrieu, Mary, 61, 64
Latino treatment programs. See cultural
specificity in treatment programs
Lawson, Jack, 157, 168
learning disabilities/disabled
civil rights of, 32
in general population versus
justice system, 19, 20-21
identifying offenders with, 32,
180-81
Lexington Reformatory (South Carolina),
98
Lindsey, Michael, 164
Louisiana, civil rights litigation, 28
Louisiana Correctional Institute for
Women, 63
Louisiana: The Children's Initiatives,
61-65
Love, Faith, 157-60

M

MacLaren Youth Correctional Facility
(Oregon), 156
Marion County (Indiana) Office of Family
and Children, 56
Marion Superior Court, Juvenile
Division, 56
Martin, Emily, 158, 164
McDonough, Sharon, 80
medical/health care issues. See also
mental illness
civil rights of offenders, 28, 30
special needs populations, 30
in transitioning populations,
44-45
Ventura Youth Correctional
Facility services, 51
violent offenders, medicating, 5
well-child care, 61
Mental Health Association of Marion
County (Indiana), 56
mental health disorder identification,
175-84
attention deficit /hyperactivity
disorder (ADHD), 177
bipolar disorder, 179

comorbidity of, 183-84
conduct disorder, 176-77
delusions, 183
depression (major), 177-78
disorganized behavior, 183
dysthmic disorder, 178
hallucinations, 182
learning disorders, 180-81
mental retardation, 179-80
oppositional defiant disorder, 176
posttraumatic stress disorder (PTSD), 181-82
psychotic disorders, 182-83
mental illness. See also emotionally disturbed youth; medical/health care issues
Alborada Intensive Treatment Program (California), 48-49
civil rights issues, 30, 33
Dawn Project (Indiana), 55-58
early offenders, 31
intake/assessment systems, 31-32
intensive treatment programs for, 48-49
isolation and, 33
medication appropriateness, 32
self-mutilation, 33, 182
statistics on incarcerated juveniles, 31
suicide, 31, 178, 182
mental retardation
boot camps and, 32
in general population versus justice system, 19, 20, 22
identifying offenders with, 179-80
intake/assessment systems, 31-32
mentors. See also modeling
teen parents as, 63
Writing Our Stories program, 80
Mexican Americans. See entries beginning with Hispanic
minority confinement
overrepresentation, 1-2, 163-68. See also cultural specificity in treatment programs; specific populations, for example, Hispanic
Minority Youth Transition Program (Oregon), 157-60

Mira Loma Female Drug and Alcohol Abuse Treatment Program (DAATP), 49-50
Missouri Department of Elementary and Secondary Education, School Improvement Plan, 44
Missouri Division of Youth Services, 39-46
aftercare
case management system of, 41-42
day treatment programs, 43-44
family therapy, 45
health care services, 44-45
intensive care supervision, 43
Jobs Program, 44
sex offender therapy, 45
sheltering/sanctioning strategies, 46
facility design for individualized treatment, 40-41
mission statement, 40
services and approaches, 41
modeling. See also mentors
adolescent development skills, 112
appropriate/consistent behaviors, 16, 115
by trackers in aftercare programs, 43
by veteran staff in training, 7
work behaviors of society, 68, 70, 112-16
Mt. Meigs facility for boys, 77, 79, 81
Murray, Albert, 143

N

National Council on Crime and Delinquency, 54-55, 146
National Gangs Research Project, 153
National Highway and Traffic Safety Administration, 108
National Institute of Government Purchasing, 63
National Institute of Justice, Office of Science and Technology, 9
National Juvenile Detention Association Center for Research and Professional Development, 153

National Law Enforcement and
Corrections Technology Advisory
Committee, 9
National Youth Court Center, 104, 108
National Youth Gang Center, 153
Native American Advisory Committee,
161-62
Native American treatment programs,
157-60, 163. *See* also cultural specificity
in treatment programs
NERPAC (NorthEast Rescue Plan Action
Committee), 162
New Jersey, youth courts system, 104
New York, Colonie Youth Court, 104-8
New York State Division of Criminal
Justice Services, 104
New Zealand, restorative justice
conferences, 122
Newman, Scott, 124
nonviolent offender probation options,
100-101. See also child delinquents
NorthEast Rescue Plan Action
Committee (NERPAC), 162
Northern Mariana Islands, civil rights
litigation, 28

O

offender populations
African-American statistics,
157-60
civil rights entitlement to safety,
28
poverty statistics, 98-99
single-parent family statistics,
98-99
substance abuse statistics, 98
temperament/characteristics, 68,
69, 72, 90
offender-staff relationships, 15-17, 68,
114-15, 118, 158-59
offenders with disabilities. *See* also
specfic disabilites, for example learning
disabilities
conclusions, 23
in general population versus
justice system, 19-22
statistical estimating difficulties, 22-23
Office of Juvenile Justice and
Delinquency Prevention (OJJDP)
Auxiliary Probation Program, 102

civil rights protections, 36
Colonie Youth Court funding, 105
contact information, 102
Field-Initiated Research and
Evaluation Program, 122
juvenile drug courts, 102
mandate, 101
Minority Youth Transition
Program (Oregon), 157-60
National Youth Court Center, 108
statistics of societal influences,
98-99
Study Group on Very Young
Offenders, 121
oppositional defiant disorder
identification, 176
Oregon Office of Minority Services,
151-73
culturally specific treatment/
services, 156-57
ethnic advisory committees,
161-63
Gang Tattoo Removal Program,
156-57
Hispanic Advisory Committee
relationship, 161-62
Minority Youth Transition
Program (Oregon), 157-60
mission/goals, 152
Native American Advisory
Committee relationship, 161-62
Oregon Youth Authority Juvenile
Justice Training Academy
(OJJTA), 160
Oregon Youth Authority
relationship, 152, 161-63
Oregon Psychiatric Association, 156
Oregon (State) programs
crime prevention, 166-68
Intensive Aftercare Program,
168-72
Statewide Structure Committee,
168
Oregon Youth Authority, 151-73
Community Resources Unit, 161
cultural competency principles,
152-53, 161
Employee Services, 161
gang intervention/treatment
services, 154-56

Governor's Summit on the
Overrepresentation of
Minorities in the Juvenile
Justice System, 163?68
history, 151
Indian tribal governments
relationship, 163
Juvenile Justice Training
Academy (OJJTA), 160
Juvenile Policy Committee,
152-53
mission, 151-52
Office of Minority Services
relationship, 152, 161-63
organic impairment in violent
offenders, 5

P

parental involvement
civil rights requirements for, 35
Dawn Project (Indiana), 56-57, 58
in Head Start, 64
Program for Caring Parents
(Louisiana), 63, 64
parenting skills training, 61, 62-63, 64
parole, facility design in successful, 9
parolee programs, 67-75
Payne, James, 124
Pennsylvania
Bethlehem restorative justice
experience, 124
Juvenile Act of, 111
WorkBridge program at Cornell
Abraxas, 111-19
Pfizer Corporation, 62
Philadelphia WorkBridge program,
115-16
physical management techniques, adult
versus juvenile, 33
Pittsburgh WorkBridge program, 115-16
postcommitment supervision. *See*
aftercare; transition to the community
posttraumatic stress disorder (PTSD),
181-82
Poteet, Matt, 157
pregnancy, factors affecting juvenile
violence, 5
Prevent Child Abuse Louisiana, 62
prey or predator concerns, 29, 84
probationer programs

auxiliary probation, 100-101
Safer Foundation's Youth
Empowerment Program, 67-75
Program for Caring Parents (Louisiana),
63
psychotic disorder identification, 182-83
psychotropic medication
for mentally ill offenders, 32
for violent offenders, 5
PTSD (posttraumatic stress disorder),
181-82
Puentes, Christina, 157-60
Puerto Rico, civil rights litigation, 28

Q

quality assurance programs, for civil
rights compliance, 36

R

Ramirez, Rolando, 156
Rapides Foundation, 62
recidivism
early offenders, 121-22, 124,
136-37
Indianapolis Restorative Justice
Experiment, 136-37
reintervention training and, 72-73
sheltering/sanctioning strategies,
46
recidivism prevention
Communities that Care model,
146
reintegrative shaming in, 123-24
restorative justice conferences,
123-24, 136-37
Safer Foundation's Youth
Empowerment Program, 67-75
socialization in, 123-24
WorkBridge program
(Pennsylvania), 116
Rehabilitation Act of 1973, 19
rehabilitation opportunities, 112-15, 118.
See also restitution (offender)
Reintegrative Shaming Experiments
(RISE), 124
religious/spiritual services, 50, 157
reparation. See restitution (offender)
restitution (offender). *See* also
rehabilitation opportunities

contracts for, 113
early offenders and, 122-24
restorative justice conferences,
122-23, 130-31
WorkBridge program
(Pennsylvania), 112-13, 116, 118
youth courts in, 103, 107
restorative justice conferences. *See* also
Indianapolis Restorative Justice
Experiment
benefits/effectiveness, 123-24
Bethlehem, Pennsylvania
experiment, 124
early offender challenges, 122-23
process, 123-24
purpose, 123
Reintegrative Shaming
Experiments, 124
restorative justice models. *See*
restorative justice conferences; Work
Bridge program (Pennsylvania)
restraint techniques, adult versus
juvenile, 33
Rhode Island, youth courts system, 104
RISE (Reintegrative Shaming
Experiments), 124
The Rose That Grew From Concrete
(Shakur), 81
Rousch, David W., 153

S

Safer Foundation's Youth Empowerment
Program, 67-75
safety (staff). See staff safety
Scholastic Publications, 63
school violence statistics, 4
security enveloping, defined, 90
security systems
envelope concept
defined, 90
facility design, 91-92
materials, 94
operations/scheduling in, 90-91
staffing, 91, 93-94
technology, 91, 94
facility design, 14, 84, 86, 91-92
fixed versus fluid posts, 93
juvenile versus adult, 84, 86
teaming/cross-training in, 89

youthful offenders in adult
facilities, 89-95
self-mutilation
isolation and, 33
posttraumatic stress disorder
(PTSD), identifying and, 182
sentencing alternative programs. *See*
also incarceration options
restorative justice conferences,
122-24, 137-39
WorkBridge program
(Pennsylvania), 111-19
sex offender treatment, 45, 156
Shakur, Tupac, 81
Sherman, Lawrence, 122-23
short-fuse syndrome, 5
Six Pillars of Character, 63
Small-Mart Clothing closet
(Louisiana), 63
socialization
behavior management systems,
14-15
day treatment programs
(aftercare), 43-44
delinquent behavior and, 68
Gang Intervention/Youth
Empowerment Treatment
Services, 155-56
Intensive Aftercare Program
(Oregon), 171
in recidivism prevention, 123-24
restorative justice conferences
in, 123-24
societal trends affecting juvenile
corrections, 1-2
Solano, Griselda, 156
Song, Kara, 157-60
South Carolina
family courts collaboration,
100-102
juvenile justice system history,
98
South Carolina Department of Juvenile
Justice, 100-102
South Carolina Family Court system,
100-102
Southern Oregon Indian Center, 157
special education disability
assessing, 34-35
civil rights requirements, 34-35

juvenile versus youthful offender statistics, 19-20
in public education, 20
Special Litigation Section, Civil Right Division, 27?29
special needs populations. *See* by specific population, for example, mental illness
spiritual/religious services, 50, 157
staff (correctional)
    abuse by, 16
    boundary/limit setting, 16
    modeling of adult behavior, 16, 112-16
    technology versus, 9, 94
    in youthful offender security, 93-94
staff-offender relationships, 15-16, 68, 114-15, 118, 158-59
staff safety
    behavior management systems, 14-15
    conclusions, 18
    management responsibility for, 13
    offender relationships and, 15-17
    the physical plant in, 13-14
    policies/procedures in, 17
    security systems for, 14
    specialized program units for violent offenders, 7-8
    supervision/training in, 17-18
staff supervisor responsibilities, 17-18
staff wellness, 7-8
staffing issues. See also training (staff)
    diversity in hiring practices, 161
    fixed versus fluid posts, 93
    hiring/ retaining qualified, 2, 17-18, 161
    staff-to-offender ratios, 5
    turnover (overcrowding related), 30
    in units for violent offenders, 5
Stalder, Richard, 61
Steiner, Hans, 4
Steps to Success (Louisiana), 62?63, 64
"Straddling Two Worlds: The Visit" (Foster), 81
Street Law Incorporated, 108s
team approach to treatment

Kansas, community planning initiative, 145-46
mental health disorder identification, 183-84
Minority Youth Transition Program, 157-60
Ventura Youth Correctional Facility, 47
WorkBridge program (Pennsylvania), 115
teaming/cross-training for staff training, 7, 18, 89
technology
    in research/evaluation, 9
    security, youthful offenders, 86
    staff versus, 9, 94
    youthful offender program security, 94
teen courts. See youth courts
teenage pregnancy prevention, 62-63
Thompson, Jeannie, 77-82
Thornton, Julia, 62
training (community)
    character building, 61
    parenting skills, 61, 62-63
    well-child care, 61
    youth court programs, 105-6
training (offender). See also academic/ vocational programs (institutional)
    cultural specificity for gang members, 155
    Hands On Parenting (Louisiana), 63
    parenting skills, 63, 64
    youth court programs, 105-6
training (staff). See also staffing issues
    Breaking the Barriers (Indiana), 58
    juvenile versus adult practices, 33
    for mental illness/mental retardation screening, 32
    on-the-job, 7, 18
    recognition component, 7
    in reform efforts, 36
    as safety issue, 17-18
    teaming/cross-training in, 7, 18
    transfer of learning methods, 18
    veteran staff roles/needs, 7
    violent offender units, 5, 7-8
    for youthful offenders, 86

youthful offenders in adult
facilities, 84-85
transition to the community. *See* also
aftercare
auxiliary probation, 100-101
civil rights requirements in, 35
Dawn Project (Indiana), 57-58
for emotionally disturbed youth,
58
facility design in successful, 9
family involvement, 58, 158-59
incentives/sanctions in, 159
individualized plans, 158, 171
Juvenile Transition Program
(Indiana), 54-55, 57-58
lifeguard services, 73-74
Minority Youth Transition
Program (Oregon), 157-60
Missouri Division of Youth
Services, 42-46
reintervention training in, 72-73
Safer Foundation's Youth
Empowerment Program, 67-75
violent offenders, 6-7
treatment programs (institutional).
See also academic/vocational programs
Alborada Intensive Treatment
Program (California), 48-49
creative writing, 77-82
culturally specific treatment/
services, 156?57, 166-68
dramatics/performance, 79
Gang Intervention/Youth
Empowerment Treatment
Services, 155-56
Gang Tattoo Removal Program
(Oregon), 156-57
individualized, needs-based,
40-41
juvenile versus adult needs,
84, 86
for mental illness, 48-49, 51
Mira Loma Female Drug and
Alcohol Abuse Treatment
Program (DAATP), 49-50
Missouri Division of Youth
Services, 39-40
photography, 78-79
substance abuse, 49-50
for violent offenders, 5-10

Writing Our Stories (Alabama),
77-82
treatment team approach. *See* team
approach to treatment
trends affecting juvenile corrections,
1, 1-2
Truth-in-Sentencing programs, 8

U

The United Way, 62
U.S. Constitution, 28
U.S. Department of Education, Early
Childhood Development Division, 62
U.S. Department of Justice, 27
U.S. Department of Juvenile Justice
Auxiliary Probation Services
Sustainment and Expansion Plan, 100
U.S. Department of Transportation,
National Highway and Traffic Safety
Administration, 108

V

Vacca youth facility (Alabama), 78
VanMeter, Joe. *See* also transition to the
community
Ventura Youth Correctional Facility
(VYCF)
academic/vocational programs
(institutional), 50
Alborada Intensive Treatment
Program (California), 48-49
Buenaventua Specialized
Counseling Program, 48
described, 48
female offender treatment, 47-51
medical services, 51
Mira Loma Female Drug and
Alcohol Abuse Treatment
Program (DAATP), 49-50
population statistics, 51
psychiatric/psychological
treatment, 51
religious services, 50
volunteer program, 50
victim satisfaction. *See* restitution;
restorative justice conferences; youth
courts
violence in schools, 4
violence prevention, 77-82

Violent Crime Control and Law Enforcement Act, 27
violent index crimes statistics, 4
Violent Offender Incarceration program, 8
violent offender treatment programs
    academic/vocational, 6
    behavior management programs, 48
    conclusions, 10
    medication in, 5
    specialized program unit components, 5
    staff/offender interaction, 9
    staffing issues, 7?8
    target goals, 6
    for women, 48
violent offenders
    arrest statistics, 4
    assessment strategies/ limitations, 4?5
    causes of impairment, 5-6
    civil rights protection from, 28, 29
    early offenders as, 121
    facility design for, 8-9
    intergenerational transmission concept, 6
    prevention programs, 77-82
    school violence statistics, 4
    temporal lobe functioning in, 5
    transfer effects, 8-9
    transition to the community, 6-7
violent offenders (female), 48. See also female offenders
visitation programs for parents, 63
vocational programs. See academic/vocational programs
volunteer programs
  auxiliary probation officers (South Carolina), 100-101
    The Children's Initiatives (Louisiana), 64
    Kansas, community planning initiative, 143-50
    sweatlodge ceremonies, 157
    Ventura Youth Correctional Facility (VYCF), 51
    youth courts, 103-9
Volunteers of America, 63
vulnerable juveniles, 29, 84

W

Walker, Frank X., 80
weapons at school, 4
Weaver, Ron, 156
Williams, Charles "Andy", 3
Williams, Charles "Andy" (violent offender), 10
Wood, J. Walter, Jr., 81
WorkBridge program at Cornell Abraxas, 111-19
    community service component, 113-15
    employment initiative, 112-15
    introduction, 111-12
    summary, 118-19
    testimonials, 116-18
    work crew project, 113-14
Writing Our Stories, creative writing program, 77-82

Y

Youth Correctional Facility. See Ventura Youth Correctional Facility (VYCF)
youth courts. See also juvenile justice system
    benefits obtained and waived rights, 107-8
    cases accepted/sentencing, 103, 106-107
    Colonie, New York, 104-108
    operating budgets, 108
    participant benefits, 106
    participatory roles/training, 105-106
    purpose, 103
    structure and models, 103-104
Youth Empowerment Program (YEP), 67-75
youthful offenders in adult facilities. See also juvenile versus adult, differing needs
    concerns/issues common to, 83-84
    institutional concerns/solutions, 84-86
    security systems, 89-95
    staffing issues, 93-94
    summary, 86-87
youths with disabilities, 19

Francisco "Frank" J. Alarcon is the second-in-command of the Florida Department of Juvenile Justice, one of the largest juvenile justice systems in the nation. He was appointed deputy secretary in March 1999. He is a twenty-eight-year veteran in public service and has more than twenty years of experience managing juvenile justice organizations. Prior to his current appointment, he was the director of the California Youth Authority, the largest youth correctional agency in the United States. While director, Mr. Alarcon convened a National Panel of experts that resulted in a 1998 published report, *Violent Youthful Offenders: A Practitioner's Plan for Action.*

Lisa Melanie Boesky, Ph.D., is a clinical psychologist and specializes in the identification and management of juvenile offenders with mental health disorders, including suicidal and/or self-injurious youths. She has designed several mental health training programs for correctional staff and trains juvenile justice staff on a national basis. She has helped develop a mental health screening tool for juvenile correctional facilities and consults on mental health policy and programming to juvenile justice agencies across the country. She is the author of *Juvenile Offenders with Mental Health Disorders: Who Are They and What Do We Do With Them?* (available from the American Correctional Association, Lanham, Maryland). She can be reached at (206) 979-5792 or www.drlisab.com.

Kurt M. Bumby, Ph.D., received his doctorate in forensic clinical psychology from the University of Nebraska-Lincoln as part of the Clinical Psychology Training and Law-Psychology programs. Currently, he serves as the assistant deputy director for the Missouri Division of Youth Services and is a frequent guest lecturer, trainer, and consultant. Dr. Bumby has published several articles and book chapters on a variety of topics including juvenile delinquency, child maltreatment, sexual offender management, and other forensic issues.

Jesse W. Doyle has more than twenty-eight years of experience working in the field of juvenile justice. He has directed programs for over twenty years and is presently vice president of Youthtrack, Inc., Western Region Operations in Littleton, Colorado. Additionally, he is a national trainer and consultant.

Michael J. Elmendorf, II is special assistant to New York Gov. George E. Pataki. Elmendorf is a member and acting chairman of the New York State Juvenile Justice Advisory Group, a founder of Colonie Youth Court, and currently serves as executive vice president of Colonie Youth Court, Inc. He is a graduate of Union College in New York, where he prepared a thesis on the youth court program.

Lili Frank Garfinkel has been an advocate for underrepresented populations for thirty years. She joined PACER (Parent Advocacy Coalition for Educational Rights) in 1984 to start the "Let's Prevent Abuse Project" and started PACER's Juvenile Justice project in 1994. She joined the EDJJ project at the University of Maryland in 1999. Garfinkel coauthored the book *No One Saw My Pain* (W.W. Norton) with Dr. Andrew Slaby and has written a manual on youth with disabilities in the juvenile justice system, as well as numerous articles.

Kit Glover is the treatment and education coordinator for Missouri's Division of Youth Services. She holds a master's degree from the University of Missouri-Columbia in curriculum and instruction. Her focus is programmatic and technical development of the agency's education component. She spent nineteen years in public education prior to working for Youth Services.

Salvador "Tony" Godinez is the juvenile field services administrator for the Illinois Department of Corrections. He also is a former warden in Illinois, Nevada, and Pennsylvania, and former deputy director in Michigan. Having taken a circuitous route in his career with stops in Nevada, Michigan, Puerto Rico, and Philadelphia, he finds himself back where he started twenty-five years ago. And, like many of his peers, he is pondering how the system got to the point of housing so many juvenile offenders in adult correctional facilities.

Earlene Green, D.D., L.S.W., C.A.C., is a native of Philadelphia, Pennsylvania and a graduate of Temple University, School of Social Administration. She is currently employed by Cornell Companies, Inc. as a program director for WorkBridge and Services to Children in Their Own Homes programs in Philadelphia.

Anne Hasselbrack, an editorial assistant at the ACA, earned a bachelor's degree in criminal justice from the University of Maryland, College Park. She writes fiction, nonfiction, and poetry, and her novel *Extra-Curricular: A Novel of Rape on Campus* is being made into a stage play at the University of Northern Iowa under a grant from the Department of Justice, Violence Against Women Office.

Lonnie Jackson is the statewide director of Minority Services for the Oregon Youth Authority. He is the author of *Gangbusters: Strategies for Prevention and Intervention*, which is available from the American Correctional Association.

Charles J. Kehoe, ACSW, LCSW, currently is vice president for business development for Securicor New Century, LLC, in Richmond, Virginia where he is responsible for developing prospects in the management and operation of juvenile correctional facilities and provides training, technical assistance, and consulting services to adult and juvenile correctional programs. He has authored and co-authored several articles pertaining to corrections, and he has been called upon to be an expert witness in Federal and state courts and provide consulting services in the master planning and design work for new facilities. He is a member of several organizations including the National Council of Juvenile and Family Court Judges, the Fraternal Order of Police, and the American Correctional Association, where he is president-elect.

Ron Leffler has been employed by the Indiana Department of Correction for the past twenty-two years. He began his career with the department as a parole agent, then assistant district supervisor, and then to his current position of director of juvenile transition programs, twelve years ago. Prior to coming to the department, Mr. Leffler was a juvenile probation officer for five years. Mr. Leffler holds a bachelor's degree in criminology and a master's degree in public administration. He has been a member of ACA for twenty-seven years.

Brent Matthews is a director with Indiana Behavioral Health Choices, Inc. He has a master's degree in clinical child and youth work After serving the Dawn Project for four years, he is now director for the Action Coalition to Ensure Stability (ACES), serving homeless persons who are mentally ill and/or substance abusers. Mr. Matthews has spent more than twenty years in the field of child, youth, and family work and is a presenter at many local, state, and national conferences on strength-based practices in the system of care.

Edmund McGarrell is an adjunct senior fellow of Hudson Institute and director of the Institute's Crime Control Policy Center. He is also the director and professor of the School of Criminal Justice at Michigan State University. He has been a fellow at the National Center for Juvenile Justice and was formerly director of the Washington State Institute for Community Oriented Policing and has taught at Indiana University and Washington State University. Dr. McGarrell has directed a number of large scale research projects including an evaluation of a fear and crime reduction program in public housing and a study of the effects of directed police patrol on firearms crime, both sponsored by the National Institute of Justice. His current research includes the use of crime information in strategic planning in the Indianapolis Violence Reduction Partnership, problem solving approaches to the issue of inmate reentry, and the study of the use of restorative justice conferences for juvenile offenders. He received his Ph.D. from the School of Criminal Justice, Nelson A. Rockefeller College of Public Affairs and Policy, State University of New York at Albany.

Albert Murray was appointed commissioner of the Kansas Juvenile Justice Authority (KJJA) in May of 1997 by the governor of the State of Kansas. As a newly created agency, he was the founding commissioner of the Kansas Juvenile Justice Authority, using a mixture of resources from other state agencies and new resources. Commissioner Murray is a seasoned professional in juvenile justice of more than thirty years. Most of his career was spent in his native home state of Tennessee, where he held numerous roles within the Tennessee juvenile system, to include the role of assistant commissioner. He presently serves on the ACA Board of Governors, conducts accreditation audits, and is chairman of ACA's Juvenile Corrections Committee.

Jennifer M. O'Mara is currently employed as an evaluation supervisor in the Department of Research and Evaluation at Cornell Companies, Inc. She is primarily responsible for managing and maintaining an internally developed portfolio of client evaluation instruments used within various Cornell treatment programs. She has a master's degree in research methodology from the University of Pittsburgh.

Al Palomino is a parole agent III and public information officer for the Ventura Youth Correctional Facility in Camarillo, California.

Scott B. Peterson is former director of the Colonie Youth Court and executive director of Youth Courts of the Capital District, Inc. He is currently employed as a program manager at the Office of Juvenile Justice and Delinquency Prevention, Office of Justice Programs, U.S. Department of Justice. Mr. Peterson's responsibilities include national projects such at the National Youth Court Center, National Resource Center for Safe Schools, and the upcoming National Guidelines for the Juvenile Court with the National Council of Juvenile and Family Court Judges. He can be reached at peterson@ojp.usdoj.gov.

Jeffrey Poirier is a Research Assistant at the American Institutes for Research where he contributes to research related to education, juvenile justice, and children's mental health. Mr. Poirier earned a B.A. in sociology from the University of Pennsylvania and is currently completing a Masters in Education Policy Studies at George Washington University. He is particularly interested in the equity and adequacy of education finance, as well as the cost effectiveness and benefits of preventing juvenile delinquency.

Mary Magee Quinn, Ph.D., is a senior research analyst at the American Institutes for Research in Washington, D.C., and an associate director of the National Center on Education Disabilities and Juvenile Justice. Her research interests include disabilities, education, and behavior problems.

Steve Rosenbaum is chief of the Special Litigation Section in the Civil Rights Division of the U.S. Department of Justice, and has served in that position since 1996. The Section is responsible for enforcing the Civil Rights of Institutionalized Persons Act (CRIPA), which are federal laws that prohibit a pattern or practice of misconduct by law enforcement officers, and the Freedom of Access to Clinic Entrances Act. Mr. Rosenbaum joined the Civil Rights Division in 1978, and has served as the Division's lead counsel on some of its most demanding and complex litigation. He received his B.A. in history, with honors, from Harpur College, SUNY Binghamton in 1975, and was enrolled in Phi Beta Kappa. He attended the University of Michigan Law School and received a J.D., cum laude, in 1978.

Robert B. Rutherford, Ph.D., is professor of special education and associate director of research and graduate programs in curriculum and instruction at Arizona State University. He is also an associate director of the National Center on Education, Disability and Juvenile Justice.

Kathryn Scott is an evaluation supervisor in the Department of Research and Evaluation at Cornell Companies, Inc. Her primary responsibility is to implement projects within Cornell's companywide data standardization project. Following her 1997 graduation from Duquesne University with a bachelor's degree in psychology, she went on to receive a master's degree in research methodology from the University of Pittsburgh.

William "Bill" Sturgeon has more than twenty-five years of experience in the criminal justice field. During this time, he has held management positions in both law enforcement and corrections. He is the coauthor of *No Time to Play: Youthful Offenders in Adult Correctional Systems* and *Recess is Over: A Handbook for Managing Youthful Offenders in Adult Systems* (both of which are available from American Correctional Association). He has been a consultant for the U.S. House of Representatives, the National Institute of Corrections, numerous state and local governments, the Republic of South Africa, and The Netherlands. He has also consulted for many private companies. Mr. Sturgeon received an associate degree from Berkshire Community College, a bachelor's degree from Southern Vermont College, a master's degree from Goddard College, and training in conflict management and mediation from the Harvard School of Public Health.

Claudia Thorne is a regional director for Cornell Abraxas' Northeast Region. In this capacity, she oversees the development and operations of community-based programs serving youths and their families, including Work-Bridge. Ms. Thorne has a bachelor's degree from Boston University and a master's degree in social work from Howard University in Washington, D.C.

Ron Tonn is the Safer Foundation's Associate Vice President for Public Development. Since 1976, he has been instrumental in the development and articulation of the Safer Foundation's Basic Skills Training methodology, an innovative educational counseling design specifically for former offenders. He has served as the director of the Safer Foundation's educational services for over a decade. He previously directed all Safer Foundation service provision units and is currently responsible for agency diversification through new program design. Mr. Tonn has designed and written methodologies for employment, education and supportive services, case management, and prevention programs for adult and juvenile offenders. He earned degrees in psychology/sociology from Purdue University.

Gina E. Wood is the state director of the South Carolina Department of Juvenile Justice (DJJ). Since her cabinet appointment by Governor Jim Hodges and unanimous confirmation by the South Carolina Senate on March 31, 1999, she has made significant improvements at the Department of Juvenile Justice, an agency with an annual budget of more than $100 million and nearly 1,700 employees. Ms. Wood's accomplishments are grounded in her vision "to build and maintain a balanced and restorative juvenile justice system to include a safe and secure environment that ensures rehabilitation and prevents delinquency."

Daniel Zarecky has been the director of the Cornell Abraxas WorkBridge Program in Allegheny County, Pennsylvania since 1997. He has a bachelor's degree in criminal justice from Gannon University in Erie, Pennsylvania, and has been working in the field of juvenile justice for the past thirteen years.

Cage Your

Cage Your Rage for Teens:
A Guide to Anger Control Workbook
Murray C. Cullen and Joan Wright
Based on the principles outlined in the best selling ACA book, *Cage Your Rage*, this workbook is designed to help juveniles understand and deal with anger. By recording their feelings and actions, teens learn to recognize and control their anger. Chapters discuss what causes anger, growing up with anger, how emotions develop, relaxation and managing anger. Additional topics include calming others, compromise, staging and signposting, self talk, and feeling and action controls. *(1996, 100 pages, 1 56991 036 7)*

Setting the Stage: How To Deliver An Anger Management Program
This instructor's manual provides invaluable assistance for leading teens through this excellent program. *(1996, 95 pages, 1 56991 037 5)*

Cage Your Rage For Juveniles Video Program
This program complements the *Cage Your Rage for Teens* workbook and examines four critical areas in helping juvenile offenders to identify and control the anger that triggers their rage. Part One assists juveniles in examining themselves and the roots of their anger, because anger learned is anger repeated. Part Two works with juveniles to understand how their anger turns into rage and leads to aggressive behavior. Part Three provides juveniles with the knowledge to analyze situations and develop appropriate responses to their anger by using self talk. Part Four offers juveniles alternatives to help them manage their anger properly. *(2000, three videotapes, 52 minutes, comprehensive leader's guide, and workbook)*

To order or to request an ACA product catalog, call 1 800 222 5646, ext. 1860
American Correctional Association
4380 Forbes Boulevard
Lanham, MD 20706 4322
www.aca.org

FOUNDED 1870

MUST READ
JUVENILE RESOURCES

Juvenile Offenders with Mental Health Disorders: Who Are They? and What Do We Do With Them?
Lisa M. Boesky, Ph.D.
The number of individuals entering the juvenile justice system with some form of mental health disorder continues to grow. Those housed in juvenile correctional facilities provide new challenges to those in charge of their care. This book is a guide for professionals working with this population. Whether you are a officer, administrator, mental health counselor, physician or anyone working with offenders with mental health disorders, this book is for you. Topics discussed include: Diagnosis of Mental Health Disorders, Mood Disorders; Attention Deficit/ Hyperactivity Disorders (ADHD), Substance Abuse Disorders, Suicidal Behavior, Screening and Assessment; and more. *(2002, approx. 300 pages, 1 56991 154 1)*

Reality Therapy and Choice Theory:
Managing Behavior Today, Developing Skills
for Tomorrow

David A. Jackson, M.A., RTC and
Lawrence G. Myers, M.A., CCA
Many resources focus on how to make juvenile offenders behave a certain way. How to walk, talk and act. However, when these same juveniles are returned to their normal life, they are unequipped to successfully analyze situations and act appropriately. *Reality Therapy and Choice Theory* will provide you with methods to help juveniles understand why they do the things they do. It takes therapy from behind closed doors and into the real world. This resource will also help you teach juveniles how to focus on the present, as opposed to living in the past. *(2002, 216 pages, 1 56991 162 2)*

To order or to request an ACA product catalog,
call 1 800 222 5646, ext. 1860
American Correctional Association
4380 Forbes Boulevard
Lanham, MD 20706 4322
www.aca.org